*Race and the Making of
American Political Science*

AMERICAN GOVERNANCE: POLITICS, POLICY, AND PUBLIC LAW

Series Editors:
Richard Valelly, Pamela Brandwein, Marie Gottschalk, Christopher Howard

A complete list of books in the series is available from the publisher.

Race and the Making of American Political Science

Jessica Blatt

PENN

UNIVERSITY OF PENNSYLVANIA PRESS

PHILADELPHIA

Published by
University of Pennsylvania Press
Philadelphia, Pennsylvania 19104-4112
www.upenn.edu/pennpress

Printed in the United States of America
on acid-free paper

10 9 8 7 6 5 4 3 2 1

Library of Congress Cataloging-in-Publication Data

Names: Blatt, Jessica, 1970- author.
Title: Race and the making of American political science / Jessica Blatt.
Other titles: American governance.
Description: 1st edition. | Philadelphia : University of Pennsylvania Press,
    [2018] | Series: American governance: politics, policy, and public law |
    Includes bibliographical references and index.
Identifiers: LCCN 2017036428 | ISBN 9780812250046 (hardcover: alk.
paper)
Subjects: LCSH: Political science—United States—History. | Race. |
    Political science—Study and teaching (Higher)—United States—History. |
    Racism—United States—History.
Classification: LCC JA84.U5 B49 2018 | DDC 320.0973—dc23
LC record available at https://lccn.loc.gov/2017036428

For Rosa, Leo, and Sean

Contents

Introduction   1

Chapter 1. "The White Man's Mission": John W. Burgess and the Columbia School of Political Science   13

Chapter 2. "All Things Lawful Are Not Expedient": The American Political Science Association Considers Jim Crow   35

Chapter 3. Twentieth-Century Problems: Administering an American Empire   53

Chapter 4. The *Journal of Race Development*: Evolution and Uplift   72

Chapter 5. Laying Specters to Rest: Political Science Encounters the Boasian Critique of Racial Anthropology   90

Chapter 6. Finding New Premises: Race Science, Philanthropy, and the Institutional Establishment of Political Science   116

Epilogue   138

Notes   149

Index   193

Acknowledgments   203

Introduction

A few years ago, the *Journal of Theoretical Politics* featured a startling announcement: The results of a new analysis of genetic and attitudinal data heralded "the end of ideology as we know it." The philosophers, the implication went, having only interpreted ideology, had been missing the point. Science was finally poised to offer a rigorous, empirical account of its wellsprings. Our ideologies were in our genes.

Specifically, an interdisciplinary team from political science and behavioral genetics claimed to have shown that most conventionally understood sources of ideology were instead a "cultural veneer" overlaid on a "potentially divergent underlying structure of genetic differences."[1] Put simply, the idea was that in important instances our genes determine which of the available political preferences we are likely to choose. Even more simply, certain kinds of bodies are predisposed to certain kinds of politics.

The article (the title was, in fact, "It's the End of Ideology as We Know It") was part of a special issue dedicated to research on "genes and politics," or what practitioners call "new empirical biopolitics."[2] This vein of political science research goes back to the 1970s but has only recently achieved greater visibility.[3] A high point came when a 2005 article on the heritability of political attitudes made the cover of the *American Political Science Review* (*APSR*), the discipline's flagship journal, and attracted a respectable amount of media attention.[4] Since then, a small but prolific group of researchers has been claiming to identify genetic bases for our attraction to liberalism or conservatism; levels of social dominance; likelihood to join political parties, vote, or employ particular decision strategies; gender differences in political behavior; feelings of political efficacy; receptiveness to populism; negative attitudes toward out-groups; and even "Machiavellianism."[5]

Much of this work is ambitious, calling on us to radically revise our understanding of political life. For one writer, the "shopworn," "competing

... paradigms of behavioralism and rational choice are in their last throes," to be replaced by a new, "sociogenomic" synthesis.[6] The *APSR*'s editor was particularly struck by the popular media attention accorded the 2005 cover article, musing that it might someday "emerge among the most important articles the *APSR* has ever published."[7] And while few political scientists have rushed to retrain in genetics, the continued appearance of work on the biology of politically relevant differences in respected political science journals suggests that other editors and peer reviewers remain interested in this approach.[8]

The 2005 study and others that followed have of course come in for criticism. Critics such as the geneticist Jon Beckwith and the political scientist Evan Charney fault "empirical biopolitics" for often reifying political categories in ways that do violence to the historical record. They also note that its claims often require us to resort to tortured logic to accommodate previously intelligible phenomena, such as the emergence within a generation of a solid, small-government Republican bloc in the American South (where support for the New Deal had been strong). Finally, critics point to methodological issues, including that these claims seem to rely on an outdated, genes-as-blueprint paradigm, rather than on newer understandings in which DNA is part of a dynamic, epigenetic system.[9]

Moreover, while genes and politics researchers distance themselves from the suggestion of racial implications, the deeply racialized dynamics of American political life make racial implications hard to avoid. If preference for liberal policies is significantly genetic, the pervasive attachment of African Americans to the Democratic Party, for example, could seem to imply that racial distinctions, rather than being "socially constructed," map on to meaningful biological differences. Similarly, if genes and politics researchers are right, "gender gaps" in voting behavior constitute powerful evidence against feminist briefs for the social construction of gender. In short, all sorts of observed racial, gender, and other disparities might be biological in origin and, by implication, less susceptible to change than liberals (in thrall to their genes, no doubt) might like to believe.

Specific arguments aside, it is clear that this literature is part of a larger resurgence in biological determinism in the United States in the twenty-first century. That resurgence has taken the form of bald-faced racism, as in the newfound prominence enjoyed by white supremacists (the so-called "alt-right"). It also takes more benign-seeming forms, such as the commercialization of racially specific medicine, a thriving ancestry-testing industry, and the column inches given to deterministically minded science writers like Nicholas Wade.[10] Many scholars fear that this cultural and scientific moment bodes a return to past follies, as when early twentieth-century eugenics advocates wrote confidently of hereditary "unit characters" for everything from "pauperism" to "ability in literary composition" and "thalassophilia" ("love of sailing").[11] Claims about innate social and political characteristics can also seem to open a door to the rehabilitation of long-discredited theories of innate race and sex differences or even a "backdoor" to ethically murky human engineering efforts.[12]

This book focuses on the early years of U.S. political science, not its current state. I discuss the discipline's recent, partial embrace of biological determinism here because, just as it evokes an earlier, troubling moment in the history of science, it also recalls ideas central to U.S. political science at its origins. Now we are told that radical new research shows that "a correlation exists between political involvement and physiological predispositions" or that political liberalism is substantially determined by a genetic predisposition to "seek out new experiences."[13] However, the idea that our politics are born into us—indeed, specifically that some people are innately cut out for self-government and progress while others are by their very constitutions more suited to traditional forms of authority—was in a real sense the precept on which U.S. political science was founded in the late nineteenth century.

The Victorian scholars who formalized the study of politics in the United States in the 1880s did not have the language of "genes."[14] What they had was "race." John W. Burgess and Herbert Baxter Adams, who between them founded the first two doctoral programs in politics in the United States, taught that Anglo-Saxons were the bearers of a "Teutonic germ" of liberty. It was Anglo-Saxons who created, and were fit to enjoy, democratic institutions. It was also they who carried forward the potential of civilization. As for the rest, some might eventually be assimilated, but most were more suited to authoritarianism (at home) or colonial domination (abroad). The first U.S.-trained cohort of political science PhDs learned that adhering to a priori fictions of equality and social contracts had only resulted in the disaster of the Civil War. Avoiding such a calamity in the future would require more reliable political judgment, based in a hard-headed appraisal of the truths of nature—particularly the truths about innate human difference. "Ethnology," Burgess affirmed, constituted "elevated ground," a "standpoint" from which researchers could get a clear view of the political world.[15]

If "Teutonic germ" theory had been idiosyncratic, the resonances with "empirical biopolitics" would be telling enough. However, as I will argue, the racial ideas it invoked were central to the paradigmatic theory around which the discipline was coalescing, uniting scholars who disagreed about much else. What's more, these background racial assumptions long outlasted the specific tenets of "Teutonism." Well into the twentieth century, major political scientists understood racial difference to be a fundamental shaper of political life. They wove popular and scientific ideas about racial difference into their accounts of political belonging, of progress and change, of proper hierarchy, and of democracy and its warrants. And they attended closely to changing scientific accounts of human difference, viewing these as basic to their own work. The impulse to describe political differences as natural ones, then, runs deep, and won't seem to go away.

From National Soul to Independent Variable

The central argument of this book is that race thinking shaped U.S. political science at its origins far more profoundly than has previously been recognized. From the late nineteenth century and well into the twentieth, scholars of politics defined and continually reoriented their intellectual work in response to changing scientific notions of race and to the political imperatives of the racial order at home and abroad. Racial thought informed ongoing efforts to frame political science as a "real" science, and it was deeply implicated in major intellectual and institutional innovations as the discipline established itself within the American academy. This includes what may be the defining development for the study of politics in the United States: a gradual, and at times fitful, shift from a legalistic, historicist framework to liberal accounts of politics as the play of individuals, groups, and interests. In this sense, changing notions of racial difference were constitutive of a model of political life itself that continues to exert a powerful hold on our political imagination, outside the academy as much as within.

Some elements of this story have been told. For example, few if any recent considerations of late nineteenth-century American political science fail to note that it is rife with "essentially racist conclusions."[16] However, these are usually treated as regrettable ephemera—either secondary to more central contributions or shameful mistakes that were eventually left behind, leaving little trace. This is changing, particularly with regard to scholarship on international relations, thanks to important interventions by Robert Vitalis, Brian Schmidt, and others.[17] Nonetheless, much work remains before we can fully appreciate the role of racial ideas and particularly the role of race science in the study of American politics, and the ways in which the racialized premises driving the study of international relations shaped U.S. political science as a whole.

Race and the Making of American Political Science contributes to that project by examining how racial ideas figured in a number of settings in which pioneering U.S. political scientists sought to stake out their intellectual territory and define their methods. These include Burgess's Columbia University department in the 1880s and 1890s; the meetings, publications, and other activities of the American Political Science Association (APSA) in the decade following its founding in 1903; the pages of the first U.S.-based international relations journal, the *Journal of Race Development* (founded by George Blakeslee and G. Stanley Hall at Clark University in 1910); and, finally, in the 1920s, efforts by Charles E. Merriam and others to bring scientific methods to bear on political questions and to integrate the study of politics into an interdisciplinary social science matrix.

Chapters 1 through 4 show that, particularly at the discipline's early, founding moments, notions of "race" and "politics" were often so deeply intertwined as to be hard to distinguish. As political science began to take shape within the academy, leading practitioners put racialist premises at the heart of their accounts of democratic legitimacy and sovereignty, the dynamics of political change, and the propriety and limits of political reform. For the founding generation, led by Burgess and deeply influenced by German political philosophy, this took the form of the Teutonic "state." Burgess taught that American political institutions and particularly the American legal system represented the highest form to date of the development of the Anglo-Saxon "genius for liberty," and he framed political science as the task of understanding and safeguarding that development. Subsequent cohorts of political scientists distanced themselves from the legal focus and idealist trappings of Burgess's approach, seeking to bring greater realism and empirical rigor to their science. Despite these shifts, however, younger political scientists such as Woodrow Wilson and Henry Jones Ford continued to ground their accounts of political life in an evolving racial unity. Like Burgess and along with many of their contemporaries, Wilson and Ford treated political community as an aspect of racial life. They also saw "recognition" of racial difference—or what Ford called the "natural history" of politics—as fundamental to any "realistic" science or sound project of political reform.[18] Similarly, members of both generations shared in a wider consensus that the legal and administrative principles appropriate to governing "backward" races abroad applied as well for the government of racial others at home.

If these ideas crossed theoretical and methodological divides, so too were they shared across political ones. For example, Burgess, along with many of his contemporaries, opposed McKinley-era colonial expansion on the grounds that it would expand government power and saddle the developing American state with new race problems when it could barely handle the ones it already had. The Wilsonian generation, by contrast, accepted both more active government and U.S. colonialism as pragmatic responses to new economic and geopolitical realities. Leading scholars active in the APSA and elsewhere sought to craft models of domestic and imperial governance that would accommodate American values to scientific knowledge about racial difference. For many of these writers, different levels of evolutionary progress meant that the "darker races," both at home and abroad, would most likely require a semipermanent subordinate status appropriate to each group's degree of evolutionary progress. Others saw racial evolution as a field for intervention and uplift. However, commentators on all sides of this debate agreed that what Blakeslee and Hall's pathbreaking international relations journal would dub "race development" was at the heart of the question.

That is, until roughly the beginning of World War I, multiple, distinct intellectual and political projects rested on the assumptions that "races" were the primary units of political life and that racial evolution was an appropriate framework in which to understand political change. Again, these projects differed in their political prescriptions and their degrees of optimism about the possibility of more egalitarian relationships between racial groups. However, in each of them the idea of essential racial capacities or traits marked both the grounds and the limits of that possibility.

Chapters 5 and 6 trace a break with this consensus, and the emergence of new understandings of both racial and political difference. After World War I, notions of organic unity were harder to sustain. One response came from "pluralists" such as Harold Laski, who put internal differentiation at the center of democratic theory. Many political scientists, too—particularly a group that coalesced around the brilliant academic entrepreneur Charles E. Merriam, the University of Chicago, and the Social Science Research

Council (SSRC)—began to perceive organic, racialist accounts of political difference as "traditional" and "authoritarian" and to cast about for suitably scientific alternatives. Merriam and his colleagues were less centrally preoccupied with issues of white supremacy and colonialism than were many of their predecessors. Nonetheless, it was again to race science that this group looked for new accounts of human difference more suitable to a usable, empirical science of politics.

As they groped for conceptions of political life more consonant with the ferment they saw in interwar American life, Merriam and the group he gathered around him put great stock in the idea that scientific methods could anchor political judgment and point to possibilities for "social control" in the face of rapid social, economic, and political change. They correctly perceived, however, that for all its attempts, the discipline had thus far failed to break free of teleology, historicism, and what one writer called "race mysticism."[19] To complete this break, they turned to new theories of race and historical change coming out of other fields. They showed particular interest in a critique of race-based "stage" theories of civilizational development that was being elaborated by the anthropologist Franz Boas and his students. From the Boasian critique, Merriam and others drew the lesson that the modern state was the product of contingency and change. This suggested that modern political processes and institutions could be studied on their own terms, independent of racial essences or deep historical-evolutionary analysis. It did *not* lead them to abandon the idea of innate racial difference. (Neither, incidentally, did it lead all of the Boasians to do so, at least not immediately.) It did, however, open up the question of additional bases for the differences, political and otherwise, between groups.

Along with many of his students and colleagues, Merriam saw tantalizing possible answers to that question in frameworks and technologies of human measurement coming out of psychology and biology. Several of them showed special interest in the large-scale, World War I army intelligence-testing program designed by Yale University psychologist Robert Yerkes, as well as in studies of racial difference carried out under the auspices of the National Research Council (NRC). In those settings, difference assumed a new form. What psychologists and race researchers seemed to be finding weren't essential group characteristics, exactly, but instead uneven distributions of traits (such as "intelligence") within and between populations. Moreover, racial differences were not the only kinds identified.

The intelligence tests, for example, produced seemingly useful knowledge about intra-racial difference (such as the finding that white officers showed a higher "mental age" than white draftees).

These findings offered intriguing possibilities for understanding and managing difference within a pluralistic democracy, and a number of political scientists sought to capitalize on those possibilities. Many political scholars (most of them close to Merriam in some regard) found in "differential psychology" and "social biology" inspiration for a renovation of political science. If intelligence and other traits could be measured and mapped between and within populations, many reasoned, other, more properly political qualities might be treated in the same way. And if this were possible, a quantitative, methodologically rigorous science of politics might be poised to offer reliable diagnoses of what ailed the polity and to prescribe cures.

This hope was both intellectual and political. But it was also connected to local, institutional concerns—it was not lost on this group that psychologists and natural scientists had secured major funding for their efforts, and political scientists, for the most part, had not. Chapter 6 documents a series of attempts to replicate or latch onto the successes of those fortunate colleagues. Some of those experiments bore fruit in terms of both knowledge and institutional success—early research in political psychology is one example. Others, such as an abortive bid to bring the social sciences into research funding structures created to foster the natural sciences, did not pan out as hoped. However, I show that, successful or not, in the course of these efforts political scientists began to articulate new visions of political difference. (In many cases, they also secured sizable amounts of foundation money for political research.)

In short, as they engaged with innovations in anthropology, psychology, and the natural sciences, a number of important political scientists began to talk about politics in a new way and to elaborate new structures in which to do their work. Political institutions—once a reflection of the character and evolution of monolithic, racialized "peoples"—began to appear instead as the more or less contingent product of interacting historical, sociological, psychological, and biological factors. It wasn't always clear where those differences came from (biology, society, psychology, etc.), or how stable they were. But the job of answering those questions was properly left to other disciplines. Political science could busy itself with mapping, analyzing, and thinking about how to control them.

A Note on Race, Political Science, and Disciplinary History

As John Gunnell points out, when we are not tracing our origins to Plato or the Enlightenment, U.S. political scientists have traditionally consumed our own history in the form of intradisciplinary debates—narratives about how the perspective or methods with which we identify emerged from earlier, flawed ones, for example; or how the currently dominant tendency has overtaken some earlier, more promising one. These accounts certainly enrich our understanding, but, as Gunnell also observes, they are perhaps better understood as "events *in* the history of political science," rather than as satisfactory treatments *of* that history.[20] Fortunately, in recent decades they have been supplemented by a rich body of serious, far-reaching disciplinary histories, with Gunnell as perhaps the leading scholar and with key contributions from Dorothy Ross, James Farr, John Dryzek, and Richard Adcock, among many others.[21]

At the most basic level, this study is animated by questions of how racial ideas shape American political thought and politics, and vice-versa. For that reason, I make no pretense of offering a comprehensive disciplinary history. Instead, I focus here on a series of founding moments or transitions identified in previous historiography and on how in those settings political scientists addressed racial topics or, alternatively, addressed the kinds of questions to which "race" is often an answer. Racial ideologies tell stories about how the social world is configured, the sources of those configurations, and how permanent or susceptible to change they might be. To get at how these stories have figured in political science, then, this book looks primarily at political scientists' explicit and implicit accounts of the deep sources of political difference and hierarchy, the forces driving political change, and the bases of political solidarity.

In that sense, political science is as much the site of this study as it is its object. All the same, *Race and the Making of American Political Science* speaks to a number of historiographical questions about the discipline. Most obviously, it speaks to the place of race in the discipline's history (and, to an extent, in its present). The last decade or so has seen an explosion of scholarship on the ways in which anthropology, sociology, criminology, and other social sciences at once responded to and helped to shape racial ideology and the U.S. racial order.[22] Vitalis and others writing about the racial entailments of international relations scholarship have brought political science into this conversation; a few more granular analyses of particular figures or institutions have begun to do the same for the study of U.S. politics.[23] However, the role of racial ideas in U.S. political science's history more generally has not received extended, systematic attention until now.

This may be because U.S. political science is often tightly identified with liberalism. Bernard Crick's early, pathbreaking history of the discipline depicted American political science as shot through with a liberal "moralism" that sought, in his words, to "take the politics out of politics."[24] For Ross, political science, like the American social sciences more broadly, was born of a liberal, exceptionalist impulse to "naturalize the historical world."[25] Gunnell in turn sees "defining, explaining, and evaluating the United States as a democratic society" as "the defining mission of political science"; for Adcock, U.S. political scientists served to "Americanize" European liberalism by adapting it to the social and industrial realities on their side of the Atlantic.[26]

This focus on the liberal and democratic strains of U.S. political science is warranted and revealing. At the same time, it may obscure the ways in which illiberal ideologies, too, mark our history and shape our practice. Ido Oren explores this theme, showing that at important moments major U.S. political scientists have only taken issue with authoritarian or even fascist regimes when those regimes came into conflict with the American state.[27] *Race and the Making of American Political Science* shows that racial ideologies underwrote authoritarian and exclusionary doctrines within political science and also that racialism shaped the technocratic strains of American liberalism that Crick and others find at the heart of U.S. political science.[28]

If the identification of political science and liberalism may have discouraged attention to the discipline's racial commitments, so too may the fact that it has often been set apart for its relative *inattention* to racial topics. Specifically, critics take the discipline to task on the grounds that for much of its history, and to a degree still, U.S. political science has failed to take "race" seriously as an element and product of political life. In Rogers Smith's gloss, after a late nineteenth-century "period of explicit disciplinary racism," students of politics in the United States "devoted less attention to race" than did their counterparts in other disciplines, and certainly less than was warranted by the profoundly racialized dynamics of U.S. politics.[29]

This narrative captures an important truth. There is no question that for much of the twentieth century the political science mainstream failed to view racial oppression and hierarchy as problems that fell within its bailiwick. In 1970, Mack Jones and Alex Willingham found that political scientists excluded both the African American experience and systems of racial oppression from "fundamental political questions about the nature of society."[30] The following decade saw African American political scientists arguing that the study of race was "an academic graveyard" in a field for which African American politics were largely "invisible."[31] In 1985, Ernest J. Wilson III published an article titled, "Why Political Scientists Don't Study Black Politics, But Historians and Sociologists Do."[32] Twenty-two years later, he found that, despite progress, "African American issues" were "still at the margins" of political science. Similar patterns have been documented for people of color more broadly.[33]

For Smith, this marginalization of racial topics dates to around 1920, when the "explicitly racist" scholarship of the founding generations began to give way to the idea that "race" was "pre-political," "generated at root by biology and/or economics and/or culture and/or history and/or often unconscious or at least informal social psychological process and social activities."[34] This conforms to the findings of a 2011 discipline-wide task force that found that political scholarship still "tends to treat identity as given and outside of analysis" rather than "as a core analytical category for understanding important aspects of political behavior, social movements, and the development of public policies."[35] That is, Jones and Willingham's observation of almost half a century ago—that political scientists to a troubling degree fail to treat "race" as integral to the realm of "politics"—still holds.

In one sense, the story this book tells runs counter to this narrative by showing that the racialism of political science's founders marked the discipline more profoundly than we have acknowledged.[36] In my account, the "explicit disciplinary racism" that Smith and others have noted in fact signaled a deeply racialized worldview that helped to give form and content to the practice of political science at its origins. At a deeper level, however, my account documents the origins of the disconnect these critics note. That is, if "race" was expelled from "politics" to some "pre-political" sphere, it was not because race suddenly came to seem insignificant. Rather, this shift was connected to an intense engagement *with* the idea of race.

This part of my account also situates political science within a broader process of the co-production of racial politics, race science, and the social sciences more broadly. For George Stocking Jr., the Boasian turn in anthropology in many ways constituted the condition of possibility for the social sciences as we know them. Specifically, he argues that the social sciences themselves only achieved their modern form when the holistic, organic, "shuttling" between "nature" and "culture" that characterized Victorian race theory was replaced, in large part through the efforts of Boasian anthropologists, with a meaningful distinction. In this new paradigm, the social appeared as something like an autonomous domain, built on a substrate of biological possibility and constraint. The latter, too, was more clearly delineated, meaning that just as "the social" achieved independent status, the life sciences saw their own questions and territory sharpened and defined in the same process. If this shift in racial thought was key to bringing into focus the modern projects of anthropology, sociology, and even biology, my account suggests that it played a similar role for political science, contributing to new conceptions of the discipline's purpose, methods, and scope—a scope that, not incidentally, often excluded "race" by consigning it to those other realms.[37]

"The White Man's Mission": John W. Burgess and the Columbia School of Political Science

Much of the credit for establishing the study of politics as a distinct learned discipline in the United States goes to John W. Burgess. A constitutional scholar, teacher of future presidents,[1] and prominent commentator on domestic and foreign affairs, Burgess "more than anyone else . . . established the disciplinary, professional, and intellectual foundations" of political science in the United States.[2] He articulated the paradigmatic theory of the emerging discipline, taught its first cohort of American-trained PhDs, helped to found its first U.S.-based scholarly journal and association, and fought successfully to establish specialized, nonprofessional graduate education of the kind that characterizes doctoral programs in the liberal arts and sciences today.[3]

Burgess was also an especially committed and vehement racist, even by the standards of late nineteenth-century America. With his colleague (and one-time student) William A. Dunning, Burgess "played a powerful and disreputable part" in cementing the image of Reconstruction as a "hideous tyranny" of "negro domination," which was later popularized by Thomas Dixon's Reconstruction novels and D. W. Griffith's film, *The Birth of a Nation.*[4] Burgess described the black-led Reconstruction legislatures of South Carolina and Louisiana as "the most soul-sickening spectacle that Americans had ever been called upon to behold," and the legislators themselves as "ignorant barbarians."[5] He held firmly that "American Indians, Africans, and Asiatics" ought never to "form any active, directive part of the political population" in the United States and was skeptical about the wisdom of extending the suffrage to many non-Aryan whites.[6] He thought

Anglo-Saxons had a "world-duty of carrying civilization into the dark places of the earth," justified the removal of native populations everywhere with the remark that "there is no human right to . . . barbarism,"[7] and characterized even the most cautious statements of possible racial equality as "great sophism." Even slavery, to which he described himself as "strongly hostile," he saw as having been justifiable in its time "as a relation which could *temporarily* produce a better state of morals in a particularly constituted society than any other relation."[8] The "white man's mission," he wrote, "his duty and his right," was "to hold the reins of political power in his own hands for the civilization of the world and the welfare of mankind."[9]

Burgess's attitudes are no secret. While he has been lauded as the "father" of American political science, commentators in recent decades are highly likely to note the racism that suffused his work. Particular attention has been paid to his leading role in constructing the harshly negative portrayal of Reconstruction that until recently dominated historiography on that period, and his racial views are invoked in debates over the significance of racism to American imperialism and in discussions of elite responses to the prospect of World War I.[10] (Burgess was horrified at the idea of conflict between Anglo-Saxons and their Teutonic cousins, and he retrospectively described the U.S. declaration of war on Germany as "a grievous blow . . . my life's work brought down in irretrievable ruin all about me.")[11] Until very recently, however, his ideas about race, Reconstruction, and imperialism have not been more than passingly explored in the historiography of political science or the discipline's core concepts. That is, most considerations of Burgess's role in formalizing the study of politics in the United States have treated his ideas about race and racial hierarchy as an unfortunate artifact of his times—a stain on his legacy and a problem for the contemporary relevance of his work, certainly, but little more.

However, this limits our understanding of Burgess and, more important, of how systematic political inquiry came to occupy a distinct academic field in the United States. The problem is not that recent commentators have been insufficiently indignant or embarrassed about Burgess's racial ideology.[12] It is, rather, that by failing to take it seriously as a fundamental aspect of his thought, we miss how his racial ideas shaped his political science and the vision for the discipline that he did so much to realize.

Burgess saw political progress as the expression of a racially specific national soul (which he called "the state"). From this perspective, national homogeneity and Anglo-Saxon ("Teutonic") domination were necessary to American (and, by extension, civilization's) advance. More generally, Burgess saw historical development, political sovereignty, and the possibility of democracy itself as determined in basic ways by racial inequality and difference. Burgess, his students, and his colleagues also invoked the seemingly scientific status of "race" to bolster the most basic claim to intellectual authority they made in this period. This was the idea that they were freeing political and historical theory from abstractions that they believed had previously dominated it and rooting it instead in objective science, practiced according to rigorous methods by credentialed professionals.

Scientific Politics and the Gilded Age "Crisis"

Before the Civil War, higher education existed in the United States primarily to train clergy and to hone the character and morals of young gentlemen of the upper classes. Advanced science and technical education became available with the founding of the Rensselaer School in 1824,[13] and these fields saw rapid expansion in midcentury. But it was not until the decades after the Civil War and Reconstruction that anything like the modern, specialized, secular university appeared in the United States.[14] Serious works of social and political analysis had certainly been produced before that period, and some were even by college professors. Particularly influential was the German immigrant scholar Francis Lieber, whose marriage of German historicism to a liberal, nationalist account of American history was carried forward in Burgess's work.[15] However, the social sciences as such—distinct, professional enterprises with identifiable institutional affiliations, specific barriers to entry, and aspirations to scientific status—only began to take shape in the United States in the late nineteenth century, with political science among the first to establish a home in the new university system.

For Thomas L. Haskell and Dorothy Ross, among others, the social sciences, the new universities, and the intellectual style associated with each of these were in significant ways products of "crisis," brought about by the disruption and social ferment of the Civil War and its aftermath.[16] For Haskell, the ideal of the academic as belonging to a specialized "community of the competent" was a response by the northeastern upper classes to a society that seemed increasingly disinclined to defer to its authority. For Ross, this period saw the dissolution of an elite consensus about the bases of knowledge and the course of American history, as science challenged theological authority and rapid change threatened comforting notions of America as an "exceptional" nation. On an institutional level, Stephen Skowronek sees the new universities as part of the "rise of the new American state" in this period, meant to create and rationalize a modern administrative apparatus in response to the realities of an industrialized, urban, and interconnected economy.[17]

The story of the institutionalization of political scholarship in the United States conforms to these largely complementary accounts. Although not born to the northeastern gentry, Burgess spent his professional life in institutions dominated by men of that group and even at times identified as a northerner.[18] Certainly his anxiety about popular economic and political demands was palpable—so much so that Daniel Rodgers numbers Burgess among a cohort of new political and legal professionals in this period seeking to "wrest the language of political legitimacy away from the people" and put a "new set of constitutional limits" around their powers.[19]

In fact, Burgess's politics were complicated, combining a commitment to nationalism with deep suspicion of active, centralized government. He thought that a homogeneous population and a strong judiciary were the keys to producing a robust and ordered polity without the incursions on liberty that would result from powerful democratic government. He was also deeply concerned that America might veer off its "true path . . . toward despotism on the one side or anarchy on the other."[20] To avert these catastrophic alternatives, political knowledge and governing practices had to be grounded in sound, scientific principles rather than a priori, philosophical speculation about natural rights or social contracts. Burgess's scholarship and the School of Political Science he founded were explicitly dedicated to those purposes, and the impulses to rationalize politics and assert upper-class authority animated them both.

A case in point is civil service reform, the public cause with which Burgess and the School of Political Science were most visibly associated in the 1880s. Burgess originally envisioned the school as a training ground for public administrators and officials along the lines of the (then-private) École Libre des Sciences Politiques in Paris.[21] Its graduates were to supply enlightened public servants to replace the machine bosses and patronage appointments controlling many of America's government institutions at the time. When the school was launched in 1880, the Columbia newspaper published a cartoon captioned "True Civil Service Reform." It depicted

Burgess leading his colleagues in full medieval battle gear, commanding a cannon labeled "Political Science" and trained on ramparts emblazoned with the words "To The Victor The Spoils."[22]

The imagery was apt. Like many reformers, proponents of civil service reform were class warriors of a sort, seeking to displace corrupt mass politics with administration by what Burgess's one-time student Richard T. Ely called "a natural aristocracy" drawn from respectable society and educated in enlightened governance. This group alone, Burgess agreed, possessed the "intelligence, skill and fidelity" to competently identify and carry out the common weal.[23]

Moreover, again as with much of the Gilded Age and Progressive reform tradition, this class politics was bound up with racial ideology.[24] White elites had mostly looked with horror at the black-led administrations of the Reconstruction South and many saw depoliticizing government functions as a hedge against the consequences of black suffrage.[25] Similarly, despite the fact that political machines long predated the "new" immigration of the late nineteenth century, these things were conflated in the minds of many reformers. As a result, the arguments for civil service reform were often made in explicitly racialized and anti-immigrant terms. James Bryce, an eminent British politician and student of American politics,[26] argued that political machines existed because of the "ignorant and pliable voters" supplied by the recent wave of immigration, which brought "primitive people, such as the South Italian peasants," suited only to "quasi-feudal relationships."[27] A civil service chosen on merit and by exam would eliminate the patronage that greased the machine's gears, reducing corruption and, with it, any incentive for these groups to interest themselves in political life. Burgess, likewise, saw any participation in government of non-Teutonic people as a recipe for "corruption and confusion," since only "the Teuton" possessed a "superior political genius." That is, not even all white men could be counted among the custodians of "the welfare of mankind." Rather, that role was to fall to the best men of "Teutonic" or "Aryan" stock, elite members of what he called "the political nations par excellence."[28]

Burgess's vision of a school for enlightened public service proved premature. While Burgess was optimistic that the school might "place its students in immediate connection with the Civil Service examinations, so far as they now exist" and also "exert its influence . . . for the extension of same," the committee charged with evaluating his proposal was skeptical. They endorsed his plan in substance, but noted that it was unlikely that "the possession of superior qualifications will necessarily afford the aspirant . . . any very substantial . . . advantage." Still, they agreed with Burgess that "a class of men better prepared in the principles" of political economy, politics, law, and history than were "most of those who control the destinies of our people at this time" was "greatly wanted."[29]

As it turns out, the committee had the right side of the argument, at least in the short term. The Pendleton Act, which had aimed to depoliticize the civil service, covered only 10 percent of government jobs when it was passed in 1883, and that percentage was to rise only gradually for several years. As a result, the immediate demand for graduates of the Columbia School of Political Science was to come less from government institutions than from colleges and universities, as institutions of higher education expanded their enrollments and the doctoral degree came to be sine qua non for professors. Nonetheless, this case lends support to the argument that the university project was bound up with concerns about the transformation of old hierarchies. Similarly, it bears out Skowronek's linkage of universities to the rise of modern administrative practices—if not as a response to state demand for personnel and expertise, then as a site for ideological and political organization, as well as what today's schools of management and administration would call "capacity building." It also hints at the ways in which the university model was shaped by racial ideas and anxieties circulating in its infancy.

While Burgess's school may have done little to reform American government institutions in the short term, it did much to transform the study of politics, creating a new set of homegrown credentials and a shared, scientific language. Confronted with the economic upheaval, demographic shifts, labor conflict, and radical movements of the Gilded Age, the political professionals at Columbia sought to keep the "reins of government" in the right hands. "Humanitarian outbursts," the narrow interest claims of everyday democratic practice, and majoritarian rule alike were inadequate to the challenges of the moment. Burgess and his colleagues sought to meet them with stronger stuff. A central component of this was to be a sound account of human difference.

The "Most Serious and Delicate Task"

The rapid pace of immigration lent urgency to this effort. Like many American intellectuals in this period, however, Burgess and his students were primarily concerned with coming to terms with the country's—and their—recent past. It was a past that seemed to call for a radical rethinking of American political life. The democratic experiment had not been meant to erupt in a bloody conflagration. Nor did the rapidly expanding and often ruinously volatile economy of the post–Civil War era fit the picture of the sturdy producers' republic that previous theory had painted. The faith of the founders seemed "absurdly obsolete" and replacing it would require understanding the causes and consequences of the war.[30]

Burgess's political science was committed to this project. For him, the "most serious and delicate task in literature and morals" was to write the history of the United States from 1816 through the outbreak of the Civil War. A new and correct understanding of this period was to his mind the key to developing a "national opinion upon the fundamental principles of our polity" and to beginning to settle political questions on the "merits" rather than through the lenses of sectional prejudice.[31] Burgess also had a personal stake in coming to terms with the conflict and in reconciling Northern and Southern perspectives. Born in 1844 to a slave-holding, Unionist family in Tennessee, and spending his adult life among the Northeastern elite, he more than once characterized his life's work as a response to his firsthand experiences of the Civil War and the (to his mind) catastrophic experiment in racial equality that followed it.

Burgess retrospectively described his Civil War experiences in terms of persecution, exile, and finally revelation. According to his 1934 memoir, he was driven from his home as a teenager by thuggish, secessionist "freelances" who "took this occasion to wreak their vengeance upon their unionist neighbors for every personal grudge which existed between them, as well as for political differences." Threatened with conscription into Confederate forces, he was forced to flee on a half-hour's notice, under cover of darkness and alone save for "a beautiful mare" that his father had "ordered . . . a negro" to prepare for him. After a grueling journey (the horse didn't make it), he reached Federal lines and volunteered as a scout for the Union Army, painfully aware that he would be executed as a traitor if Confederate forces captured him.[32]

It was during this "frightful experience" that he divined "the first suggestion" of his future calling. His memoir recounts a night of sentinel duty, overlooking the aftermath of a battle and straining his "eyes to peer into the darkness" and his "ears to perceive the first sounds of an approaching enemy": "I found myself murmuring to myself: 'Is it not possible for man, a being of reason, created in the image of God, to solve the problems of his existence by the power of reason and without recourse to the destructive means of physical violence?' And I then registered the vow in heaven that if a kind of Providence would deliver me alive from the perils of the existing war, I would devote my life to teaching men how to live by reason and compromise instead of by bloodshed and destruction."[33]

Deliverance came not long after, in the form of a discharge followed by a northward journey to take up undergraduate studies at Amherst College. At Amherst, Burgess met the Hegelian philosopher Julius Seelye, whom Burgess described as "the man for whom I had been all my previous life looking." Seelye taught him that universal reason was the "substance of all things" and that "it was the duty of man and the purpose of his existence to bring the precepts of reason to consciousness and . . . embody them in . . . thought and conduct, law and policy."[34]

Only a handful of doctoral programs existed in the United States at the time, and they were restricted to the natural sciences. For an advanced degree in any other field, ambitious Americans were forced to go to Europe. American students were attracted to German universities over French and English ones for intellectual reasons—including the exciting atmosphere of the "romantic rebellion against the Enlightenment," the comparatively freewheeling nature of German intellectual debate, and the prominent role that scholars enjoyed in German public life at that time—but also for the financial inducements they offered and their relative profligacy with degrees. French universities required nine years of study with annual examinations. In Germany, however, matriculation was "a formality" and a student could return to the United States with a doctorate after studying for just two years and producing a brief thesis.[35] In 1871, Burgess set off on the latter path, deepening his immersion in German idealism and social thought with courses in philosophy, political science, public law, and ethnology at the Universities of Göttingen, Leipzig, and Berlin.

During the course of his studies, Burgess observed firsthand both the return of the victorious imperial troops to Germany after the Franco-Prussian War and the ouster of President Adolphe Thiers that brought the conservative Patrice de Mac-Mahon into power in France. Burgess considered these political experiences to have been as educational as his studies. He thrilled to see "the power of the new Germany make its triumphal entrance into the new imperial capital" and felt privileged to have "practically [seen] the German Empire constructed, both militarily and civilly."[36] Moreover, despite some initial republican concern that France might be on course for a return to the monarchy, he soon saw that Mac-Mahon's ascension "signified, happily for France . . . that the radical tendencies of the Revolution had been checked and that the Republic had been saved from threatened anarchy."[37]

Burgess's European sojourn lasted two years, after which he returned to the United States determined that the life's mission he had glimpsed during "that awful winter's night" in 1863 would be furthered by implementing German-style advanced academic training at home.[38] A first attempt at Amherst College was rebuffed by the administration. Columbia offered better, if still not glowing, prospects. He found the place "a small old-fashioned college" and the student body mainly "rich loafers."[39] If the college itself was slight and old-fashioned, its law school, where Burgess also had an appointment, was "technical" with a "stiff, required course of study" useful only for "imparting a knowledge of existing law."[40] Columbia's trustees, however, held the "promise of the future," and allies on the board warmed to his vision of a school "for developing and improving the law as a science."[41] With their help, and after four years of strenuous politicking, the school was finally established in 1880.

Ultimately assuming a deanship, Burgess oversaw the institution of many now-typical aspects of modern PhD programs, including distinct academic departments and the predominance of the seminar.[42] More important for present purposes, he created the conditions for an academic discipline of politics in the United States, supplying it with an institutional home and exemplary form, a "core" intellectual framework and standard of rigor, and a cohort of American-trained scholars qualified to teach it at the college and graduate levels.[43]

In many ways, then, the study of politics as it took shape in the university setting in the United States was an explicit attempt to meet the challenges of the Gilded Age with better ideas and a wider perspective than those that had seemingly failed antebellum America so spectacularly. Burgess, his colleagues, and his students were particularly focused on understanding the causes of the Civil War and the lessons of its aftermath. At a deeper level, avoiding the mistakes of previous generations appeared to require new answers to the urgent questions the conflict had raised: What binds a nation? Where does sovereignty lie? What does it mean to be self-governing? What are the limits of self-government?

Several things seemed clear: No fictitious social contract was capable of creating a solidary national community, and rights claims could be profoundly dangerous when asserted by parts against the whole of society. Moreover, grand statements of human equality and rights in the Declaration of Independence and abolitionist doctrine, however noble in the abstract, were not objective descriptions of reality but rather exemplified the sort of a priori reasoning and "mystical enthusiasm" that the late nineteenth century could ill afford.[44] These articles of an earlier political faith needed to be tempered by a sober appreciation, based in historical experience and scientific advance, of the source and limits of rights, and of how human difference shaped historical development and political life.

It was an article of scientific consensus at the time that one way human difference mattered was in determining who could thrive in which parts of the world. Indeed, what Robert Vitalis has called the "first law of international relations theory" was the conviction, popularized in the antebellum period by Robert Knox's *The Races of Men*, that whites could thrive only in temperate zones, and blacks only in the tropics.[45] Gilded Age students of American history and politics placed this law, in Bryce's phrase, "at the bottom" of the Civil War. Bryce, for example, saw the importation of slaves as a natural response to the fact that Southern winters were "cool enough to be reinvigorative, and to enable a race drawn from Northern Europe to thrive and multiply," but the summers were "too hot for such a race." Unfortunately, the "industrial and social conditions that were due to climate" had set up an irresoluble conflict with the North.[46]

Burgess held that American slavery had come to the North as one of many "social customs," based originally on the "firmly and universally established opinion of the time." However, like Bryce, he subscribed to the theory that the "chief causes" of its eventual concentration in the South and the sectional conflict that followed lay in the interplay of geography and biology. Slave labor was unproductive in the North, where it was "too cold for [negroes] to thrive" and where difficult farming conditions "required a great deal . . . of intelligence, thrift, and industry in the laborer." The southern colonies, on the contrary, had "vast, level areas of good soil," "warm, uniform climate," and "simple crops." These provided "conditions favorable to the employment of negro labor" and ultimately to the development of a society and an economy fatally incompatible with the northern system.[47]

Slavery had not been an unqualified error, however. Because Africans were "proof against" the malaria and hot climate that debilitated whites in the tropics, slave labor had in fact been necessary for the United States to realize its "manifest destiny." As Burgess wrote in the second of a three-volume American history,

> It is not easy to see how the rich-swamp lands of [the southern and southeastern] colonies could ever have been reclaimed and made tributary to the civilization of the world in any way but by the employment of negro labor. And it is not easier to see how the negro could then have been brought to do this great work save through slavery to the white race . . . under the direction of the superior intelligence of the white race, to the realization of objects determined by that superior intelligence. . . . And the pure negro would not at that period of his development labor voluntarily.

As Burgess saw it, slavery had served a useful dialectical function on the level of consciousness, as well. The "excessive nationalism" of the slave system called forth abolition, which, however misguided in his view, contained progressive elements that helped to shake the country out of its philosophical impasse.[48]

For Burgess, then, the problem was not simply the fact of slavery, or even that race and geography had combined to unleash dynamics that culminated in inevitable conflict. It was that natural rights theory had been inadequate to illuminate and direct those dynamics, with disastrous consequences. The correct course would have been for North and South to come together around a common understanding that, by the mid-nineteenth century, "the time had come for a modification of the existing form of negro slavery in the South."[49] However, because abolitionists clung to their abstract ideals, and Southern slaveholders to their material self-interest, progress had come too drastically and at far too high a price.

For Burgess, Reconstruction further showed that the Civil War had not broken the hold of misguided ideals or base materialism among those who controlled the nation's destiny. Just as the fiction of a social contract had provided a rationale for secession, the fanatical passion of abolitionists for an (in Burgess's mind) illusory ideal of equality had led the Republican Party to its "great mistake" of granting suffrage to the emancipated slaves. This meant subjecting whites to the "political control" of "ignorant barbarians" and to the profiteering of northern "carpet-bags."[50] Indeed, if Burgess's life's work began to come clear to him on the Civil War battlefield, it crystallized again in an encounter with Reconstruction-era Tennessee. That "mournful experience" appears in his memoir as follows: "My own parents as well as all my former friends were living in more or less of distress and poverty, and the entire political and social structure was demoralized. It was in the midst of the so-called carpet-bag era, when the respectable and intelligent white people were disenfranchised and ignored, and the negroes, led by Northern adventurers, ruled and plundered the land. Neither property nor life nor chastity was safe, and men and women of the better sort longed to be laid at rest."

In Burgess's retelling, this spectacle prompted him to resolve "again that if the Providence which conducts the affairs of men would only sustain and direct me, I would give my life to the work of substituting reason for passion in determining the course of States and nations." A "thoroughly impartial" accounting of the Civil War and Reconstruction would be part of this work, helping to elicit from the north a "sincere and genuine acknowledgement" that Reconstruction had been blundered. This was necessary to secure "real national brotherhood" between southern and northern whites. Burgess saw the Hayes-Tilden compromise, which effectively ended Reconstruction, as the first step toward just such an admission, however tacit. As he put it, the North was "learning every day by valuable experience that there are vast differences in political capacity between the races."[51]

Furthering the work of this anything but "impartial" accounting were Burgess's junior colleague, the political theorist and historian William Archibald Dunning, and a group of younger, mostly Southern historians whom the two men trained at Columbia.[52] One of Burgess's prize pupils, Dunning did his doctorate at Columbia and remained there for the rest of his career, rapidly rising to the Lieber professorship of history and political philosophy. Thirteen years younger than Burgess, and a northerner by birth (from Plainfield, New Jersey), educated at Dartmouth College and in New York and Berlin, Dunning shared neither Burgess's firsthand experience of the Civil War battlefield nor his personal stake in Reconstruction. All the same, perhaps even more than his older colleague, Dunning was responsible for elevating the study of that period to a central place in American historiography and political analysis and for constructing an image of it that commanded widespread scholarly acceptance for most of the twentieth century. Burgess and Dunning's students produced a raft of state-level studies that, with varying degrees of vitriol, denounced the corruption of "carpetbaggers," "scalawags," and black legislators and glorified the efforts of white "redeemers" to resist "Africanizing" the southern states.[53] For their part, Burgess and Dunning contributed sweeping, synthetic interpretations of Reconstruction as the tragic misadventure of a Radical Republican Congress in thrall to delusions of natural equality.[54] As both made clear, these were not conclusions of purely historical interest. Each was adamant that the lessons of 1816 through Reconstruction needed to be applied to pressing, current questions of immigration, the emerging regulatory state, and world affairs. And Burgess put his understanding of Reconstruction at the heart of the account of history, political change, and the sources of sovereignty and democratic legitimacy on which he built his political science.

The Teutonic "State" and the Science of History

Bryce observed, not without apprehension, that "one of the greatest achievements of science" up to his lifetime had been "making the world small."[55] This meant, above all, a new world of migration and contact between races. Burgess, too, viewed this development with alarm. He saw that his generation had paid the price for the failure of unenlightened nationalism and eighteenth-century philosophy alike to appreciate properly the sources of national cohesion, the significance of racial difference, and the place of each in the progress of history. The new professional political science he sought to lead would, he hoped, avoid the same mistake for the twentieth century.

For Bryce, scientific advances may have been contributing to the problem, but scientific inquiry also promised to reveal solutions, or at least proper responses.[56] And for scholars of politics in the United States at the time, "science" signified above all the science of history. Both Burgess and Bryce were steeped in "Teutonism" or "Anglo-Saxonism." This school of historical interpretation, much in vogue in England and America in the mid-nineteenth century, emphasized the continuity of history, holding that English and American institutions reflected an unbroken line of evolutionary development from antecedents in the ancient Germanic forests. Bryce was schooled in this tradition by the English historian E. A. Freeman, and his work reflects the Teutonist emphasis on both Anglo-Saxon supremacy and the centrality of race to political life more broadly.[57] However, Bryce himself was more interested in the newness and innovations to be found in America, and his celebrated *American Commonwealth* moved away from

Teutonism's emphasis on continuous development in favor of dense description of the country as he found it.

Burgess, however, put Teutonism front and center as he elaborated what was to become the dominant theoretical framework for university-based political science in the United States in the Gilded Age. This was the idea, laid out most thoroughly in *Political Science and Comparative Constitutional Law*, that sovereignty and legitimacy were to be found in an organic, racialized unity termed "the state" that stood in "back of" and "distributed" its power to institutions of governance.[58] Midcentury northern publicists, notably Lieber, had used similar language to recruit Anglo-Saxonism to the cause of the Union, basing the Constitution's authority in an "ethnoracial nation" deeper than and previous to any contract between states.[59] This idea was to hold great appeal for scholars in the 1880s and 1890s. Indeed, for Burgess, "the state" was the key to a scientific study of politics, and racial homogeneity was the key to the state's development.

The state was at once spiritual and material, universal and embodied—Hegelian idealism infused with late nineteenth-century racial anthropology and social evolutionism.[60] It represented "the gradual and continuous development of human society . . . [and] of the universal principles of human nature" but was at the same time rooted in the "ethnologic concept" of the "nation" and "relations of birth and race-kinship." Only the Teutonic (or Aryan) nations inherited the capacity to realize the highest form of the state. Latin and Greek civilizations had more limited political genius; Asia and Africa were home to only "unpolitical nations."[61]

There was little that was original or idiosyncratic in the basic outlines of Teutonist state theory. Anglo-Saxonist history was well established, and the Gilded Age "saw Anglo-Saxon chauvinism pervade the upper reaches of American scholarly and political life."[62] Burgess's achievement, which he shared to an extent with the Johns Hopkins University historian Herbert Baxter Adams, was to modernize this tradition, pursuing it with the zeal for rigorous, empirical methodology that was the hallmark of German historiography and embedding it in a newly professionalizing discipline.[63]

The German approach involved above all commitment to a Rankean reconstruction of the past "as it really was" through painstaking work with primary sources as well as archaeological, geographic, philological, and other scientific investigation.[64] And, indeed, both Burgess and Adams grounded their work in voluminous, careful, legal and historical research. They were also affected by the excitement that a progressionist version of

Darwinism, along with Herbert Spencer's application of it to the social world, generated among late nineteenth-century scholars, who were evolutionists "almost to a man."[65] As a result, Adams and Burgess produced versions of Teutonism that differed from their predecessors' in being more pronouncedly laced with metaphors and assertions from ethnology and biology.[66] And of course the fact that they operated within universities where they were able to establish graduate programs meant that their Teutonism became the basis for training a generation of younger American scholars.

In Adams's case, scientific history translated into minute excavations of the evolution of this or that New England tradition (town forms, traditional offices, etc.) from early Germanic prototypes, an enterprise that came to be known as "Teutonic germ theory."[67] Proud to have established his history seminar in a converted biology lab, Adams likened his library of legal and historical documents to a natural history museum and argued that his methods extended the insights of evolutionary biology into the field of history. The "science of Biology," he wrote, "no longer favors the theory of spontaneous generation. Wherever organic life occurs there must have been some seed for that life," and a Teutonic "germ" taking root in American soil was the seed of its democratic institutions.[68] Scholars could illuminate the natural history of this process by "dissect[ing] government documents" and generally using "the laboratory method of work."[69]

While both scholars operated within a Hegelian framework and both located sovereignty in an organic community with Teutonic roots, Burgess's program was perhaps more ambitious than Adams's. Burgess sought to understand and vouchsafe the future of liberty. To do so, he thought, required specifying its past and tracing its development. In *Political Science and Comparative Constitutional Law*, he compared the fundamental political institutions of the United States, Germany, Great Britain, and France, measuring each in terms of its contribution to the great problem of "reconciling government with liberty;" that is, of combining strong national sovereignty with the greatest measure of individual autonomy. This synthesis would be the chief characteristic of "the national State . . . the self-conscious democracy, the *ultima Thule* of political history."[70]

The Teutonic state was nothing less than the developing self-consciousness toward which all political history was groping, and it was in this national consciousness that the truth of sovereignty could be found. It, and not any aggregate of individuals, was the "self" in "self-government";

true liberty arose not from "mere ideas" about "the things . . . called natural rights" but only "through the action of the national State inscribing these ideas of individual immunity against governmental power" in fundamental law.[71]

The United States and its institutions represented the apogee of the state thus far achieved, and continuing its development was the "prime" and special "mission of the ideal American commonwealth."[72] However, as recent history had so vividly demonstrated, success was not assured. A "correct and profound appreciation of the historical development of the state" was the "only protection" against the ever-present "danger of diverging from the true path" to its successful realization.[73] In other words, since Burgess's political science was devoted to explicating the historical development of the state, the discipline was charged with nothing less than stewarding the future of democracy and the possibility of liberty.

Fortunately, in the United States political scientists had good material to work with. The revolutionary basis of the American republic meant that with traditional encumbrances swept away, Americans had "seen the state organized" in its purest form in the Constitution, with its system of balanced, separated powers at once ensuring democracy and guarding against its excesses.[74] This self-organization of the state—not any compact of preexisting subjects or commonwealths—produced the Constitution. The Constitution, in turn, provided the basis for the legal doctrines and institutions that emerged as the state evolved toward its most perfect realization.

We have seen that this account provided a strong argument for the Union: If the states (plural) were created by a preexisting, sovereign unity ("the state," singular), secessionist demands based on claims of a prior independent existence were nonsensical. Burgess's account also constructed democratic legitimacy on the basis of a distinctly limited democracy. If the development of the state was to be seen in laws and legal institutions, judges and legal scholars—those Burgess admiringly called "the aristocracy of the robe"—would be better suited to maintain it on its course than any mechanisms of popular democracy.[75] That is, democratic legitimacy was grounded in the organic law produced by the nation's historical development rather than in natural rights, social contracts, electoral processes, or any manifestation of popular politics whatsoever.[76] From this perspective, the state itself, and not the people (in any mundane sense), was the subject of popular sovereignty.

The preeminence of state and "Teutonic germ" theory, however thorough in its moment, was relatively short-lived. As late as 1903, a young Charles E. Merriam, then a recent graduate of Burgess's department, was still referring to Burgess's version of state theory as "the new system" and the culmination of "a change from the rather haphazard style of discussing political theory in earlier days to a more scientific way of approaching the questions of politics."[77] Already by that point, however, Burgess no longer occupied a place at the center of the discipline—he was conspicuously absent from the leadership of the newly organizing American Political Science Association (see Chapters 2 and 3)—and many of Adams's students were growing weary of laboriously researching foregone conclusions.[78] Worse, two decades later, a report on the Second National Conference on the Science of Politics (in which the very same Merriam, by then having assumed a Burgess-esque place in the discipline, played a leading role), categorized Burgess's work and Teutonism more generally as "Pre-Scientific Studies" based on "speculation."[79]

How that happened, and what happened to Burgess-style race thinking in the process, is the subject of the rest of this book. For now, it is enough to imagine how maddening Burgess must have found this characterization, given that state theory was meant precisely as the antithesis of speculation. Burgess explicitly understood himself as engaged in a scientific revolt against what Elisha Mulford (something of a transitional figure between Lieber's group of nationalist writers and Burgess's contemporaries) called the "formulas and abstractions" that had seemingly dominated American political discourse since the Revolutionary generation. The condition of political science," Mulford wrote, was the "apprehension of the nation as an organism": "It involves the distinction of an art and a science; there may be, for instance, an art in building heaps of stones, but there is no science of stoneheaps. The unity and identity of structure in an organism, in which a law of action may be inferred, form the condition of positive science."[80]

For Burgess, race (that is, "relations of birth and race-kinship") was the basis of the "unity and identity of structure" in the "organism" that was the state. Social contracts and natural rights belonged to the realm of philosophy. "History and ethnology" offered "elevated ground," a "standpoint" from which to make valid political judgments.[81] For example, as we have seen, Burgess located both the source and limit of popular sovereignty in the state. The basis for this apparent anomaly Burgess found on precisely that "elevated ground."

From this vantage point, it appeared clear to Burgess that it would not be safe for "the popular or democratic form" to "exert its greatest influence" until America had "perfected its nationality." That is, a truly "national" state would "permit . . . the participation of the governed in the government" because in a Teutonic state the population would support only "the enactment and administration of laws . . . whose effect will be the realization of the truest liberty."[82] However, in the late nineteenth century, "the ethnic character" of the American population was "very cosmopolitan . . . , conglomerated, so to speak, with other elements, numerically quite strong," such as "Celts," "Mongols," and "negroes." To make matters worse, the United States was fairly "prodigal" with suffrage.[83] Therefore, it remained necessary to limit legislative power and other instruments of popular control in favor of a strong federal judiciary.

Burgess worried that even in the heyday of his theory, its implications were never sufficiently appreciated by many readers. He lamented in his memoir that his work was misunderstood as "the 'Leviathan' of modern political science," and that his critics never recognized that the state as it developed would *limit* government, not glorify it.[84] Indeed, Burgess exhibited a clear antipathy to the emerging regulatory apparatus of government, which he saw as an unwarranted intrusion of mass whims on the sphere of liberty guaranteed by the state.[85]

This, too, was racialized, in that Burgess viewed those demanding economic regulation as "foreign" or corrupted by "foreign elements" and therefore as outside that protected sphere of liberty. In an 1895 essay titled "The Ideal of the American Commonwealth," Burgess characterized America as "already based upon ideal principles" and as having "advanced many stages in an ideal development." For this reason, he wrote, "we are compelled" to view people favoring a "revolution" of that system "as the enemies in principle of the American republic and of the political civilization of the world."[86]

Three sources threatened such revolution: sectionalism, "pollution" by "non-Aryan elements," and "so-called socialistic movements." Sectionalism, while largely defeated in the Civil War, had demonstrated its terrible power in that conflict and still threatened in the form of Populism. For their part, the threats of non-Aryan pollution and socialism were linked by the fact that "looking to government" was a (Southern- and Eastern-) "European habit." The strength of socialism in the United States, then, was owed to "the immense immigration into our population of that very element of Europe's population to which such propositions appeal." [87]

These threats led Burgess, despite his suspicion of regulatory measures and zeal for liberty, to embrace a draconian interpretation of government's police powers in some cases.[88] The element that threatened American liberty by importing socialistic ideas also constituted a threat by its very nature—the disorder to which those non-Aryan European populations were prone might be a justification for increased governmental capacity on a permanent basis. This meant that the "conclusions of practical politics" that followed from state theory included the "prime policy"—indeed, "duty"—of a modern constitutional government "to attain proper physical boundaries and to render its population ethnically homogeneous," thereby following "the indications of nature and aid[ing] the ethnical impulse to conscious development." Similarly, government could permissibly "insist . . . upon the use of a common language and upon the establishment of homogeneous institutions and laws." This could include the use of force, which when put to such ends, was "not only justifiable . . . but morally obligatory." Government might, for example, "righteously deport" any "ethnically hostile population," and ought to secure borders against "deleterious" foreign influences.[89] Identifying "disorderly" with racialized groups allowed Burgess to embrace both liberty (for the uncorrupted Teutons) and authoritarianism (for everyone else).

One of Burgess's prize pupils, Richmond Mayo-Smith, took a similar position in his extensive work on immigration. This is perhaps even more striking in Mayo-Smith's case. While no radical, Mayo-Smith took far more moderate and labor-friendly political stances than his mentor. So his views are harder to dismiss as a pure rationalization of reactionary ideology.

A statistician and political economist, Mayo-Smith was among the founders of the American Economic Association (AEA). Richard T. Ely had founded the AEA in 1885 in order to create a home for institutionalist economics, an alternative to neoclassical theory that was friendlier to state-led reform efforts. As Ely put it in an early mission statement for the group, the neoclassical principle of laissez-faire was "unsafe in politics and unsound in morals."[90] Mayo-Smith was a moderate figure—in fact Ely recruited him, along with E. R. A. Seligman, another moderately reformist Columbia-affiliated economist, in part to soften any image of the AEA as a home for left politics. Still, Mayo-Smith viewed the question of government regulation as a matter of expediency more than principle, seeking to develop statistical methods that could evaluate policy initiatives on a case-by-case basis. He also evinced considerably more solicitude for the working classes than Burgess did, developing close ties to labor and to the settlement house movement.[91] Nonetheless, this solicitude only applied to racially acceptable members of the working class, and especially to those who were already present on U.S. soil.

Mayo-Smith deployed the framework of state theory against the claim that universal, natural rights claims might be relevant to immigration policy. Like Burgess, he cast the very notion of such rights as a misunderstanding, born of a narrowness of vision that mistakes the present state of things for eternal truth. In his view, rights and liberties were "merely historical," a grant conferred by a state that "may also withdraw it." And even if such rights had developed, they would be trumped by America's "duty to humanity" to exclude "the depraved dregs of European civilization" and thereby to see to it "that civilization progresses."[92]

Indeed, America's immigrant past could only properly be understood within this framework of progress. In its earlier, lower state of civilization, America needed foreign population to claim the continent's vast resources. The harshness of the early period of settlement mitigated the danger of welcoming that labor since the difficult conditions of the early years fortunately "kill[ed] off a large number of those consigned" to them. Even so, as a nation progressed, Mayo-Smith argued, it lost its "capacity of absorbing the lower elements of other civilizations," and America was "getting to the limit set by nature" for the "work" of offering "opportunity to the poor and degraded of Europe." This did not represent a loss, however, because humanity's interest did not lie in the fate of its degraded members but rather in that of its elite: the "duty of every nation" was "to see to it that the higher civilization triumphs over the lower" by "preserving its own civilization against the disintegrating forces of barbarism."[93]

A similar logic explains why Burgess, who pronounced fulsomely on the duties of the Teutonic nations to have "a colonial policy," opposed expansion of American empire overseas when that became a practical possibility.[94] Burgess described the Spanish-American War and subsequent annexation of the Philippines as "the first great shock" of his professional career and, along with his colleagues, devoted many pages of the Columbia-based *Political Science Quarterly* (*PSQ*) to arguments against such a premature adventure.[95] In a typical passage, Burgess wrote, "So long as we do not inhabit two-thirds of the territory on this continent; so long as we have not explored, much less exploited, its resources; so long as we remain in large measure a mixed population of Americans, Europeans and Africans; . . . so long as we have an Indian problem and a Mormon problem and a negro problem, to say nothing of many less important questions—so long, it seems to me, we should more nearly follow the natural order of things, if we should remain at home and attend to our own domestic affairs."[96]

Burgess's "despondency and despair" at the American declaration of war was a response also to what he perceived as the eagerness of the business class to promote war "for the sake of profiteering by the vast increase of governmental expenditures." Quite apart from the greed this displayed, Burgess believed those expenditures and the demands of war would occasion an unwarranted increase in government (as opposed to "state") power. Also, much like the greedy nationalism to which the antebellum South had fallen prey, this fervor for war would divert from the progress of American liberty by adding the burdens of colonial administration and a new, racially inferior population. Particularly distressing was "to see that Americans were, after all, a warlike people, superficially informed, and easy to incite on Quixotic enterprises." That is, the best representatives of the American nation had not, as expected, advocated limited government and the further Aryanization of the American population as a principled stand, irrespective of baser motives.[97]

Burgess's shock that the American business class might put profit over principle may seem naïve (even if the principle in question was a commitment to racial purity). At the same time, it highlights the degree to which Burgess saw the world in racialized terms—the Teutonic genius was meant to show itself in that race's best men, and if America's upper classes couldn't be trusted to make sound and sober judgments, even in the face of recent experience and scientific advance, this would be a serious blow. However, the point is not to evaluate the strength of Burgess's analysis. It is, rather, that Burgess's "attempt to apply the method, which has been found so productive in the domain of Natural Science, to Political Science and Jurisprudence" relied centrally on the idea that historical progress was racial progress.[98]

By the turn of the twentieth century, Burgess's work would come to seem increasingly old-fashioned. A younger generation of political scientists, including future U.S. President Woodrow Wilson, would reject Burgess's intellectual style and many of his conclusions. Nevertheless, many of the racial ideas shaping the older man's thought would recur in his successors' work, and others would be only subtly recast. As the next chapters will show, the idea that organic, racialized "peoples" were the protagonists of history and the true subjects of democracy would outlive the Hegelianism in which state theory had embedded it. And no less than their teachers, many younger political scientists would put the racial "lessons" of the Civil War and Reconstruction at the center of a scientific account of politics.

"All Things Lawful Are Not Expedient": The American Political Science Association Considers Jim Crow

For all John W. Burgess's influence, his elaborate theoretical edifice did not long survive intact, and elements of it were subject to challenge even as he remained the discipline's leading figure. One of the sharpest such challenges came as early as 1891 from future U.S. President Woodrow Wilson. At the time, Wilson was newly teaching jurisprudence and political economy at Princeton University, having completed his studies under Herbert Baxter Adams at Johns Hopkins and published his thesis, *Congressional Government*, to wide acclaim.[1] Wilson took unpitying aim at Burgess in a review of *Political Science and Comparative Constitutional Law* in the *Atlantic Monthly*. The review blasted everything from the older man's "mechanical" style to his "extraordinary dogmatic readiness to force many intricate and diverse things to accommodate themselves to a few simple formulas." If that weren't enough, Wilson continued that it was "characteristic of [Burgess] to have no doubts; to him the application of his analysis seem[ed] the perfect and final justification of it." Burgess's "thoughtful readers," Wilson predicted, would "experience much more difficulty and have many more doubts."[2]

Wilson's screed signaled what would shortly become a pervasive critique of Burgess's mode of political science. Wilson and like-minded scholars, such as Henry Jones Ford, Albert Shaw, Frank Goodnow, and others seeking to further professionalize the discipline in the early twentieth century, found Burgess-style political science to be legalistic and unmoored from any empirical foundation. They also affirmed that the past, so central to Teutonism, was an inadequate guide to the rapidly shifting world they sought to understand. That new world might not be as desired, but the old one could not be recovered. Nor did it hold the keys to the future. As Leo Stanton Rowe was to exhort in 1897, a modern, scientific study of politics would have to come to terms with "new relations" whether one liked them or not.[3]

All the same, none of these scholars rejected Burgess's racialism. Wilson's work was typical in this respect. Wilson sought to move away from the older man's idealist, historicist intellectual style but maintained many of Burgess's fundamental precepts, including a racialized conception of the collective shaping and authorizing government. (Indeed, his one concession to Burgess in the 1891 review was that Burgess's formulation of "the state" as the "more enduring . . . entity . . . , which gives to the government its form and vitality" was "serviceable."[4]) Wilson's well-received 1889 text-book, *The State*, for example, rehearsed all the familiar elements of state theory: the Aryan origins of the Anglo-American political tradition; a link between Teutonic history and the development of individual liberty; an explicit rejection of universalizing, natural law or social-compact theory; and a notion of the "organic political life" of a community as the source of sovereignty.[5]

Wilson's fundamental issue with Burgess seems to have been that state theory left little room in American political life for creativity or any real novelty. As Wilson saw it, Burgess's work cast political progress as "unconscious and unintelligent," leaving "nothing for us to do."[6] To be relegated to such passivity was anathema to a fast-rising public figure such as Wilson, who saw great changes afoot and imagined an active role in directing them for great, visionary men (such as himself). Thus, in his hands, "the state" shed much of its prescriptive, normative thrust.

The full title of Wilson's book on the topic gives an indication of the direction in which the concept of "the state" was to move in his work, and subsequently. First subtitled *Elements of Historical and Practical Politics*, the book bore a second, distinctly government-centric subtitle: *A Sketch of Institutional History and Administration*. Wilson was already a leading voice in the newly popular study of administration, and his treatment of the state gave prominent attention to the practical principles of governing, which he presented as significantly continuous across government systems. So throughout the book's nearly 700 pages, government and its functions received more attention, and the Teutonic state appeared less as a singular, world-historic actor and more as one kind of state among many. Moreover, the organic will behind government also appeared in altered form, with the word "state" substituted by the broader "society."[7]

In this, Wilson resembles James Bryce, whom he much admired (and eventually resembled, in that both enjoyed illustrious and internationally significant careers in practical politics). Bryce, too, had focused on the living institutions and quotidian practices of American politics, the nature of which he attributed to "opinion," "character," and material "circumstance." The same year *The State* appeared, Wilson praised Bryce's *The American Commonwealth* for demonstrating that American institutions were "the expression of the national life," which was shaped both by "forces permanent in the history of the English race" and "peculiar influences . . . operative in our separate experience."[8] That is, as much as Wilson and Bryce privileged the real over the ideal—government itself over "the state"—each maintained the link between political institutions and a racial collectivity. Similarly, both men sought to show history as at once "a record of the progress toward civilization of races originally barbarous" in accordance with their innate capacities *and* meaningfully shaped by contingency and "circumstance."[9]

The State was meant for students, a "general clarification" of "systems of government and the main facts of institutional history" arrived at "through the use of a thorough comparative and historical method."[10] Not surprisingly, then, it presented the conventional wisdom in political science, inflected with newer currents in political scholarship, in particular the imperative to look past legal forms to the practices of political life. Likewise Bryce, a generation older, had begun to give a realistic slant to a traditional approach by disdaining the niceties of state theory while preserving much of its thrust, including the linkage of national character, race, and political institutions, as well as the suggestion of a collective political subject residing outside, and breathing life into, formal institutions.

However, while both men retained the idea that a collective consciousness shaped and animated government, in their work this collectivity was beginning to take a less specific form and to lose much of its particularly political character. Where race had once been the essence that political forms expressed, in their work and subsequently these things increasingly appeared in dynamic relationship to one another. Moreover, these authors, like many who would follow them, sought to shift the discipline's focus away from the source of sovereignty and the justification of democracy and toward the day-to-day workings of institutions in an actually existing democratic polity. Crucially, this would include the practical "reality" of racial difference.

Reform and Racial Difference

At the turn of the twentieth century, U.S. political science lacked a central institutional home outside Columbia's Academy of Political Science, which was dominated by students, faculty, and alumni from that university. However, the idea of an independent, national, professional organization gained traction as the PhDs trained there, at Johns Hopkins, and at even younger graduate programs (notably the University of Wisconsin and the University of Chicago) spread to teach courses in political science in colleges and universities nationwide.[11] A series of planning sessions in 1902 culminated the following year at a meeting of the American Historical Association (AHA) with the announcement of a new American Political Science Association.[12] The political science group selected Columbia's Frank Goodnow as its first president and held its first independently organized meeting in Chicago in 1904.

The original plan had been for a society of "comparative legislation," but the APSA's founders aspired to understand the "actual practices" of politics beyond what Wilson, borrowing a term from Walter Bagehot, had disparagingly called its "literary" (i.e., legal) forms.[13] Accordingly, it was decided that the association would encompass the "entire field of political science."[14] After attending the first planning meeting in 1902, Burgess disappeared from any important role in the new association, which came to be spearheaded primarily by younger men representing a range of institutions, not exclusively academic.[15]

Exactly how Burgess was sidelined is murky. What is clear, however, is that the leadership of the new APSA wished to chart a new course. When Goodnow gave APSA's first presidential address, he put his listeners on notice that from then forward the discipline would not "permit" the "political philosopher . . . to roam at will, subject to no check on the exuberancy of his fancy or caprice." Rather, political scholarship would attend scrupulously to "the extra-legal customs and extra-legal organizations" that shape the "actual political system of a country."[16]

This shift would leave the discipline less explicitly anchored to a theory of American democracy as Aryan *Volksgeist* and as a result would authorize a more experimental and pragmatic view of American institutions. Interpreting the development of the state and remaining true to its spirit had been Burgess's central preoccupations. For many younger political scientists, "science" and "spirit" were antithetical terms. To qualify as the former, political scholarship had to offer a hardheaded appraisal of the facts, uncorrupted by preconceived philosophical frameworks, and point to real-world solutions to urgent problems of the day.

As we have seen, amid this increasing insistence on an inductive, empirical orientation to political life, "the state" did not disappear but began to shed some of its prescriptive force. Where once the term had been central to professional political analysis, signifying the soul of the race and the source of sovereignty, after the turn of the century the idea of a state standing behind and authorizing government increasingly came to signal the more prosaic notion that governing forms and practices reflected, and ought to be appropriate to, the character of a "people."[17] Less concerned with discerning the normative content of history, political scientists like Wilson and like-minded colleagues sought to describe and understand the functioning of American institutions and were open to the idea that those institutions might need fundamental alteration if they were to continue to serve American ideals.

Nonetheless, a racialized conception of "the people" persisted and helped to lend a conservative cast to political scientists' reformism. For example, Wilson no less than Burgess held up Reconstruction as the prime example of a failure to grasp the basic facts of political life and of the ways in which the American system could fail to safeguard the people's will. For many of Wilson's contemporaries, too, Reconstruction served as a cautionary tale about both racial difference and the dangers of political action guided by principle rather than by a dispassionate, scientific estimation of political life as it was. To be scientific, political science would have to attend less to doctrine. Its task, rather, would be to discern how the *practice* of politics could accommodate not only new economic and social realities but also lasting "anthropological" truths.

Both this more pragmatic, experimental attitude and the sense that racial issues were of prime importance put political scientists firmly in the intellectual mainstream at the turn of the century. The Progressive Era in the United States and elsewhere was animated by an intense faith that scientific knowledge could solve social problems. And while progressivism had a left flank that engaged structural economic questions, among many

American progressives, "social problems" often served as shorthand for the existence of people different from themselves and/or operating for whatever reason outside the bounds of familiar norms and hierarchies. Racial (and what were coming to be distinguished as "ethnic") differences received special attention.[18]

Of course the term *progressive* is now applied to a broad range of tendencies, and many intellectuals and other elites at the turn of the century didn't fit the label at all. However, as Rogers Smith puts it, the era nevertheless saw an "elite convergence" on certain ideals and a strong push for government to enact reforms guided by them. In Michael McGerr's gloss, the progressive tendency centered on four "quintessential" ends: "to change other people; to end class conflict; to control big business; and to segregate society." Similarly, Smith connects the various strains of progressivism through a common vision of a "modern democratically and scientifically guided nation that was also culturally ordered, unified, and civilized due to the predominance of northern European elements in its populace and customs."[19]

It was in many ways a frightening period for the educated middle and upper classes. William McKinley's victory over William Jennings Bryan in the 1896 presidential election ended the threat posed by Populism and the radical, farmer-worker alliance that had propelled it. But it did not resolve the issues underlying that insurgency and others like it: the rise of unprecedentedly massive corporations and consolidation of wealth at the top that seemed to threaten republican ideals; a breathtaking pace of urbanization and immigration that transformed the landscape and population; crippling, repeated economic depressions that fueled intense, often violent episodes of labor protest and repression.[20] The cities seemed to be exploding, and at times they actually did—revolutionary anarchists and others bombed and otherwise targeted political and business figures, factories, railroads, and other symbols of capitalist power at the turn of the century regularly enough to make such attacks "a central preoccupation of American politics and culture."[21] The acquisition by the United States of overseas colonies likewise presented challenges to traditional notions of the country's place in the world.

Nonetheless, it was also a time of wild, even utopian hopes among many elites. Where economic, ideological, and demographic changes threatened anarchy, progressives of various political stripes had great faith that scientific insight and the power of the state could be wielded in concert to produce a harmonious, well-ordered society. In *The Promise of American Life*, perhaps the paradigmatic statement of centrist progressivism, Herbert

Croly argued that American prosperity, free political institutions, and the "worthier set of men" these would create offered "the highest hope for an excellent worldly life that mankind has yet ventured."[22] Unlike Burgess and Adams, who looked to the past to guide the present, progressives were predisposed to see modernity itself—big, efficient institutions, including government, corporations, and labor unions; expanded trade; and, for some, overseas territory—as American democracy's best hope for deliverance from the scourges of economic depression, socialism, and general unrest. Fueled by support from industrialists interested in promoting scientific and technical progress, an explosion of professional societies, universities, and specialized journals promised new platforms for a newly self-conscious intellectual class eager to put its expertise at the service of this project.

In this context, many of the first homegrown PhDs in political science in the United States thought that the time was ripe to expand the purview of political scholarship and to make themselves useful to a government that had recently taken on new functions, including the management of an overseas empire. The rapid transformation of the American economy and society since the mid-nineteenth century had, they affirmed, delivered a world qualitatively different from that of the previous generation. The old formulas simply no longer applied.

Burgess's political science sought to legitimate and proscribe, depending on the idea of "the state" to authorize American democracy while simultaneously marking its limits. The dominant tendency among the political scientists who would assume disciplinary leadership after Burgess, however, would be to see the workings of democracy as more pressing than its warrants. Goodnow, along with Wilson and others, consistently emphasized that things like democratic legitimacy and what Goodnow called "that elusive thing called sovereignty" had been problems for a post–Civil War age.[23] "Efficiency" and "administration" were to be the watchwords of the new century, and the organization of the APSA was meant to put political science in step with the times.

To accomplish this, political scholarship would need to move away from the legalism and teleology of earlier years, and toward what appeared to be firmer scientific (that is, realistic, empirical, and inductive) footing. According to Shaw, twentieth-century political science would consist of "the orderly presentation of facts and the formulating of conclusions . . . of practical benefit to the perplexed legislator in time of his need."[24] As a result, things like the search for the Teutonic origins of liberty came to seem much less urgent, even quaint. Political scientists, Wilson urged, needed to focus on how to "*run* a constitution," something that "was getting harder . . . than to frame one."[25]

It is one thing to announce a new course for political knowledge and another to chart one, however. The frequency of calls for empiricism at APSA meetings over the years suggests that many continued to have misgivings about the discipline's progress on that front. And not all observers were left with the impression that the APSA offered anything new or unusual. For example, when *Political Science Quarterly* reviewed the first issue of the *Proceedings of the American Political Science Association*, it affirmed that the "association's field of activity" was to be the "study of the state," with perhaps a novel emphasis on administrative law.[26]

Certainly around this time it became less common for every commentary on a given political event or institution to sweep through the centuries in search of origins and explanations. The valorization of inductivism and fact-gathering, moreover, meant that the writing in political science journals was drained of much of its drama. Page after page of the profession's journals would be stuffed with matter-of-fact reports of legislative and judicial action, political developments, and administrative organization in the United States, Europe, and colonial possessions, often with little in the way of analysis and even less of the lofty pronouncements that Burgess had favored and that Goodnow would mock as "empyrean . . . speculation."[27]

Nevertheless, these shifts masked significant continuities, particularly with regard to questions of racial difference and democratic unity. When Burgess was its leading light, political science had rested heavily on the tenets that races were organic and naturally separate units, that whites (and particularly "Teutons") were superior, and that political interference with the natural racial order was doomed to fail. As we shall see, this did not change as his influence waned. Nor, even as political scientists sought to distance themselves from philosophical generalization, were grand pronouncements about the relative capacities and proper hierarchy of races subject to much in the way of empirical scrutiny. On the contrary, as they had in Burgess's work, invocations of racial difference continued to serve almost as talismans anchoring propositions about political life to seemingly basic facts of nature.

Moreover, if there was a generational break in political science, it was one without an explicitly ideological edge. Despite the general recognition that both new modes of political analysis and governing would be required, most prominent political scientists of Wilson's generation followed Burgess in viewing active government more as a danger than as the democratizing force some left progressives championed.[28] During the Gilded Age, political economy and sociology attracted many young, reform-minded scholars steeped in "dissenting evangelical piety and social millennialism" and seeking new solutions to the "social question." Their political commitments often put them sharply at odds with more conservative colleagues, resulting in hard-fought contests for control of departments and professional associations.[29] However, whereas many aspiring economists and sociologists were animated by alarm at the harms to the masses wrought by capitalism, the group that led APSA tended to view the problem the other way around. In general, political scientists of this generation concerned themselves more with the damage that ill-conceived or excessive democracy might do to a modern, industrial state.[30]

However, there was a general sentiment that a doctrinaire commitment to limited government would no longer suffice. It would be the task of a science of politics and administration to guide government's pursuit of social goals while keeping that pursuit within reasonable limits. Wilson's one-time Johns Hopkins classmate Albert Shaw captured this general feeling in his presidential address to the APSA just a few years after Goodnow's, affirming that, "for better or for worse," new forces—particularly calls for economic regulation—were transforming the country. He was unenthusiastic at this prospect—he preferred "no rules of the game" to "very bad ones" that might "discourage wealth production." Still it was evident that "everywhere there is . . . a powerful determination to make use of . . . governmental power and agency." If, as he believed, this could not be stopped, then the APSA's task was to bring a "moderating" and "scientific spirit" to bear on when and how such power might be used.[31]

Stephen Skowronek casts Wilson's presidency in this light. For Skowronek, Wilson's liberal reforms as president were motivated less by a desire to transform society or its basic hierarchies than to preserve the essence of an old social and racial order in new circumstances.[32] An examination of the racial entailments of Wilson's political science lends support to this view. His scholarship was consistently animated by the sense that the old institutions of American politics had failed and only new arrangements could guarantee the kind of society those institutions had once sustained. However, this was not at all unique to Wilson. An orientation to reform as a method of conservation or recuperation of old values and hierarchies was a common theme in political science journals and meetings during this period.

Wilson's influence probably played a part in promoting this orientation. *Congressional Government*, which was published in 1885, had been an argument for just such a program of reform. That work pointed to a radical disjuncture between the constitutional theory of balanced, separated powers and what Wilson saw as the post–Civil War reality of "congressional supremacy." For Wilson, the central problem with American government was exemplified by the ability of a minority in Congress to enact radical policies, such as Reconstruction (that "extraordinary carnival of public crime" that resulted when freed slaves were thrust into "unnatural" ascendancy over whites).[33]

For most constitutional analysts, the fragmentation of the American system was its defining democratic feature, in that it hindered a potentially tyrannical concentration of power at the top. Wilson saw attachment to this idea as backward-looking and sentimental, arguing that in a context where the real threat came from tyrannical minorities, a strong executive better guaranteed liberty. His model was the British system in which a ruling party controlling both parliament and the prime minister's office provided clearer lines of accountability and democratic control.

Wilson's argument was provocative. In advocating a fundamental reordering of the constitutional system, it displaced Burgess's "ideal American commonwealth"[34] from the pinnacle of political development. It suggested that the flowering of Teutonic liberty might be off course in America or, worse, that no course might be charted at all. Wilson's empiricism was certainly limited—it has been widely noted that he never actually visited Congress while conducting his research. Still, the book was exciting in that it sought to analyze "actual practices" of politics, and not just juridical forms. It received praiseful notice for the sharp contrast it drew between the ideal and the real, as well as for its sense that present politics were more dynamic than previously suggested.

Still, *Congressional Government* was far from a radical screed. As it happened, the terms of present politics were not good, and the changes Wilson advocated were meant to recuperate what could be salvaged of a lost past. Crucially, this included a racial order that had been disrupted by the Civil War and Reconstruction. In Wilson's estimation, after Lincoln's death, organized minorities who controlled the committee system in Congress—

notably the Radical Republicans pushing Reconstruction policies—had run roughshod over the weak executive, resulting in such tyrannical measures as federal election inspectors enforcing black voting rights over the objections of southern whites and the officials whites had elected.[35] For Wilson, the fragmentation of government meant to keep it in check instead provided opportunities for an extremist minority to gain unwonted power and to foist an alien people onto the American electorate.

In the 1885 book, the (mostly implied) remedy was a more deliberative legislature, closely integrated with the executive branch. In his 1908 *Constitutional Government*, Wilson would place more emphasis on the executive, looking "to the President as the unifying force in our complex system, the leader both of his party and of the nation," and as a prudent antidote to an unreflective, minority-driven Congress.[36] As Wilson saw it, the executive reflected the naturally conservative will of the (white) "people" as a whole. That is, the executive embodied or gave expression to something quite akin to Burgess's "state," still identified with the Anglo-Saxon element of the American population but now residing in the presidency rather than in the judiciary. Burgess had looked to the "aristocracy of the robe" to act as the state's check on the capricious power of the legislature.[37] For Wilson, a stronger, more integrated presidential government would take on this role, protecting tradition and safeguarding (whites') liberty against alien influences and the misguided crusades of ideological minorities. Wilson's proposed radical restructuring and strengthening of American government was a way to direct and temper government action in the service of existing hierarchies—the forms and methods would be new, but they would be deployed for old purposes.

"Not Factitious but Anthropological"

Wilson sought constitutional reordering in order to safely accommodate new realities—including, especially, the reality of a free African American population. The question of how to accommodate American institutions to a new, post-Reconstruction racial settlement loomed equally large at APSA meetings and in political science journals. Some commentators, like Wilson, would recommend new political arrangements. Others would turn primarily to administration, suggesting that if racial others had (against all scientific principles) been given a formal, legal grant of equality, some flexibility in the application of those laws would be called for.

Across generational and theoretical divides, political scientists were united in a near-consensus that African Americans were inferior, politically incompetent, and unsuited to live under a legal system constituted by and for Anglo-Saxons.[38] There was also general agreement that by their very presence in the United States African Americans challenged social peace and the viability of constitutional principles, and that any attempt to integrate them into American democracy necessarily stemmed from a catastrophic misunderstanding of that basic truth.

In an early volume of *PSQ*, William Chauncy Langdon articulated a principle that would go largely unchallenged in political science for some time. As he saw it, "The negro [was] not an Anglo-Saxon, or a Celt, or Scandinavian—only undeveloped and with a black skin. . . . The African [was] on the contrary a wholly distinct race, and the obstacles to social equality and political co-efficiency" with "our own" race were "not factitious but anthropological."[39] These judgments stood through the early years of the twentieth century (and beyond), and were voiced at APSA's meetings and in its publications no less than they had been at Columbia and in *PSQ*. That is, as much as the first generation of U.S.-trained scholars may have sought to radically reorient their discipline, they were united with the founding generation in their sense that no account of politics could be scientific without an understanding of the significance of racial difference.

Even a cursory examination of *Political Science Quarterly* shows that the Burgess/Dunning/Wilson line on Reconstruction reigned unchallenged there for years. *PSQ*'s monotony in this regard certainly owes much to Dunning's and Burgess's influence at Columbia. However, the birth of the APSA and the launching of the *American Political Science Review* in 1906 led to no slackening of interest in these topics, nor did it lead to any real stirrings of dissent from the reigning estimation of Reconstruction, African Americans in general, or the prospect of racial equality on almost any front. What developed instead was a consensus that the emerging Jim Crow regime of racial segregation and stratification represented a moderate, pragmatic response to the realities of racial difference. The fact that it might occasionally do violence to constitutional strictures simply demonstrated that those strictures had been based on an inadequate and misinformed political theory that the new century could ill-afford.

In some representative examples drawn from the late nineteenth century and into the twentieth, black people appeared in *PSQ* and, later, in papers presented at the APSA and articles in the *APSR,* as the "half-civilized,"[40] "alien" element within the American population. At best, blacks were depicted as the "permanent[ly] . . . indolent and thriftless,"[41] "spoil of the politician,"[42] "unfit" to vote,[43] lacking "initiative and inventive genius," and prone to chicken-stealing[44]; at worst, "savage"[45] and determined to "outrage and murder" Southern whites' "young daughters."[46]

On occasion, commenters referred with relief to the idea that negro unfitness might be a self-limiting problem. For example, in a *PSQ* review, Columbia's Gary N. Calkins found grounds for optimism in Frederick Hoffman's "convincing" thesis that "the American negro" was so racially feeble as to be headed for extinction. To Calkins's cautious relief, "the race of negroes['] . . . downward grade," meant it was less likely to "menace our republican institutions."[47] Another author noted approvingly that "a very large proportion of the negroes born in this country die in childhood," thus mitigating the "danger" that whites might be "overwhelmed."[48] (Bryce made a similar observation in the *North American Review* in 1891, commenting sanguinely that, troubling as the negro problem might be, demographic data suggested that "time [was] on the side" of "the white race.")[49]

A review of these two main political science journals and the proceedings of APSA meetings up to and including 1910 yields no counters to these images of black inferiority, and just one sympathetic, extended treatment of Reconstruction and black voting rights.[50] That sympathetic treatment was a 1905 address to the American Political Science Association by Albert Bushnell Hart. Hart, a German-educated Harvard historian who (like Dunning) would go on to serve as president of both the American Historical Association and the APSA, occupies an ambivalent position in Reconstruction historiography. He invoked the abolitionists as his spiritual "ancestors" and at Harvard mentored W. E. B. Du Bois, whom he invited to read a paper favorable to Reconstruction at the 1909 AHA conference.[51] However, Hart also edited the series in which Wilson and Dunning's scurrilous histories of Reconstruction appeared, and in a 1910 book he displayed a more settled belief in black inferiority (at least in the medium term) as well as what an approving *APSR* reviewer characterized as healthy "acceptance of the inevitable" with regard to the racial order in the post-Reconstruction south.[52]

Whatever his ambiguities, in 1905 Hart took an extreme minority position on Reconstruction, suggesting to listeners at the APSA that Reconstruction governments had been unfairly maligned. As Hart saw it, black suffrage during Reconstruction had been incomplete and brief and had ended via a "violent and irregular process," leaving scholars with little real evidence as to "the capacity of the negro to exercise discretion in his vote."[53] Again, however, this position put Hart well outside the mainstream. When he delivered his paper to the APSA, he was paired with Baltimore Attorney General John Rose, whose talk on "Suffrage Conditions in the South: The Constitutional Point of View" was harshly critical of calls to enforce black voting rights; all three discussants at the panel took a similar stance.[54] Rose's address (without Hart's) was published in the inaugural issue of the *APSR* under the more direct title, "Negro Suffrage: The Constitutional Point of View"; a sympathetic account of "Racial Distinctions in Southern Law" appeared alongside it.[55] Clearly, these were not marginal issues—with only two other full-length pieces in that issue, exactly half of the articles in the *APSR*'s first issue were justifications of disenfranchisement and segregation. Moreover, aside from Hart's cautious defense of Reconstruction, the journals and meetings featured no dissent from the proposition that sentimental ideas about equality or moralistic attachment to constitutional guarantees had no place in the scientific treatment of those issues, which was to be governed instead by pragmatic considerations and scientific dispassion.

Rose's *APSR* article offers a particularly clear formulation of the pragmatic realpolitik that characterized this discussion. He acknowledged that political distinctions based on race were clearly unconstitutional and that measures such as literacy tests and "grandfather" clauses were nothing more than subterfuge. They were, nonetheless, necessary. Echoing Wilson's faith in the wise conservatism of national opinion, Rose urged deference to prevailing norms, even when they conflicted with what Wilson had called the "literary" form of the law. The important point, to Rose's mind, was that law that got ahead of the population was doomed to fail. As he put it,

> St. Paul has said that all things that are lawful are not expedient. . . . Let those who believe that whether his skin be white, yellow, red, brown, or black, a man's a man for a' that, be of good cheer. Either they are right or wrong. If the latter they will some day be thankful that their brothers in the South have not been able to see with their eyes. . . . Those who do not share the present feelings and convictions of the overwhelming majority of the white people of the South must walk warily. At the best, they can do only a little to hasten the coming of the day they long for. They can do much to postpone it.[56]

One discussant at the APSA meeting where Rose presented his argument was more extreme, positing black savagery as a permanent impediment to African Americans' political inclusion. But the others matched Rose's sense that civil rights for African Americans might be viable in principle, but only if they were achieved slowly and "organically" (and largely as a result of changes in the character of the African American population). John Martin, for example, agreed with Rose, arguing that "the ex-slave, unused to directing his own actions and incapable of coping with his old masters, could not retain possession of the weapon that the North had thrust into his hands; still less could he use it for his own advancement in civilization." On this basis, he asked, "Of what use would it be, then, once more to confer upon him this gift at present?"[57]

Gilbert T. Stephenson took a similar stance in "Racial Distinctions in Southern Law,"[58] the article that appeared alongside Rose's in the inaugural issue of the *APSR*, and again a few years later with "The Separation of the Races in Public Conveyances." Stephenson characterized segregation laws as "scarcely more" than the legalization of "existing and widespread custom." And while he professed to be neutral as to the propriety of legal discrimination, he gave over almost the entire last page of one article to a passage from an 1867 decision by the Pennsylvania Supreme Court that upheld segregation by a private railway, blandly commenting that the passage "gives . . . clearly and concisely the reasoning that those have adopted who believe that . . . racial distinctions are justifiable."[59] The thrust of it was that "separation of the white and black races upon the surface of the globe is a fact . . . apparent. . . . A distribution of men by race and color is as visible in the providential arrangement of the earth as that of heat and cold. The natural separation of the races is therefore an undeniable fact, and all social organizations which lead to their amalgamation is repugnant to the laws of nature."[60] The moral in almost all these cases was that constitutional dogma could not and must not be allowed to overweigh "anthropological" realities.

Because of the constitutional issues they raised, legal distinctions based on race were the aspect of the "negro problem" that captured the most professional interest from political scientists, who for all their protestations remained very interested in the legal forms of American politics. However, they also devoted attention to the phenomenon of lynching, and their treatment of the topic was clearly shaped by their sense that law must be made to accommodate racial difference. According to a 1952 Tuskegee Institute report, there were 3,179 confirmed press reports of lynchings—defined as mob murders "under pretext of service to justice, race, or tradition"— between 1882 and 1902. Most (but by no means all) victims were black men. Similarly, a majority—but not all—took place in the South.[61] These crimes were worrisome to political scientists in that they seemed to indicate a population at odds with the law, and to open the doors for yet more lawlessness. However, in the political science journals, racial coexistence itself appeared to be the cause of the problem, and as such to pose an intrinsic, existential challenge to the U.S. constitutional system.

Again, political scientists devoted little extended study to the topic. Still, they were interested. Books on lynching featured in the *APSR*'s "Index of Recent Literature," and *PSQ*'s "Record of Political Events," which ran in each issue, included a recurring section on the topic.[62] *PSQ* reported incidents of and statistics on mob vigilantism (as well as "more or less formal race conflicts"[63] and "race war"[64]) and made special note of particularly notorious lynchings. In general, these reports were spare, simply reporting the attacks and their outcomes. Occasionally, such violence was denounced as "evil" or "lawless." However, on the few occasions when the topic received deeper treatment, it became clear that the source of the lawlessness was to be found in the victims, not the perpetrators.

In this, political writers were working in the Dunning School tradition. (Dunning was in fact the author of several of the earliest reports in *PSQ*.) That is, lynching and vigilantism appeared in that historiography as yet another unfortunate consequence of the Reconstruction policies themselves. When the law was on the side of "unnatural"—that is, equal— relations between people of different races, it lost its hold on otherwise law-abiding whites. (This was the case that Wilson made for the rise of the Ku Klux Klan in his *History of the American People*, characterizing that organization as "the price of the policy" of Reconstruction, and an enforcer of the "*real* laws" of the southern states.)[65]

Perhaps the clearest exposition of this logic had come in 1891 from Henry Cabot Lodge, then a congressman (with political science training from Harvard University), in an article in the *North American Review* criticizing what he viewed as ill-considered immigration policies. "Lynch Law and Unrestricted Immigration" condemned the lynching that year of a group of Sicilian immigrants, which, as *PSQ* also noted, had triggered diplomatic tensions. The remedy, however, required excluding the victims rather than constraining the perpetrators. Lodge advocated reforming immigration law to slow the entry of those "classes of immigrants" that provoked native-born Americans to such behavior.[66]

Discussion of lynching in the post-Reconstruction south in the political science journals around the turn of the century almost invariably echoed this perverse reasoning, implying that forcing southern whites to live with blacks on any terms approaching equality made it impossible for them to behave in a civilized fashion.[67] However, even when whites were the victims, a version of this logic reigned—conditions of lawlessness forced the perpetrators' hands. In the South, that lawlessness stemmed from inevitable "race conflict"—white victims were in a sense collateral damage. In the west, race conflict could contribute to a similar set of conditions (as in the case of massacres of Chinese laborers). Nonetheless, lynching was foremost conceived as an aspect of the negro problem. As Alvin Johnson summarized the consensus in a 1906 book review, the "fundamental reason for [lynching's] existence, in the South at any rate, is . . . that a system of criminal law which has evolved under the conditions of Northern Europe is not adapted to the task of checking criminal tendencies in an inferior race."[68]

In this again, Albert Bushnell Hart was an exception. Even in his more conventionally racist 1910 book, *The Southern South*, Hart pointed out that lynching dates to revolutionary times and insisted that "lynching did not originate in offenses by Negroes, is not justified by any increase of crime, and is applied to a multitude of offenses, some of them simply trivial." Moreover, he fixed the responsibility on whites, "that race which has the habit of calculated and concerted action: reckless Negroes can always make trouble by shooting at the Whites, but the laws, the officers of justice, the militia, the courts, are in the hands of white people."

For Hart, the solution was improved race relations, led by the white upper classes, "the upbuilders of the commonwealth, the educators, the professional classes, the plantation owners, the capitalists, most of whom wish the Negro well, and oppose violence and injustice." Together with "the best element of the Negroes" these virtuous white elites could engage in an uplift program that, in reducing racial tension (by correcting the defects and deficits of African Americans), might free the South from its "two worst enemies—the black brute, and the white amateur executioner." In the meantime, improved policing was in order, including "rural police . . . to make prompt arrests and protect prisoners" and new methods of choosing sheriffs, since those chosen by election often displayed "no backbone" in the face of white demands for mob rule.[69]

For others less convinced of the prospect of uplift, however, the solution was, as Johnson put it, "a legal system which should differentiate between races."[70] That is, for figures like Johnson, Lodge, Rose, Stephenson, and Wilson, in the absence of fundamental constitutional reform, administrative workarounds and pragmatic accommodation of the facts on the ground were necessary to ensure social peace and order under conditions of racial heterogeneity.

A theoretical grounding for American democracy had been an urgent desideratum for a generation of political scientists that had witnessed the near-destruction of the Union. Burgess, like so many of his contemporaries, had found one in a racial right to self-government, elevating white supremacy to an ethical principle and a world-historical mission. Wilson and his generation were no less convinced of white supremacy, but they tended to frame their task in more grounded, practical terms. Changing relationships between racial groups, such as those imposed by colonial expansion abroad and Reconstruction and immigration at home, appeared as problems for administrators and as questions for the kind of realistic, inductive political science that would help administrators with their work.

This pragmatic attitude led many political scientists to break with Burgess as well with regard to American imperialism. A growing government role in the economy and constitutional barriers to formal racial discrimination were new realities to be managed as well as possible, however one might feel about them. So too was the fact that, with its acquisition of tropical "dependencies" after the Spanish-American War, the United States was ruling overseas colonies.[71] Burgess's state theory could not accommodate this development; his response to it was shocked despair. For the younger generation, it was yet more proof that old frameworks were obsolete. Indeed, Wilson's colleague Henry Jones Ford would attack Burgess's work precisely on the basis that it had attended *too little* to racial difference, leaving political scientists poorly equipped to advise the rulers of an imperial power.[72] As we shall see, Ford's remedy was a sweeping research effort to discover the political tendencies and capacities of racial groups across the globe. In the meantime, many of his colleagues in the emerging field of colonial administration thought it prudent to apply to any lingering commitment to American-style democracy the lessons of what one of them called that "part of our national experience" that had been "supplied by the negro question and Chinese immigration."[73]

Chapter 3

Twentieth-Century Problems: Administering an American Empire

The "Forethought" to *Souls of Black Folk* contains what is probably W. E. B. Du Bois's best-remembered line: "The problem of the Twentieth Century is the problem of the color-line." This will be news to almost no one. At the time of this writing, a Google search for this observation-turned-aphorism returns more than 120,000 results. In the essay itself, however, the line is something of a throwaway. Du Bois delivers it and moves along without elaboration.[1]

Presumably this is because Du Bois was calling readers' attention to something perfectly familiar to them. But what, exactly? This phrase has been given many readings—Adolph Reed Jr. points out that Du Bois's work has been recruited in the service of a number of divergent interpretive and political agendas over the years, including, among others, racial nationalism, socialist universalism, liberal pluralism, and "militant integrationism."[2] An address Du Bois gave to the first Pan African Convention in 1900, a few years before *Souls* came out, may indicate what he expected his contemporaries to make of his remark. In that speech, he used the same phrase, going on to remind listeners "that in this age when the ends of the world are being brought so near together the millions of black men in Africa, America and the Islands of the Sea, not to speak of the brown and yellow myriads elsewhere, are bound to have a great influence upon the world . . . by reason of sheer numbers and physical contact." That is, like Bryce, Du Bois saw the world becoming "small" and thought that contact and conflict between groups on different sides of "the color line" would be central to the problems it was likely to face in the future.

Much in Du Bois's work challenged conventional wisdom at the turn of the century. And Du Bois in his 1900 address framed the problem in starkly moral terms—asking "how far differences of race . . . will hereafter be made the basis of denying to over half the world the right of sharing to utmost ability the opportunities and privileges of modern civilization."[3] However, his beginning premise was a commonplace of turn-of-the-century thought: that interaction between racial groups was increasing, and increasingly problematic.[4]

This consensus held among the most racially liberal of the reformers, diplomats, and others who had been gathering to promote international cooperation and the welfare of nonwhite peoples at Lake Mohonk conferences and elsewhere since the 1880s.[5] It was equally strong among the most chauvinistic advocates of imperialism, who, with Theodore Roosevelt, felt themselves engaged in a larger struggle for "civilization over forces which stand for the black chaos of savagery and barbarism."[6]

That is, regardless of where their sympathies lay, intellectuals and public figures around this time could generally agree that "the races" were the fundamental units of world politics and that relations between them were to be a, or even *the*, defining question for the world in the new century. For many prominent figures in the American Political Science Association, this translated into intense professional interest in the dynamics of imperialism as well as in the administrative problems the United States faced in its role as a newly minted colonial power. The APSA's leading colonialism scholars brought to these questions the same pragmatic empiricism that on the domestic front seemed to suggest that constitutional structures might have to be relaxed in order to accommodate racial, economic, and other realities. Their answers paired a Jim Crow theory of race relations with an internationalism marked by the progressive faith that the right kinds of organizations were the key to transcending political conflict.

Those answers also highlight a shift in orientation to political change that was occurring around this time. For Teutonists, political life was linked to its origins by a slow, organic unfolding of its essential nature—what mattered was to stay true to the through-line of development that the analyst could discern underneath the violent upheaval of the ages. However, where Teutonism saw a slow unfolding of racial destiny, many younger political scientists partook in the "growing distrust of simple progressionism," and (partial) "loss of faith in the inevitability of progress" that characterized new visions of both social and biological change emerging in this period.[7] As a result, their work implied a more active role for statesmen, administrators, and intellectuals in shaping political arrangements and accommodating them to racial difference.

Knowledge Problems

In political science, *realism* is a term of art for post–World War II theories of international power politics. As Robert Vitalis points out, however, the first international relations expert to self-identify as a "realist" may have been Lothrop Stoddard, the author of *Rising Tide of Color Against White World Supremacy.*[8] The theme of that book, like many of Stoddard's, was that "the key-note of twentieth-century world-politics" was to be "the relations between the primary races of mankind." Stoddard is remembered now chiefly as a virulent proponent of scientific racism who sought to protect the "white world" from being overrun by the nonwhite "worlds." This does him no personal injustice—Stoddard was a hard-line biological determinist and, according to at least one account, a "hero" of Adolf Hitler's,[9] whom he met while reporting a book subtitled "A Sympathetic Report from Hitler's War-time Reich."[10] However, Vitalis notes that in the early decades of the twentieth century, Stoddard was a prominent commentator on international matters, with a Harvard pedigree and publications in professional journals.[11]

Vitalis's observation is aimed at a disciplinary memory that casts most early twentieth-century scholarship on international relations as "formalist" or "idealist." As potted textbook histories would have it, scholarship on international affairs in this period focused on legal questions to the exclusion of hardheaded accounts of international realities.[12] For Vitalis, this story may only be maintained through a massive act of "forgetting"— specifically, forgetting that from the turn of the century through the interwar period, political scientists engaged in intensive study of colonial administration and empire.[13] Moreover, while it is true that many of these figures put great stock in international organizations (of which they conceived empire to be an example) to bring order and peace to international affairs, they also saw themselves as revising legalistic doctrines in the light of empirical realities—particularly what they saw as the realities of racial difference.

If the early APSA leadership followed Wilson in finding the teleological, "literary" theory of politics inadequate to the challenges of governing the

United States in the twentieth century, it brought the same ostensibly no-nonsense attitude to scholarship on world affairs. Teutonism had been cautiously optimistic that the Anglo-Saxon "state" would eventually perfect itself. The rest of the world would eventually assimilate the newly realized ideal or submit to forcible "organization" at its hands. As a result, places and people outside that rarefied sphere held primarily historical interest. However, the Spanish-American War had largely made that stance moot. Serving as a pretext for the annexation of Hawaii (already controlled by American landowners) and formally bringing the former Spanish colonies of Cuba, Puerto Rico, the Philippines, Guam, and parts of the West Indies under U.S. administration, the war meant that, like it or not, the United States needed to attend to the "unpolitical nations." Political scientists courted irrelevance if they did not contribute scientific insight into the problems of governing those colonies and of jostling for influence with other major powers in far-flung regions.

In this context, discussions of political change began to draw more on Darwin than on Hegel, emphasizing processes of branching and differentiation rather than progress toward a universal goal.[14] From this viewpoint, difference appeared as a permanent and defining feature of human life and an urgent subject for political analysis. A true science of politics would require an empirical accounting of "the racial characteristics and political capacities" of people outside the apogee of political development that earlier theory termed "the state."[15]

Henry Jones Ford made this case forcefully. A prominent newspaperman and political scholar, Ford would later be recruited by Wilson first to teach at Princeton and then to serve in Washington; in 1918, Ford became president of the APSA. Throughout his career, he linked a critique of American political institutions to a call to widen the scope of political science. To his mind, nineteenth-century teleological universalism was as limiting as the eighteenth-century social-contract theory it had purported to replace. As Ford put it in his 1898 book, *The Rise and Growth of American Politics*, political science was to abjure "any abstract law of human development" and instead account for "local circumstance."[16]

Developing such alternatives would require political science to shed its theoretical blinders and turn a critical eye to American institutions as well as to the rest of the world.[17] Ford's critique of U.S. politics shared much with Wilson's. As Ford saw it, "The working of the constitution" had been transformed, while "the theory . . . remained almost intact"; he decried

America's combination of a weak executive with a Congress in thrall to local interests through its "monstrous" committee system.[18] Only a strong, responsible executive could tame the excesses of narrow interests and the whims of mass democracy to successfully lead a complex industrial power such as the United States. As one contemporary later summarized Ford's views, "The chief faults of government in the United States he traced to a common rootage in a false interpretation of democracy whereby, in the language of fable, the donkey has been encouraged to put his foot in the stirrup."[19]

To replace the antiquated American system with a more efficient one and to determine the fitness of American institutions for "other races," political scientists had to understand "the nature of public authority whatever forms it may assume." Crucially, this would require analysis of all the "states mentioned in handbooks and gazeteers," not just "one class of states which alone" were recognized as "having attained political organization." That is, by narrowing the study of politics to "a particular phase of development which has resulted in special forms embodied in positive law," Burgess, Adams, Dunning, and others had forged a science that "gather[ed] its concepts from the mental deposits of our own race experience" and excluded the "very states whose activities [were] the chief centers of disturbance in world politics," such as China, Russia, and Turkey.

In Ford's view, no truly inductive science could afford to ignore vast areas of subject matter. It also needed to take its naturalism seriously. In contrast to the Teutonists' use of biological references, Ford's commitment to a natural-science account of politics was far more than metaphorical. Fully the first half—just under 150 pages—of Ford's 1915 book, *The Natural History of the State: An Introduction to Political Science* is devoted to a discussion of the scientific evidence on biosocial evolution.[20] As Ford wrote years earlier, that "politics have a natural history is implied by the accepted theory of the descent of man." If political science were "ever to be put on an objective basis," it would have to recognize that the modern states of Europe and America were "but one phase of a process of development governed throughout by the same general laws" and only intelligible "in orderly relation to the entire process." "Civilized" peoples were separated from "barbarous" peoples, and the West from the East, not because the advanced nations had progressed further toward a universal ideal but rather through a process analogous to "the variation of species."

In this view, "Political development . . . proceed[ed] on divergent lines, with successions of supremacy as regards particular types." Each "stem of polity" operated according to its own rules, and a proper classificatory system would allow the political scientist to discern patterns, make appropriate comparisons, and, in time, "give rational determination to the destinies of nations." Arriving at such a system would require political scientists to engage in extensive and deep study not only of Europe and America but also of those black, brown, and yellow "myriads" that Du Bois would invoke.

This "objective" approach was meant to free theory from the grip of unscientific teleology, revealing that "instability of political forms" was the true norm. Above all, it was this imperative that connected Ford's concern with comparative politics to his critique of American institutions. A natural history, unlike an idealist one, needn't read too much meaning into the past. It could recognize that "turbulent streams of influence are eroding old social strata, cutting out new channels and making new deposits," possibly forming "new strata" upon which "future polity must rest."[21]

In Ford's work, this emphasis did not translate into a rush to embrace the new. Rather, Ford framed the task of political science much as Wilson did: to discover how institutional arrangements might be rethought in order to preserve the social order in new circumstances. So, for example, he advocated a reordering of lines of influence in the federal government, concentrating power in an executive aligned with the House of Representatives and sidelining the Senate, but only in the belief that this would imbue Congress as a whole with the conservatism traditionally meant to inhere in the Senate.[22]

Ford's rejection of teleology was certainly limited. In his view, biological evolution and the homological increase of industrial efficiency militated toward progress—just slowly, and not universally. His particular domestic concerns were party responsibility and municipal corruption; he recommended careful study before any rush to actual reform. Similarly, while the systemic changes he advocated were meant to promote greater accountability and popular sovereignty, this was to occur over time, contingent on increases in the American people's capacity for self-government. Still, his rejection of both predetermined schema and universalism struck a chord with a rising generation of political scientists, many of whom were to echo his call for an empirical study of what had been known as the "unpolitical nations."

Colonial Problems

With the establishment of the APSA, the leadership of organized political science gave up the opposition to U.S. colonial adventures that had reigned in *PSQ* under Burgess's influence. For practical reasons, many U.S. political scientists exhibited particular interest in the Philippines, which many saw as the "key to America's future in Asia."[23] Consequently, its fate was at the center of much of the colonialism scholarship featured at the APSA's early meetings and in its early publications.

The U.S.-controlled Philippine Commission, under future President William Howard Taft, essentially governed the Philippines until 1916. It combined brutally repressive tactics with a strategic "policy of attraction," meant to peel off elite support for an independence struggle that landowners feared might spiral into a full-scale agrarian rebellion.[24] This policy involved law enforcement, management of relations between Christian Filipinos and "Moros," development of natural resources (particularly agriculture), public health, and education. For example, in the months following the promulgation of a 1901 law promoting a system of English-language public education, more than 1,000 American teachers came to the Philippines on U.S. Army transport ships.[25]

The commission sought to bolster U.S. public support by demonstrating the payoff in trade and access to markets that the Philippines would bring and to blunt claims that imperialism violated American ideals by distinguishing the American imperial project from the European one. Burgess and members of groups such as the Anti-Imperialist League still warned against acquiring a population with a "mix of Negro blood, Malays, and other unspeakable Asiatics by the tens of millions!"[26] On another register, perennial Democratic presidential candidate William Jennings Bryan railed against the "paralyzing influence of imperialism."[27] But discussion at APSA meetings and in the *APSR* shows that concerns in that milieu largely aligned with those of the Philippine Commission. Moreover, once the question was no longer whether to take on colonial possessions but how to govern them, the APSA began to hear calls for an organized section that would focus on the administration of "dependencies." Diplomat and colonialism scholar Henry Morris argued for a "colonial institute" at the APSA's first meeting, optimistic that "government would, undoubtedly, in time, recognize the value of such an organization and . . . soon appreciate the assistance and help offered them."[28]

No colonial institute was established, but, as Brian Schmidt has shown, the "Politics" section of the APSA became a primary site for political scholarship devoted to the topics of colonialism and imperialism.[29] That context saw lively debate about the level and type of political control of dependencies necessary to achieve U.S. objectives. But the debate took place against a background of shared assumptions: no major voices challenged the idea that race traits and differences were central issues for U.S. expansion and the problems of colonial governance.

Specialists on colonial governance primarily characterized their task as one of providing guidelines for competent and effective governance by colonial administrators. Running a close second, however, was public education as to the necessity (and often the justice) of imperialism. In a 1906 talk before the APSA ("On the Need for a Scientific Study of Colonial Administration"), Alleyne Ireland voiced the common complaint that the general public refused to give up the "uninformed" "idea that the political principles and social ideals of the North American continent afford a perfectly satisfactory standard by which to adjust the administrative policy for the governance of tropical races."[30] In a similar vein, Paul Reinsch argued that an ill-informed public, "aroused" by the brutal repression of the Philippines, had forced the administration into adopting hasty and inappropriate policies there.[31] For these writers, the public failed to understand that expansion was inevitable and could never be simply an extension of U.S.-style government; rather, it required accounting for local realities by elaborating forms of military and political control of "backward" territories that would be appropriate to their populations.

The Wisconsin-trained Reinsch was a central figure in the APSA. He participated in the discussions that launched the association, helped to write its constitution, founded its "Politics" section, and served as its first vice president. Of the many colonial experts who spoke at APSA meetings and published in its journals, he was also among the more concerned about the needs of "natives" and the more vocal in his criticism of inhumane colonial practices. Still, Reinsch was an "avowed expansionist."[32] He believed that it was simply impossible to "contain" the "forces" of "mobility, concentration, and mastery over the forces of nature" that were the hallmarks of "our own civilization . . . within national borders."[33] Harvard political scientist and Africa expert Raymond Buell, also a trenchant critic of U.S. practices, was similarly resigned that the "restless energy of the

Caucasian peoples" seemed to set them on an inevitable path toward control over the resources and territory of lesser races.[34]

Ford had fewer compunctions about colonialism's abuses than did Reinsch and Buell but agreed with them about its inexorable advance. In a 1907 *PSQ* article titled "The Ethics of Empire," Ford portrayed empire as an inevitable facet of national growth and power. While Ford allowed that in some cases, such as China's, it was "conceivable" that the power to "wield empire" might not lead to the practice, he argued that, in general, "the rise of empire appears to have the constancy of natural law." For Ford, empire was the consequence of "supremacy," and opposition to it was only misguided sentiment; indeed, there were "reasons for believing that no other kind of permanent relation between the white race and other races is scientifically possible."[35]

This logic dominated discussions of the justice of colonialism within the APSA. In its simplest form, conventional wisdom on the issue boiled down to the following propositions: (1) racial and economic forces compelled the great powers to seek new markets and new resources; (2) those resources and markets could be found among "backward" peoples; (3) backward peoples could not efficiently develop those resources or the market organization to consume the ever-increasing bounty of the modern economy; and, therefore, (4) the great powers had a responsibility to the world to develop its resources, and a responsibility to their own people to see that the benefits of doing so accrued to them and not to their rivals.

That is, empire was a fact, driven by the racial characteristics and (by extension) economic needs of the great nations. One might find it distasteful, but, as with constitutional workarounds to accommodate Jim Crow policies, to decry it on moral grounds was simply to contribute to the "great confusion" on the subject.[36] For those who would advise American policy makers and colonial officials, the questions to be argued, rather, resolved into two related areas: the extent of political control of dependencies required to achieve American purposes and how to resolve a perceived tension between the demands of efficacy and the desire to allow local self-government according to American principles.

This last was the rub, and it was where racial difference came in. Ireland took pains to emphasize that there was "in fact no problem of colonial administration in the great self-governing colonies, where the population is preponderatingly white, since the administration of such territories . . .

differs only in name from the administration of countries which are independent sovereign states." Colonial administration was defined by its attention to "such problems as arise when persons of one race are administering . . . the affairs of another race."[37]

For Reinsch, trade relations might obviate the need for colonial governance in many cases. Ireland was less sanguine. He argued that only colonization could create the conditions that most agreed offered the basic justification for territorial expansion—the efficient development of the world's resources. This task required protections for property, including "competent and impartial courts for the adjustment of commercial disputes and for the enforcement of contracts"—conditions, Ireland argued, that "native rule . . . never afforded."[38] However, even Reinsch concluded that direct political control—colonialism proper—was necessary in many cases, and he never suggested that the tropical colonies be given a simple grant of formal independence.[39] Indeed, from another angle, Reinsch and Ireland were in substantial agreement. Both thought trade relations sufficient in some cases, and both thought political control necessary in others. If they disagreed on how often the former case might arise, this reflected varying estimations of particular nations' capacity for progress, rather than any more fundamental difference.

Most commentators included the "natives' " well-being in their definition of justifiable, progressive colonialism. In these accounts, American empire would be an "empire of reform," extending the impulses of U.S. progressivism outward in a program of technocratic uplift.[40] Reinsch, for example, characterized nineteenth-century imperialism as historically "a vast aggressive movement of national selfishness," bitterly dismissed "missionary" pretensions that "the whole movement" of imperialism was one of "altruism and benevolence," and commented that "most of these races would be happier if they had never seen their civilizers."[41] However, in the twentieth century, political science was demonstrating that a "constructive" colonial policy informed by the "character and essence" of "our civilization" could serve national interests and benefit the colonized as well.[42] Ireland, in a typically less lofty vein, argued that the "object of colonization in the tropics is and always has been . . . to establish and develop a profitable commerce," and that "in the long run the best commerce may be established if the native population is prosperous and contented."[43]

However, not all subscribed to such pragmatic benevolence. Bernard Moses had taught politics and history at the University of California, Berkeley, and served a two-year stint on the Philippine Commission before moving to the University of California, Los Angeles, to found a political science department there in 1903.[44] He was a principal architect of the Philippine Commission's education policies but not, apparently, entirely willing to trust the "attraction" strategy. He wrote in a paper for the first APSA meeting that the use of "physical force" in colonization was not always to be lamented, since "to smite the barbarian with a heavy hand is sometimes the surest way to liberalize his mind."[45] Likewise, Theodore Marburg (later a founder of the American internationalist society the League to Enforce Peace, and a supporter of Wilson's during the fight for the League of Nations) thought it "important . . . to distinguish between the welfare of the present inhabitants of a country and the welfare of the country itself," asking rhetorically if the "units of the existing population should be favored as against another race who might lay a better foundation for the future welfare of the country."[46]

However, as even Moses acknowledged, whereas in the continental United States it had been "expected that the aboriginal inhabitants would disappear," in the Caribbean, Pacific, and African colonies, this "could not be presumed," and thus "they could not be ignored."[47] In a similar vein, Ford commented that "the colored races of Asia and Africa" were unlikely to be "extruded from their natural habitats" or "denatured by any ordeals to which they may be subjected by superior force."[48] For Marburg, as for Moses, this meant settlement was to be preferred if possible, and a heavy hand was necessary in any case. As Marburg put it, if Puerto Rico were opened up to "Teutonic" settlement, the mixed population there, with its dominant Spanish "element," would "be relegated to an inferior position." Far from alarming, this was a dynamic to be embraced, since, for example, the "Spaniard in California has been brushed aside in this manner; but as a result that region has developed untold riches."[49]

All the same, this was a somewhat old-fashioned position in the discipline. Moses and Marburg, after all, differed from Burgess in their practical prescriptions only in timing—for Burgess, "political nations" were to "force organization" on the rest "by any means necessary" only in the future, when they had reached a higher phase of development.[50] For Moses and Marburg, the forcible "upbuilding of civilization everywhere in all parts of the earth" could begin forthwith.[51] As Reinsch saw it, this kind of nineteenth-century rhetoric was both inhumane and impractical. But equally outmoded were the "cant" of humanitarian uplift and any notion of a universal civilization founded on the "equality and uniform virtue of human nature."[52] As he wrote in an article titled "The Negro Race and European Civilization,"

> The last few years have witnessed a great change of mind in matters of humanitarianism; the absolute unity of human life in all of the globe, as well as the idea of the practical equality of human individuals wherever they may be found, has been quite generally abandoned. Without going into the question of origins, it is clear that conditions of environment and historical forces have combined in producing certain great types of humanity which are essentially different in their characteristics. To treat these as if they were all alike, to subject them to the same methods of government, to force them into the same institutions, was a mistake of the nineteenth century which has not been carried over into our own.[53]

Reinsch and Ford were among the political scientists most explicit in their call to cast off nineteenth-century illusions about the conduct of international affairs. They were also particularly insistent in their opposition to what they called "assimilationism." This referred to the putatively futile attempt to govern nonwhites according to norms derived from the Anglo-Saxon tradition. Reinsch, for example, deplored the "fetish" of "literary instruction" in the Philippines. As he saw it, Filipinos "lack[ed] energy," exhibiting the "same psychological traits that are found among the Malays."[54] An insistence on importing American teachers to instill "our art and philosophy" would only exacerbate such Filipino ennui. As Reinsch put it in another context, "No system could have been more successfully devised for the emasculation of a race" than "learning by rote parts of an alien literature." Such training would, of course, also foster unreasonable expectations. (Reinsch was particularly concerned that such education might produce a class of people who expected but could not obtain or perform civil service jobs.)[55]

As an alternative, Reinsch suggested a system of "industrial education" along the lines promoted by Samuel Chapman Armstrong of the Freedmen's Bureau during Reconstruction and later, by his student, Booker T. Washington.[56] Through their leadership of the Hampton and Tuskegee Institutes, Armstrong and Washington had refocused efforts to educate former slaves away from the academic model championed by formerly abolitionist organizations like the American Missionary Association, which founded Hampton. Instead, they sought to prepare African American students for agricultural and other forms of manual labor, as well as to train them to teach in segregated primary schools for African Americans. Courses in civics were generally aimed at diminishing students' expectations as to their rights as laborers and at correcting any notion that the social and educational limits placed on African Americans might be unjust.[57]

Reinsch advocated a similar system—down to the secondary emphasis on teacher training—for the Philippines. In his mind, this would be more compatible with what was known of "the conditions in the country with which we have to deal" (that is, the need for agricultural and industrial development) "and the racial characteristics of its inhabitants." As it was, he thought, the educational efforts of U.S. administrators in the Philippines were part of a larger policy of "pseudo assimilation," which, in places like the Philippines where "assimilation is held to be impossible on account of racial differences . . . can only have the result of unsettling the native social life, without raising it effectually to a higher level." As he summed it up, "We shall never succeed in making Americans of the Filipinos; but we may hope by a careful, considerate, natural policy, to assist in raising their life to a higher plane, though it must remain their life and will never be ours."[58]

Reinsch similarly cautioned against destroying local customs in Africa by pointing to the moral degeneration that he perceived among former slaves and their descendants in America. Indeed, for all his differences with Burgess, Reinsch in a text written for the 1911 First Universal Races Conference echoed one of the older scholar's key contentions—that "only the fully national" could meaningfully contribute to the civilization of the world.[59] Racial difference was to be celebrated, not eliminated by thrusting things like self-government and rights down natives' throats.

Those who thought otherwise might have been fooled by American success in assimilating "Hungarian, Jewish, and Italian immigrants," who were "intimately connected with us through prior civilization." But they failed to attend to that very different part of our national experience . . . supplied by the negro question and Chinese immigration." For Reinsch, the "former ha[d] . . . taught us the lesson that deep racial differences cannot be bridged over by political institutions."[60]

Ford, too, argued that events in Cuba, Hawaii, and the Philippines indicated "that material for a sad chapter of history may be supplied by the efforts of the people of the United States to spread what they are pleased to describe as self-government and to make-over other peoples according to their own moral pattern." Also like Reinsch, Ford drew his evidence from the American experience, arguing that the ensuing disaster would be explained "in the same way in which we now shirk responsibility for our failure with the negroes—by putting the blame on their peculiar characteristics." Such logic, he argued, "is like that of the clumsy tailor who argued that the clothes he made were all right but the man did not happen to fit them."[61]

There were dissenters—Moses, unsurprisingly, had much less sympathy for native customs and traditions, remarking that the "destruction of ancient social forms and prejudices" was an "important . . . step, in preparing for the rise of a rude people to a higher stage of cultivation."[62] But, in general, the scientific position seemed to be that difference ought to be respected, even if respecting difference meant extending little in the way of respect to the actual human beings whose differences were in question. Morris drew together many strands of argument on the topic in 1906:

> The American people who solved [America's] difficulties with the aborigines by their practical annihilation and endeavored on the other hand to settle the negro question by elevating the blacks to its own level, is again confronted in the Philippines by a race problem, the more serious as it is the more complex. Shall we, in this instance, annihilate the natives . . . or eventually raise them politically and intellectually to our standards? The first solution by reason of their numbers is not probable; is the latter possible? Has not our experience with an inferior race of the East already shaken our ideal of the potential equality of all men? Has not the experiment—so far very brief but still likely long to endure—had a reflect action on our attitude toward the negro? Have not the enthusiasm and ardor of ante-bellum and civil war days for his political, social and educational equality—so greatly cooled in the succeeding forty years— been seriously chilled by the events occurring during the last decade in the Pacific and nearer at home in the Gulf of Mexico?[63]

Beyond industrial education, the cultivation of free labor and, in some instances, the devolution of certain local governing functions to native officials, APSA papers and articles were fairly short on positive policy recommendations—description and critique of existing colonial practices were the rule. However, some of the authors of these papers and articles saw chances to put their ideas into practice once Wilson became president. For example, from 1913 through 1915, Frank Goodnow was sent by the U.S. government, at China's request, to advise that country on the drafting of a new constitution. By then, Goodnow's work on the United States had moved in a more democratic direction. However, he had a different take on the Chinese case. There, Goodnow drafted two successively more autocratic constitutions, with the second calling for then-President Yuan Shikai to become emperor. (Shikai died the next year, and so did not get to take advantage of the opportunity.)[64] For his part, Reinsch supported and, as Wilson's ambassador to China from 1913 through 1919, helped to administer the Open Door Policy, which replaced formal territorial administration with trade relations on terms dictated by the United States.[65]

The concrete recommendation most often forthcoming from scientific students of colonialism was that colonies should have "autonomy." The idea of autonomy—essentially the antithesis of "assimilation"—requires some unpacking. First, it did not mean a call for independence but rather for, in Reinsch's words, "the self-determination of a society" and "the freedom to develop those customs and institutions which spring naturally from its ethnical characteristics and from the social and economic conditions under which it lives." This might involve "systems of authority," or democracy.[66] Left unspecified was how this determination was to be made. Certainly not through any democratic decision process, since such a system might well be inappropriate. By implication, determining the proper direction political development should take (determining the course of self-determination, as it were) became the task of colonial administrators and the political scientists to whom they were supposed to turn for guidance.

It almost always implied long-term subordinate status. For Reinsch, this was a paternalistic, tutelary, and mutually beneficial relationship. Ford took this idea even further, analogizing the relationship of imperial rulers and their subjects to "symbiosis": "a condition in which different organisms minister each to the other's welfare and derive reciprocal benefits from the vital associations."[67]

Both Reinsch and William B. Munro (a future president of the APSA) had kind words for changes to French colonial administration in the direction of "autonomy." In a 1909 review of two books on colonial administration, Reinsch praised the French for abandoning their "artificial policy" of "*a priori*" assimilation, which "cost them dearly in Algeria."[68] Here Reinsch echoed a point Munro made in 1907 commending France for abandoning the practice of extending legislative representation to new colonies. For Munro, bringing colonial subjects into France's "ineslastic" administrative and legislative systems constituted "excessive centralization," and the results of the more "flexible" and paternalistic stance of French authorities toward newer colonies would have "important value to students of comparative politics" eager to observe "the political development of the dependencies themselves" under conditions more closely approaching "autonomy."[69]

Imperial Problems

If this group of political scientists sought to elaborate a new, seemingly more scientific model of colonialism, they were equally eager to address inter-imperial relations. And while they were not blind to the possibility of disastrous conflict, many also found reason for optimism. Reinsch was one such optimist. In 1911, he published a brief book titled *Public International Unions: Their Work and Organization.* He billed the book as a "study in administrative international law," and, indeed, most of the book consists of careful and often technical reconstruction of the activities of various international bodies. A reader might learn for example that, at a 1905 convention of South American police officials, "the Argentinian system of dactyloscopy [fingerprint identification], together with a system of morphological description, was adopted . . . by all the administrations" for "the purpose of identifying criminals and suspicious characters," or the technicalities of distinguishing a "congress," from a "conference," or a "commission," and so forth.[70] And while the book touches on more high-minded topics such as international diplomatic cooperation through the Union of American Republics and the Hague Tribunal, for Reinsch the banality of much of these unions' work was, in fact, the point.

That is, if Buell's "restless energy of the Caucasian peoples" seemed to destine the European nations to come into conflict over the resources and territory of lesser races, Reinsch thought it might also provide reason for hope. The same energies that fueled expansion and conquest also occasioned rapid progress in the fields of science and technology. These developments, he argued, were resulting in a proliferation of prosaic, everyday forms of international collaboration and interdependence that might be turned to the service of an internationalist world order built on stronger stuff than the utopian dreams of previous theorists.

The "rationalism of the eighteenth century" had pinned its hope for world peace on the assumption that "men" were "capable of cutting loose from all the customs and interests of their traditional life, and to be directly, as reasoning beings, impelled to a world-wide unity." But this framework failed to specify which concrete "constructive force" was capable of realizing such "unity." A more "realistic and practical" age recognized that man's "nature must be raised through many degrees of institutional life . . . to the broad aims of civilization." International scientific and technical coordinating bodies, such as the Telegraphic, Metric, Seismological, and International Postal Unions promised, for Reinsch, just such a "degree of institutional life." In his view, these were concrete developments which might incrementally, organically replace "the void which the old cosmopolitan ideal left between the individual and humanity" with an "immovable and vast foundation" upon which a new internationalist ideal might be built.[71]

Reinsch was clear that his was not simply another route to the same end ("old cosmopolitanism"). This was a vision that abjured universal principles, leaving ample room for both difference and hierarchy. Just as scientific interdependence required sharing of disparate strengths and capacities, "independent nationalism" would allow "different aspects of human nature and human capacity to work themselves out." Moreover, interdependence was a phenomenon mainly of the "civilized nations of the world."[72] The lower races, along with their "extensive" and "fertile" regions[73] were to be brought into the world order as objects of "sane imperialism."[74] That is, Reinsch envisioned a loosely confederal world in which national sovereignties would be overlaid by cross-cutting networks of cooperation and control. His peaceful world system would derive not from "the absolute unity of human life in all parts of the globe" or "the idea of the practical equality of human individuals wherever they may be found"—those had been "generally abandoned"[75]—but rather from something much more like Ford's "symbiosis."

In this, Reinsch was in substantial agreement with the political scientist who did the most to put such ideas into practice in the real world— Woodrow Wilson. Stephen Skowronek points out that Wilson is often treated as a puzzlingly self-contradictory figure.[76] As a professor, Wilson ridiculed Jeffersonian ideals, lambasted Reconstruction, cited federal enforcement of black voting rights during Reconstruction as a prime example of wicked Congressional overreach, characterized imperialism as a "natural and wholesome impulse," and defended the brutal suppression of the Philippines.[77] As president, he introduced segregation into the federal civil service, blocked the inclusion of racial equality language in the League of Nations charter, and whipped up anti-immigrant sentiment. At the same time, he was the great advocate of "self-determination" and the man whose name has become a synonym (or an epithet, depending on your point of view) for liberal internationalism. In Skowronek's words, "Woodrow Wilson comes to us in starkly contrasting guises as a Southern apologist for the Ku Klux Klan . . . and as the cosmopolitan voice for 'the silent mass of mankind everywhere.' "[78]

As noted above, however, Skowronek argues convincingly that Wilson may be better understood as having turned to liberal reform as a way to safeguard old ideals and hierarchies to the extent a drastically changed context might allow. We have seen that Wilson viewed post-Reconstruction America as radically and qualitatively different from the republic of the founders. In his view, the heat of the Civil War had annihilated institutional checks on power, leaving zealots and demagogues free to push through calamitous, oppressive Reconstruction policies with no regard for constitutional constraints. And just as scholars of colonial autonomy saw in the Jim Crow order a model for "sane imperialism," Wilson found lessons for world order in the experiences of the Civil War, Reconstruction, and the post-Reconstruction settlement.

As Wilson put it, after the Civil War, "Congress pushed its way to the front, and began to transmute fact into law, law into fact." Even once, with Rutherford B. Hayes's inauguration, "natural legal conditions once more prevailed" in the South, and the "natural, inevitable ascendency of the whites, the responsible class, established,"[79] "a deep effect abide[d]," such that "all policy thenceforth wore a different aspect." There would be no return to the "delicate compromises of structure and authority characteristic of a mere federal partnership."[80] Local prerogatives were now irrevocably menaced by a government in which power was centralized but decision-making was susceptible to capture by programmatic interests.

By 1908, when he published *Constitutional Government*, Wilson had settled on professional, depoliticized administrative apparatus and a powerful president as the recipe for a "safe nationalization of interest and policy." However the attractions of these things did not, for Wilson, lie primarily in their capacity to promote national transformation. Rather, they were meant to balance and temper the forces calling for such transformations. A strong president would embody the (white) "unity of interest" that, despite momentary disturbances, Wilson (like Burgess) saw underneath the gradual evolution of national political life.[81] A professional administration would safeguard the execution of the consensual, moderate policies that would result and would insert a moderating influence between impulsive legislation and the actual use of national power.

Likewise, the League of Nations as Wilson envisioned it sought not to impose a universal regime of rights but rather to safeguard the ability of groups to develop according to their own principles—much as the southern states had demanded for themselves before (and after) the Civil War, as Burgess had insisted upon for the Teutonic nation in the United States, and as proponents of colonial "autonomy," such as Reinsch, had suggested for both "civilized" nations and colonial subjects. And, of course, Wilson's commitment to oppressed peoples was selective, focused primarily on those who had been oppressed by America's enemies, with the mandate system providing for a tutelary hierarchy that might (or might not) prove temporary, as subject peoples' capacities warranted.

In this light, Wilson appears much less puzzling and much more a typical pragmatic conservative along the lines of Shaw, Ford, and others in the APSA leadership in its early years. For this group, an empirical, objective account of politics required recognition of the central and probably permanent place of racial difference in domestic and world politics alike. And the study of political institutions would have to involve much less in the way of abstract principle and much more in the way of calculations of efficiency and the pronouncements of racial anthropology.

The *Journal of Race Development*: Evolution and Uplift

Most leaders of the young APSA doubted that reform efforts might significantly alter political and social arrangements that they understood to be rooted in deep-seated, racial characteristics. However, the first U.S.-based scholarly journal devoted specifically to international affairs did not entirely sign on to the idea that the "study of colonial development" revealed above all, as Paul Reinsch would have it, the "insistent . . . difficulty of modifying social institutions and psychological characteristics" of "an alien race" "by . . . political action."[1] Rather, for the editors and writers affiliated with the *Journal of Race Development* (*JRD*), launched in 1910 out of Clark University in Massachusetts, "political action" was a potent mechanism for uplift.

The *JRD* published much that was perfectly in line with Reinsch's basic precepts. It also contained even more extreme, hard-line colonialist rhetoric. But its primary editorial stance was a more optimistic, reform-minded take on what an evolutionary understanding of racial difference might mean for the relationship between the United States and the "backward races."

Like the APSA colonialism scholars, the *JRD*'s writers and editors embraced an expansionist role for America and sought to put social science expertise at the disposal of administrators. Likewise, the *JRD*'s writers and editors also looked to evolutionary theory to inform major questions of both international relations and U.S. politics. However, while the conservative reformers of the APSA tended to see deeply ingrained racial traits as constraining the possibility of democracy or the workability of U.S.-style political institutions for nonwhites, a dominant tendency within the *JRD* saw a role for a science of politics and administration in directing racial evolution in positive directions.

The *JRD* was co-edited by the historian George Hubbard Blakeslee and Clark's first president, the pioneering experimental psychologist G. Stanley Hall. The relatively young Blakeslee, who earned his doctorate in history at Harvard in 1903, was already among the best-known China and Latin America experts in the United States by the time the journal was launched. Under his leadership, Clark's history department added "International Relations" to its title and became one of the first departments in the country to offer courses on non-Western countries, including Liberia, Russia, Turkey, China, Japan, Siberia, the Philippines, and the Congo Free State, as well as regional courses on Africa, "the Far East," "the Near East," Latin America, and Britain's colonies. Along with Hall, Blakeslee organized the first major series of what we would now call "area studies" conferences at an American university, producing in the process a series of edited volumes on China, Japan, Latin America, Mexico, and the Caribbean, among other topics.

Blakeslee was a committed internationalist, devoted to the idea that scientific knowledge could temper conflict and foster mutually beneficial relations among the nations of the world. He brought this belief to an important career in practical politics. He served in official capacities under five presidents, including a stint advising the State Department on the post–World War II reconstruction of Japan.[2] He also served for many years in the leadership of the World Peace Foundation, which, founded in 1910 with an unprecedented $1 million from educational publisher and philanthropist Edward Ginn, brought "energetic optimism" to the tasks of applying "to international affairs the premises which guided Progressivism in its domestic programs" and of using education to convert "the masses, particularly young people," to the cause of peace.[3]

Hall, a generation older than Blakeslee, had risen to prominence at Johns Hopkins in the 1880s, founding the first formal lab and journal (the *American Journal of Psychology*) dedicated to experimental psychology. His star, and his university's with it, was to wane in subsequent decades (at least in some measure because of his reputedly difficult personality). However, for a period in the early twentieth century, Hall established Clark as a prestigious research center, bringing with him from Johns Hopkins some of the most prominent researchers in the country.[4] His particular preoccupations were education and the life cycle; he wrote extensively about adolescence (which he is alternately credited with "discovering" and "inventing") and aging. It was through these interests that Hall came to international affairs. Following Ernst Haeckel's theory of "recapitulationism," Hall thought that the development of individuals in the womb and over the life cycle essentially reprised the stages of human evolution. "Lower races," or what Hall called "race children," he understood as inhabiting the developmental level of children or adolescents, in "something like . . . an arrested childhood."⁵ From this perspective, the relationship of the "savage" to the "civilized" was roughly analogous to that of a child or student to a parent or teacher, and imperialism—at least potentially—took on a decidedly pedagogical aspect.

Although some of its editors and contributors had political science training or affiliations, the *JRD* is a precursor to the tradition of area studies, in that it sought to bring a variety of insights and methods to bear on regions of particular interest to U.S. foreign policy (and, not incidentally, on promoting U.S. interests in those regions). As such, it attracted leading Progressive Era academics and intellectuals along with civil servants, missionaries, diplomats, and others. Over the years, contributing editors included significant numbers of nonacademics as well as the sociologists W. E. B. Du Bois and Robert Park; the anthropologist and political science professor David P. Barrows; historian Payson J. Treat; economist Thorstein Veblen; anthropologists Franz Boas, Alfred Kroeber, and William Curtis Farabee; and Ellsworth Huntington, the geographer and later president of the American Eugenics Society. Contributors ranged from Japanese colonial administrators to John Dewey.

In 1919, the journal changed its name to the *Journal of International Relations*. Three years later, it moved to New York to merge with another publication and form the house organ of the Council on Foreign Relations, where it is still published today as *Foreign Affairs*. As its publishing history suggests, the *JRD* represents a tradition that is in some ways lost and in others very much with us. The journal's pages show the influence of long-discredited Lamarckian notions of heredity and crude, climate-based evolutionary theory. Moreover, the confidence with which its writers speak of "civilization" and "progress" has come to seem quaint. However, in the *JRD* we can also see the forging of a language of international development as a project of directed social change through elite scientific and political intervention that is still alive and thriving in universities, non-governmental organizations, and governing institutions.

Robert Vitalis, who unearthed the *JRD*'s publishing history, places the *JRD* within a "lost world of development theory in the United States," consisting of a complex of academics, government, and other associations (such as the APSA, Ginn's World Peace Foundation, and, later, the big private philanthropies) in America around the turn of the twentieth century. In Vitalis's account, these individuals and institutions organized around questions of "development of backward states and races . . . and what kinds of interventions if any are effective" in promoting it.[6] For him, it is in this "lost world," rather than in postwar politics and academia, that we should look for origins of the lines of inquiry and practice that later coalesced around area studies and the field of international relations. This chapter looks at the early issues of the journal to explore how the *JRD*'s writers and editors conceived of their own enterprise and the analytical tools they brought to bear on it.

The most important such tool was an indeterminate boundary between biology and society. The *JRD* returned time and again to a notion of "civilization" in which, just as for Burgess and the APSA colonialism scholars after him, race, culture, and political institutions could together be mapped onto evolutionary/developmental processes. Evolution itself appeared as both natural and cultural, the embodied accretion of influences over time. It is this slippage among nature, culture, and society that made a bioevolutionary account of politics plausible. However, if the more racially conservative elements in the APSA found reasons for semipermanent hierarchy and separation in evolutionary theory, many in the group around the *JRD* saw in the intertwining of nature, politics, and historical development the possibility for a far-reaching, even world-historical program of racial uplift.

The *JRD* was dedicated in significant ways to the proposition that the application of scientific knowledge could bring forth latent possibilities in the "blood" of peoples. That is, in common with most Progressive Era intellectuals, its contributors and editors largely understood "races" to be history's basic units and "evolution" to be its motive force. However, if Burgess's Whig historico-politics saw the progress of civilization as the flowering of a racial *telos*, "development" most often appeared in the *JRD* as an active, politically and socially directed—but still essentially racial—project. Crucially, this project depended on the mutual permeability of nature and society, particularly the idea that just as nature shaped political and social institutions, changing political and social institutions could in turn leave their mark on an evolving nature.

While the *JRD*'s personnel attests to the indistinct disciplinary matrix of early twentieth-century academic work on international relations, its editors clearly shared the ambition of many of the figures discussed in Chapter 3: to systematize international relations, the study of colonial administration, and "race development" as fields of empirical study independent of international law. In this, they and like-minded colleagues met with considerable success. By the time the *JRD* was reborn as *Foreign Affairs* in 1922, courses specifically on "international relations" were on offer from most major political science departments, and international law and international relations began increasingly to appear as analytically distinct areas of inquiry requiring specialized experts.[7]

For present purposes, the contrasts between the *JRD*'s self-conception and that of the contemporary field of international relations are more interesting than the continuities. For the *JRD*'s writers and editors, like their contemporaries and predecessors discussed in previous chapters, the biological and the political were inextricable, and understanding of political institutions was to be sought in the register of evolutionary time. But what set the *JRD* apart even in its own time was the way in which, in its pages, political institutions often appeared not only to spring from nature but also to be capable of directing nature's developmental course.

Reforming the World

The *JRD*'s high-powered cohort of writers generally expounded an expansive vision of America's role in the new century and the possibilities for worldwide progress and peaceful coexistence. For most of them, America was to lead the world in the uplift of the "backward" or "dependent" races. This was to include colonial subjects (as in the Philippines), those of sovereign states (such as China and Liberia), and "dependent" peoples within America's own borders ("the Indian" and "the Negro"). For some, this implied a sort of tutelary, temporary, paternalistic administrative/colonial endeavor; for others, it meant something closer to what we would now understand as development assistance.

It was almost always presented as a kind of reform. The idea was that even if they could not be erased, the meanings of racial differences could be changed for the better through education and political reform. Who really qualified as "backward" and how much so were points of difference. But it was an article of virtual consensus in the journal that backwardness itself could be accounted for by variations in evolutionary processes. As we have seen, this drew on conventional scientific and popular wisdom as well as on established doctrine in American social science. All the same, the *JRD*'s editors consistently positioned themselves as advocates for those subject to imperial rule. Indeed, intellectually they shared much with Pan-Africanist ideology (associated with contributing editor Du Bois), both in seeing themselves as aligned with the aspirations of "the darker peoples" and as imagining those "darker peoples" to be in need of improvement.[8]

In the editorial that opens the first issue of the *JRD* in 1910, editor Blakeslee is critical of European colonialism and tries to differentiate his own project by explaining that the journal "aims to present . . . the different theories as to the methods by which developed peoples may most effectively aid the progress of the undeveloped"; "not how weaker races may best be exploited, but how they may best be helped to be stronger." This endeavor was to be carried out on American soil as well as abroad—in the "struggle" that Blakeslee called the "key to the past seventy-five years of American history": finding "some solution for the negro problem."[9] Here Blakeslee offers a mild criticism of the American people. A few pages later, G. Stanley Hall is firmer, citing the "innumerable modes of extortion and misrepresentation that private greed is still allowed to practice upon . . . the Negro" in America.[10]

As Blakeslee's and Hall's statements suggest, while the *JRD* generally affirmed the superiority of Anglo-Saxon civilization, it rejected many of the more vicious forms of white supremacist thought that were widely accepted at the time. Often, *JRD* writers took the position that the mental and physical capacities of the races were not so deeply different; rarely, they suggested that one or another race might have the potential to equal whites. (*JRD* writers were particular fans of the Japanese, whose role as colonizers in Korea and China many saw as parallel to American efforts in the Philippines.) More generally, where others saw in evolutionary theory the scientific explanation of fundamental, permanent racial difference, in the *JRD*, evolution often appeared as a field of possibility for intervention and positive change.[11]

The *JRD* certainly published its share of jingoistic colonial rhetoric. To give just one example, in January 1911, William S. Washburn, then a recent U.S. Civil Service Commissioner in the Philippines, contributed an obituary for an American military officer who had served in the Philippines. The title was "A Worthy Example of the Influence of a Strong Man upon the Development of Racial Character," and it described the deceased as "a man who, by temperament, force of character, and training, was fitted to rule as a benevolent despot in a land where ignorance, treachery and tribal enmities bound the inhabitants to barbarism."[12] However, the journal also published articles critical of American attitudes and policies, with the occasional blistering denunciation. A 1912 article called "A Literary Legend: 'The Oriental,'" by William Elliot Griffis is a striking example. Griffis began, "Writers have created the 'Oriental' of imagination, fancy, prejudice and bigotry, who has no counterpart in reality. . . . It has become a 'vested interest,' a staple and stock in trade, a permanent and ever-promising speculation to picture 'the Oriental' as a being in human form whose nature is fundamentally different from the 'Occidental.' Such a delineation and contrast has mercantile value. It pays in what the American loves so dearly—money." It does so by enlarging "the sale of tickets at the box office [and] the circulation of the newspapers. It delights the mob. . . . The 'Orientalism' which sells . . . , which gets up periodical war scares and from nervous congressmen compels votes for big battleships, or which is set forth by politicians bidding for votes is not intrinsically different from that which was and is dearly loved in Europe. . . . Yet probably in no country more than in the United States of America, is our legacy of prejudice against 'the Oriental' so worked in the interest of dollars and cents."[13]

Some writers went so far as to contest the idea that races can be ranked hierarchically (an October 1914 article by Wilson D. Wallis of the University of Pennsylvania criticizes Hall's "race children" theories on this score) or to advocate race-mixing. (That same issue, for example, contained a piece concluding with the "hope the day may come again when the Pacific Ocean will become the intermediary for bringing together the innumerable racial globules that seem past amalgamation").[14] However, support for racial equality was never unqualified. Intermarriage was occasionally proposed as a solution to the "Indian problem," for example, but this had less to do with racial harmony and integration than with obliterating Indians by gradually turning them into white people. Intermarriage between blacks and whites was never advocated.

Taken as a whole, the *JRD* presented complex and sometimes heterodox racial attitudes that were nonetheless anchored to common understandings of the workings of race in history (or, perhaps more properly, of the workings of history through race). On the spectrum of progressive political thought, the *JRD* can, by reputation and personnel, be situated toward the left, closer to the intellectuals, settlement house workers, and socialists who sought to promote progress and civilization through transformations of the urban environment and the industrial sector than to the more center-right progressives who predominated in APSA leadership at this time.[15]

Like their counterparts in the APSA, *JRD* writers often presented their agenda as an alternative to European-style colonialism. In his first and only editorial, cited above, Blakeslee explained that the *JRD* was to be devoted to the "general subject of the control of dependencies, a field in which there has already taken place a profound change of feeling and belief." The European idea of colonies as resources to be exploited was "giving place to that recently introduced by the United States in the Philippine Islands—the policy of controlling a backward people only so long as it may be necessary to train them to carry on successfully an efficient government."[16] Even Washburn commented in 1910 that it was "essential" to "extend to the Philippines" the "reform movement . . . dominant now in America, insisting not only on clean governmental operations, but also [on] the enactment of laws for the betterment of the people, for their moral, mental, and physical elevation."[17]

Again, the inclusion of U.S. foreign relations in the reform agenda places the *JRD* in the left-progressive intellectual milieu. During the decades around the turn of the twentieth century, American foreign policy makers tended to see American possessions overseas as stepping-stones to regional markets. A chief argument of antiannexationists in the late 1890s was that trade could be maintained without the headaches (and race problems) of political control. The *JRD*'s writers certainly valued trade, and in the journal's pages uplift did not have to be altruistic. Apart from short pieces by the vice president of Miami University and the director of the International Bureau of Students (arguing for the professionalization of Latin American universities and increased exchange programs, respectively) a Latin America–focused issue in July 1914 was uncharacteristically short on the rhetoric of benevolence. For example, "The Development of Our Latin-American Trade" by American businessman John Hays Hammond emphasized what the U.S. stood to gain from access to Latin American markets; Hiram Bingham, of the Yale University history department, in "The Probable Effect of the Opening of the Panama Canal on Our Economic Relations with the People of the West Coast of South America" called for caution against overexuberant investing, noting that the Indians of the region were "not ready for a boom."[18]

All the same, more often the question of annexation versus trade appeared as beside the point. U.S. possessions were not merely means to the end of trade; they were flagships in a developmental project. Trade would be at once a contributing factor and an outcome. Echoing in many ways the anti-"assimilation" position of Reinsch and others, Hall, for example, thought that U.S. influence might help to free the "ascendant" races from misguided (European) colonial policy, allowing them to "achieve historic development along new lines." This would require a "more humane and larger policy" that would, abroad and at home, "strive to make representative colored men self-respecting . . . , in a word, to bring out the best that is in their blood, and to mitigate surely, if ever so slowly, the handicap of race prejudice, for these things alone can give the black man true freedom."

For Hall, tellingly, "race prejudice" appeared as failure to properly appreciate race *differences*. That is, rather than seeing "colored" people as insufficiently rational, for example, whites and blacks themselves should appreciate blacks' unique traits, the cultivation of which would presumably eliminate race prejudice by eliminating its basis: blacks' incomplete development. For this reason, Hall urged that the federal Bureau of Ethnology step up its efforts to document the cultures of "the red man," and that a similar "African Bureau" should highlight the accomplishments of "the African."[19]

The thrust of Hall's argument, however, and the guiding premise of the *JRD* more broadly, was that while Europe had been exploitive, the United States should pursue a policy of uplift at home and abroad that would be both beneficent and informed by science. America's qualifications for such an endeavor were linked to its exceptional history and racial makeup. The Latin America issue discussed above focused on the development of political and economic institutions and new trade opportunities with the opening of the Panama Canal. Questions of trade balances, Latin American perceptions of American intentions, natural resources, and the like were discussed. But the developmental status of Latin American civilization was central to the discussion. The issue opens with something like a call for racial indulgence from a Peruvian Envoy named Federico A. Pezet. In "Contrasts in the Development of Nationality in Anglo- and Latin-America," Pezet argues that Latin America was disadvantaged relative to its northern neighbors in its prospects for developing republican institutions and prosperous economies. For Pezet, Anglo-America was colonized by homogeneous Puritan families confronted by only relatively weak savages, leaving them plenty of virgin land. Latin America, by contrast, was settled by fortune-seekers from Iberia, who mixed with the stronger, more numerous native population, living off the latter's wealth and labor rather than establishing self-supporting colonies. Closer to Europe both geographically and climatically, North America also got the "better" western European immigrants, who were able to assimilate to the republican institutions inherited from the English.

Pezet summed up the Latin American disadvantage as follows: "Latin America, at the time of its inception into the family of nations, was a group of disassociated military nations, utterly unschooled in self-government, and inhabited in greater part by unfused races" who "from despotism and servitude . . . jumped into the most advanced form of government." He concluded with a plea for greater understanding and aid in the "common quest for human uplift."[20]

Here, the United States appeared as a potential partner with Latin American elites in the uplift endeavor. This is a twist on a more general theme in the *JRD*, in which the task seemed largely to consist of fostering an elite class. Sociologist Howard Odum's "Standards of Measurement for Race Development," emphasized class differentiation among American "negroes." He endorsed the idea that race progress can be measured by "the degree to which [a race] tended to increase the proportion of its population above the lower classes . . . to the increase of the great middle class and especially the upper half."[21]

African Americans received relatively little systematic consideration in the *JRD*. However, as we have seen, Hall and others explicitly invoked the "negro problem" as relevant to (or a species of) colonial administration. Books on the subject were frequently reviewed; these were generally commended to the extent that they identified unscientific prejudice as the chief factor condemning most black people to the lower classes and limiting the aspirations—and hence the salutary leadership—of the "better class."[22]

Similarly, articles on the Philippines in particular discussed techniques for creating "native" leadership. Training Filipinos to assume (gradually) higher positions in the civil service is the focus of Washburn's comments in the very first issue (also cited above). In it, Washburn writes that if Filipinos are "left to their own resources" they will fall into corrupt oligarchy. Hence, as "stated by President Roosevelt in one of his messages to Congress, 'It is important that this—the merit—system be observed at home, but it is more important that it be rigidly enforced in our insular possessions.'" That is, by rewarding honesty, education, and hard work, the U.S.–administered civil service could be the incubator for a class that would lead the Philippines and help to make them "in time—probably not in your day nor in mine—partially at least if not fully prepared for self-government."[23] These sentiments appear repeatedly, as when Payson Treat reviewed contributing editor David P. Barrows's *A Decade of American Government in the Philippines, 1903–1913* in 1915, highlighting with approval Barrows's emphasis on the need for the education of a political class.

Sometimes the leadership to be established was by one nonwhite group over another. A 1910 article by W. Morgan Shuster titled "Our Philippine Policies and Their Results" advocated solidifying the dominance of Christianized Filipinos over "Moros" particularly but also over "uncivilized" pagans. This was to include establishing a Jim Crow–type system of separate jurisdictions and administrations. Shuster thought that the Filipinos were "Christians and by nature peaceable" and that the "pagans" could be reached, but that "a strong, quasi-military government is the only one suited to deal with the Moro problem."[24] This view was contradicted by John P. Finley in the lead article of the April 1915 issue, "The Mohammedan Problem in the Philippines." A lieutenant colonel and former governor of a Moro province in the Philippines, Finley defended the Moros against such charges, arguing to the contrary that they were highly civilized and should be afforded a much greater level of autonomy, away from the less civilized Filipinos.

In Liberia, too, the problem appeared as establishing proper leadership and maintaining its control. Two articles on that country, one by the (African American) scholar and diplomat George W. Ellis ("Dynamic Factors in the Liberian Situation") and the other by Emmett J. Scott, both of whom had filled official U.S. government posts there, appeared in 1911. Scott's title posed the question, "Is Liberia Worth Saving?" Both articles answered in the affirmative, presenting the "Americanized" Liberians as a vanguard civilizing their race-fellows on the continent and suggesting that this experiment was threatened by European power struggles in the region as well as by recalcitrant natives. For Scott, the "Americanized Liberians" had "helped to uplift the natives—to no considerable degree, it is true, but nevertheless to an appreciable degree." To fail to support the Liberian government against both threats would have been to sacrifice those gains and also to betray the trust of the Liberian elite, who deserved support in their efforts to establish control over the countryside.[25]

Evolution, Change, and Heredity

Evolution was more often invoked than defined in the *JRD*'s pages—it operated less as a definite concept than as an interpretive grid. Like their counterparts in the APSA, *JRD* writers and editors rejected the universalism of Burgess-style teleology in favor of a more branching, differentiated model of development. However, they retained the idea that evolution was a form of progress—in this case, of progressive differentiation: from simple to complex organism; from simple to complex society. More specifically, "race development" seemed to entail moves toward a capitalist division of labor and social division based on class rather than on rank or "organic hierarchy," both of which were thought to be a characteristic of more primitive society.

Most *JRD* articles focused on differences of education, customs, and living standards rather than of biology. However, physical evolution was never far from view: many articles focused primarily on various aspects of biological evolution and even topics that would seem quite far from questions of biology were often prefaced by references to bio-social evolution. For example, a boosterish article by W. D. Boyce, the publisher of the *Saturday Blade* and the *Chicago Ledger*, titled "Advantages of Making the Canal Zone a Free City and a Free Port," brought together the notions of developmental disadvantage (particularly its evolutionary and climatic origins) with recommendations for American businessmen and policy makers. Boyce began with an overview of the history of human settlement of the Americas, noting that understanding South America's commercial development required that one "first analyze the original stock from which these people sprang." In his view, the first settlers came from Asia across the Bering Strait, and hunted and fished their way southward. Thus employed, "the Indian improved until he reached the warm country near the Rio Grande, and there in the hot climate, where life was easy he began to deteriorate." (The salubrious temperate zones of the Andes had allowed for the development of Inca civilization.) His prescription was an energetic policy of free trade and of doing business "everlastingly on the square." As to the latter, he remarked that Latin Americans were "not used to it, but they will like it once they find it genuine" and would as a result come to prefer trade with the United States to trade with Europe.[26] Articles on racial diversification in the Pacific region, the probable racial origins of the indigenous people of Latin America, the geographical origins of the peculiar racial characteristics of South Africa's "native races," and white adaptation to tropical and subtropical climates, for example, were similarly published without fuss; their inclusion required no justification, and no major discontinuity in perspective appears between writers who addressed biological or geographical topics and others whose focus was more social.

The idea that races can decline and not just develop had been at the heart of Bryce's concern about colonial expansion—specifically, the idea that America should not expand into climates where whites would not thrive. In the *JRD*, as in reform circles more generally, this notion had two important implications that underlay much of the concern about development in general. First, the opposite of "development" would not necessarily be stasis: it would probably be exploitation by more developed peoples, decline, degeneration, and possible "race war." This anxiety was invoked more often than directly stipulated, but it is nevertheless palpable, particularly in discussions of the situation in the Pacific and of what Harvard geology professor W. M. Davis called "the advance of a civilized race into the land of an uncivilized race" in Southern Africa and the Americas.[27]

The potential for whites' collective decline was a pervasive anxiety in the context of industrialization and the "closing" of the frontier—the end of the republican image of America as a land of independent small producers, immune to European decadence. Dorothy Ross argues that this anxiety produced a crisis among intellectuals, many of whom sought to replace this nineteenth-century vision of America's exceptional destiny with one appropriate to a new age.[28] This crisis produced a range of responses, from the call for imperial expansion to replace the lost frontier, to a number of populist and/or antimodernist rejections of cities and industrial production, or alternatively to the embrace of modernity that characterized most progressive intellectuals. For this last group, America's unique characteristics, and particularly its lack of European historical baggage, made it an ideal field for the development of modern society.

However, this did not mean that America's ideals would be realized automatically. What would happen to whites, for example, as they ventured into the territories of "the dark races"? (Latin America was sometimes presented as a cautionary tale on that score by Latin Americans such as Pezet as well as by North Americans.) The *JRD* writer who attended most thoroughly to this question was contributing editor Ellsworth Huntington.

Ellsworth Huntington was a leading geographer who later became the head of the American Eugenics Society. He was the author of a number of books as well as articles in nine major geography journals and more than forty other publications, ranging from the *American Historical Review* to *The Nation*.[29] In his first major book, *The Pulse of Asia*, he elaborated the "Huntington Theory," which suggested that significant and irregular climate changes, probably caused by changes in the sun, had profoundly influenced human culture.[30] In his view, weather had stimulating (storms) and stultifying (unchanging heat) effects on the human constitution; the worldwide distribution of civilization could be explained by the distribution of temperate climates. His theories, while not fundamentally original, were enormously influential, and he was responsible both for systematizing climate theory to a degree not seen before and further popularizing it among social scientists.

Huntington published four articles in the *JRD*: "Physical Environment as a Factor in Turkey," "Geographical Environment and Japanese Character," "A Neglected Factor in Race Development," and "The Adaptability of the White Man to Tropical America."[31] He argued in "Adaptability" that the riches of tropical America and Africa would be developed only with the "help" of "people of European origin." The stifling heat and evenness of the weather in the tropics, as well as the ease of life, were "conditions which for ages have acted as handicaps to every race whose lot has been cast in" the tropics. Such conditions made one "loathe to work" in general; prolonged exposure to them could turn such lethargy into a racial trait. He suggested that a few generations of habitation by whites in such regions could cause a like degeneration among them. (This would be compounded by the "fact" that "experience in all parts of the world shows that the presence of an inferior race in large numbers tends constantly to lower the standards of the dominant race.") The remedies, once again, were scientific and institutional: Huntington looked to advances in medical science to offset the corrupting effects of tropical disease and to (unspecified) advances in hygiene and institutional arrangements to prevent whites from being debilitaded by contact with their "inferiors."[32]

For Huntington, then, appropriate political action could offset the deleterious effects of climate. Others in the *JRD* took this idea further, suggesting that not only could race development be safeguarded by institutional arrangements, it might even be produced by them. That is, the right kinds of institutions could serve as the environmental conditions shaping bio-social evolution. This was not at all an idiosyncratic position. As we have seen, turn-of-the-century social thought was deeply influenced by evolutionary concepts, many of which long preceded Darwin, in which the social, cultural, and biological traits of a group developed in tandem. Left unexplained in many of these frameworks (including Darwin's) was the mechanism by which this change was effected.

Among the most prominent early answers came from Auguste Lamarck, a French zoologist and botanist writing at the turn of the nineteenth century. Known as the doctrine of heritability of acquired characteristics, Lamarckianism held that adaptation to new conditions could lead to structural modification in adult individuals; new actions, "becoming habitual" could "occasion . . . the development of the organs which execute them."[33] These new traits, or "organs," were then passed down to offspring. With the publication of Darwin's *Origin of the Species*, the spread of Mendelian ideas about heredity, and a campaign by August Weismann against Lamarckian ideas, the processes and mechanism of evolution became the subject of a protracted and often heated debate. However, Lamarckianism was not discarded wholesale, and elements of Lamarckian thought were mixed with theories of natural selection and even, as we shall see, of Mendelian genetics, both by "neo-Lamarckians" and by others who incorporated them less self-consciously.[34]

In his influential work on Lamarckianism in American anthropology and sociology, George Stocking argues, "The idea that acquired characteristics might be inherited was stated or implied in the work of so many [turn-of-the-century] writers that it is impossible to avoid the conclusion that they were primarily reflecting a widespread popular scientific attitude whose roots lay deep in the western European cultural tradition."[35] This may help explain why the logic, if not the substance, of Lamarckianism was so prevalent in the pages of the *JRD* despite the fact that, in Stocking's view, the fight in the biological sciences had been pretty much settled by the time of the journal's launch, with the heritability of acquired characteristics on the losing side.[36]

Stocking argues that the lack of an autonomous subject matter doomed American social science in this period to be tentative and ineffectual. For him, the central problem for the social sciences in the early twentieth century "was not their domination by notions of biological or racial *determinism*, but rather their obfuscation by a vague sociobiological *indeterminism*," a "'blind' and 'bland' shuttling" between race and civilization. The social sciences could not be properly "social" because the distinction between "nature" and "society" or "culture"—or "politics"—was fuzzy. The social sciences—and indeed the biological sciences—would only come into their own later in the twentieth century, when the nature–culture distinction had become "the central element" of the "modern social scientific paradigm."[37]

Stocking does not address political science or international relations specifically, but it is clear this "shuttling" was a crucial feature of what was going on in the *JRD*. In this case, however, "sociobiological indeterminism" hardly restricted the basic project. On the contrary, it was central to the uplift enterprise, as a way of simultaneously maintaining the boundaries between groups, establishing science and scientists as the authoritative source of practical knowledge about those boundaries, and giving science a clear entry point for directing change. The latter feature is what most clearly differentiates the *JRD*'s version of "race development" from Teutonism, for example. Burgess thought the role of political science was to identify the historical trajectory of civilization in order to more or less get out of its way (as by preventing the "higher races" from being diverted from their course by too many dealings with the lower ones). The editors of the *JRD* saw the civilizing process as much more dynamic, and they thought that scientific knowledge could play an active role in shaping it.

Both the indeterminate boundaries between what is natural and what is social and the confusion of Lamarckian, Darwinian, and Mendelian understandings of evolution are abundantly in evidence in a 1913 *JRD* article by contributing editor Thorstein Veblen. Titled "The Mutation Theory and the Blond Race," this article explores what Veblen describes as "two distinct but closely related captions: The Origin of the Blond Type, and the Derivation of the Blond Culture," in the light of new evolutionary theory in which change was understood to originate in mutation rather than through "usages." His thesis was that one true "dolicho-blond" existed in Europe, "in the lands immediately about the narrow Scandinavian waters," and that the other "blond groups" were in fact "hybrid types."[38] Veblen's interest in this topic and his desire to isolate the natural germ of what he in other works characterized as the most progressive world culture is notable, and consonant with his long-standing view of economic life as the result of "instincts" (a concept that he, like G. Stanley Hall, took up from William James) interacting with "institutions."[39] But of primary interest here is what Veblen makes of the biological science of the day.

As noted, a central problem for the Darwinian theory of natural selection was the "origin of the fittest"; that is, where did variation come from in the first place? Veblen perceived correctly that Mendelism held a key to that problem. However, the theory of adaptation that Veblen advanced mimicked Lamarckianism in many important respects. That is, in his view, the "Mendelian postulate that the type is stable except for such a mutation as shall establish a new type" raised "at least the presumption that such a mutation will take place only under exceptional circumstances, that is to say, under circumstances so substantially different from what the type is best adapted to as to subject it to some degree of physiological strain." In the case of the "blonde type," Veblen held, the "parent stock" entered Europe from Africa sometime in the late quaternary period, where it was "exposed to notably novel conditions of life, such as would be presumed . . . to tend to throw the stock into a specifically unstable (mutating) state." That is, external conditions called forth appropriate mutations in enough individuals that, while they inevitably had to mix with the parent stock, a new, "pure type" could in time arise. Moreover, culture itself was among these external factors: "characteristic forms" arose "in adaptation to the peculiar circumstances of environment and culture under which each particular local population [was] required to live."[40]

In this scheme, the two main stimuli for change in neo-Lamarckian theory—geography and culture—remained at the center. There was no room for the random, purposeless quality imputed to mutation by later understandings. Evolution could still be directed—if culture could prompt mutation, changes in education, administration, and industrial organization could still write new characteristics into the bodies of populations. This slippage, of course, was central to a project of uplift in which racial distinctions were entirely "real" and significant but at the same time remediable, and it pervaded the *JRD* far beyond Veblen's intervention.

This commingling of Lamarckianism with Mendelian genetics, along with the broader framework it reflects, points to several important things about the way early discipline builders in international relations and area studies conceived of the relationships among race, politics, and history. First, it highlights the ways in which, for all the ideological and methodological differences between Burgess, his successors in the APSA, and the more optimistic progressives around the *JRD*, they remained in fundamental agreement that "races" were the basic units of history and consequently the starting point for political analysis. Moreover, it underscores the lack of any clear distinction among nature, culture, and politics for all these figures, even as physical evolution and a more embodied conception of "race" took the place of a developing "spirit," or "genius." That is, despite their many differences, scholars in the early twentieth century maintained significant elements of the holistic, organic, and racialist understanding of politics that Burgess had elaborated decades earlier.

Laying Specters to Rest: Political Science Encounters the Boasian Critique of Racial Anthropology

If U.S. political science students learn only one thing about their discipline's early twentieth-century history, it is most likely that the 1920s saw an infusion of scientific rigor into the discipline. In this period, the story goes, scientific approaches began to displace "idealist" or "legalistic" ones, in turn laying the groundwork for a midcentury "behavioral revolution" that established scientific method and observational rigor as hallmarks of the disciplinary mainstream. The hero most often credited with getting the scientific ball rolling (or charged with "scientism," depending on your point of view) is Charles E. Merriam.

Born in Hopkinton, Iowa, in 1874, Merriam came from a modest but respectable Presbyterian family. His father owned a dry-goods store and served as postmaster, school-board member, and trustee of the local college, which Charles attended. After receiving a degree there, Charles moved on, first to study law at the University of Iowa and later to do his doctorate in political science at Columbia. Once liberated from small-town life and armed with academic credentials, Merriam joined the University of Chicago political science faculty. There he embarked on an impressive academic and public career, preaching the gospel of better living through technocratic management for many decades.

He quickly rose to chair of the Chicago department, became deeply involved in local politics, and entered the national arena as a player within the Progressive Party. During World War I, he helped produce U.S. propaganda at home (working for the federal Committee on Public Information) and abroad (as American High Commissioner for Public Information in Rome). On returning home after the war, he assumed new positions of academic, philanthropic, and public leadership, including significant contributions to New Deal planning efforts.

Most significant for present purposes is Merriam's work in forging new intellectual alliances, as well as institutional structures and funding models for the social sciences. While scholars differ as to the originality of Merriam's intellectual contributions, there is general agreement that he was a brilliant academic entrepreneur and a key player in promoting an orientation to political scholarship that emphasized scientific method; powerful networks friendly to that orientation; and a cadre of talented, ambitious young scholars steeped in it. Less well known, and almost entirely unexplored, however, is that in the course of these efforts, Merriam, along with many of his intellectual and institutional allies, engaged extensively with scientific debates about racial difference.

Such debates took on especially fevered tones in the 1920s. Postwar race riots, a virtual takeover of the Democratic Party by the revived Ku Klux Klan, a Red Scare fueled by fears of foreign and black radicals, immigration restriction, and the emergence of the Garvey movement were only some of the things directing public attention to "race problems." The Scopes trial and the eugenics movement meant that scientific ideas about biological evolution and human difference achieved new levels of visibility in the 1920s.[1] Elite science was also highly and publicly engaged with racial topics, as eugenics leaders and immigration-restriction advocates held forth from their perches at the top of major research institutions and bureaucracies, including the American Museum of Natural History, the Smithsonian Institution, and the National Research Council (NRC), as well as science-minded philanthropic institutions, such as the Carnegie Institute of Washington.

At the same time, the top echelons of science were confronting something genuinely novel: a sustained challenge to racism, and indeed to the idea of "race" itself, from within their own ranks. This challenge came from the anthropologist Franz Boas and his students, who advanced the claim that history and culture, not race, accounted for most differences between groups. Fierce pushback from scientific racists in the years just after the war meant that the nature, sources, and meaning of racial difference were at the center of high-profile conflicts in the human sciences.

Merriam was not a details man, but he had a keen eye for the big picture, and the significance of these debates was not lost on him. He recognized that questions of the bases and potential malleability of human behavior, the possibility of cultural and racial assimilation, and the relative and absolute capacities of human groups held profound implications for the possibility of meaningful political reform and, by extension, for the science meant to advance it. And, like many others, he was optimistic that new developments in the human sciences were poised to help settle those questions. But Merriam's engagement with race science is particularly interesting. What sets him and the political-scientific revolutionaries in his orbit apart from their earlier counterparts is that they didn't just want to be *like* natural scientists. They wanted to work *with* natural scientists, both to draw on their findings and to use their methods. Merriam in particular worked to foster relationships with leading scientists and to create institutions to bring them into collaboration with scholars working on topics of political importance.

From today's perspective, Merriam and his allies took what looks like a remarkably promiscuous attitude toward the race science of the day. Neither as personally invested in white supremacy or imperialism as some of their predecessors nor in the main committed to any kind of antiracist project, these would-be innovators were willing to take whatever seemed useful, willy-nilly, without much regard for bitter, ideologically charged fights within the science establishment. As a result, they might embrace elements of Boas's scientific critique of racial determinism while, sometimes almost in the same breath, also invoking with interest and approval the work of the very racial determinists Boas sought to undermine.

To this point, this book has traced broad continuities. For many years and across significant theoretical, political, and methodological differences, a range of U.S. political scientists had largely agreed on some version of the following premises: (1) "races" were a (if not *the*) basic unit of politics, and (2) political arrangements were (and ought to be) a function of racial characteristics. Moreover, political scientists invoking strong versions of these premises often explicitly linked them to their scientific aspirations. John W. Burgess's political "science," for example, consisted primarily in rigorously applying historical method, social evolutionary theory, and "ethnology" to questions about "the state." Woodrow Wilson, Henry Jones Ford, Paul Reinsch, George Blakeslee, and others treated "recognition" of the "facts" of racial difference as a condition for genuinely scientific political analysis. Many of them, too, grounded that analysis in versions of evolutionary theory that conflated biological, social, and political evolution.

This chapter and the next will explore a break with this perspective, focusing on the ways in which Merriam and others hoping to remake the study of politics on a natural-science model received and made sense of scientific debates about race in the 1920s. Many of these figures showed interest in the Boasian program, and particularly in its move away from organicism and teleology. At the same time, the humanistic, antideterministic implications that many Boasians took from that move appear to have been less compelling to political scientists still largely committed to the ideal of a society beneficently ordered from above. For those purposes, Merriam and several of his associates turned to more deterministic corners of the science establishment. Merriam was particularly interested in the large-scale army intelligence-testing program implemented during the war by Yale psychologist Robert Yerkes, as well as in studies of racial difference carried out under the auspices of the National Research Council. Like Teutonism and its descendants, those projects ranked and sorted the population, promising scientific purchase on politically relevant differences between groups. But they did so in more fine-grained ways, no longer dependent on "traditional," "authoritarian" stories about racial essences.[2] Rather, they offered a more modern, liberal account of difference, rooted in the characteristics of individuals and what one writer called the "proportions and averages of . . . different groups."[3]

Charles E. Merriam's New Politics

Merriam was devoted to the quest for a methodological revolution in political science. All the same, his leadership in important respects could be described as "do as I say, not as I do." Merriam's own output was not especially innovative, running to breezy surveys of political thought and/or practices, and semi-biographical explorations of "leadership."[4] Merriam made little use of new methodologies himself and produced no original, robustly scientific accounts of deep causal factors driving political life. But he was convinced that such things were possible and necessary, and he mentored a talented cohort of students who went on to do far more groundbreaking work.

The most illustrious of his students at Chicago was Harold D. Lasswell, whom Merriam eventually recruited to the Chicago faculty. There, and later during wartime service in Washington, DC, as well as from posts at Yale,

RAND, and the Hoover Institute (to name just a few of his affiliations), Lasswell did seminal work in political psychology, communications research, policy studies, legal education, and political sociology.[5] He also taught luminaries of midcentury political science, including Gabriel Almond, V. O. Key, and David Truman.

Together, Merriam, Lasswell, and Harold Gosnell, another Merriam student-turned-colleague, led the storied "Chicago School of Political Science." In a fairly representative account of its place in disciplinary history, Michael Heaney and John Hansen remember the Chicago School as the "most cohesive, productive, and influential contributor to the development of political science on a natural scientific model." They point out that its members "were among the first to use advanced empirical methods in political science, including survey experiments . . . , content analysis . . . , field experiments . . . , and correlation, regression, and factor analysis," and taught those who would go on to form "the vanguard" that "created the science of politics that became the mainstream of the discipline during the 1950s and '60s—and remains with us still."[6]

Skeptics remain, however. Most notably, John Gunnell points out that, for all his talk of "science," Merriam remained committed to an ideal of political community that harkened back to Burgess's "state." For Gunnell, the real innovation in the 1920s was a turn to a more open-ended, multifarious vision of political life by "pluralists"; the Chicago School's contribution consisted mainly of "methodological refinement."[7]

There is important truth to this characterization of Merriam's political imagination—as noted, his own work was fairly conventional. However, taken together and examined from the angle of the discipline's engagement with racial ideas, the pluralist and scientistic tendencies of the interwar era represent a clear break with the visions of political unity and difference that had animated much of the political science of earlier generations. The call for new methods, in turn, is not so easily disconnected from the new frameworks emerging at this time.

Burgess and his cohort had found comfort and guidance in "the state's" progress toward its ideal. Many who followed recast that progress as more material, diverse, and evolutionary, but they held on to it nonetheless. However, for many intellectuals in the early twentieth century, the idea of progress was becoming harder to sustain. Thinkers like Karl Pearson, Sigmund Freud, John Dewey, William James, and John Watson, as well as modernist writers and artists, had already begun to portray human knowledge as subjective and partial, and the impulses guiding human behavior as less than rational.[8] This disenchantment sharpened in the interwar years. Just as the Civil War had set a series of urgent tasks for the emerging social sciences in the Gilded Age, World War I prompted many to question more seriously the possibility of progress, as well as the bases of social order and solidarity. Perhaps most important for political science, the war furnished new reasons to reject notions of collective or evolving rationality, and the "doctrine of sovereignty, especially in German philosophy, according to which the state was not only all powerful, but also all righteous" struck many not only as outdated but as downright sinister.[9]

In this context, "pluralists" such as Harold Laski put internal differentiation rather than (racialized) organic unity at the center of democratic theory, turning away from "the state" and toward process as an ordering principle for social life. For them, groups could form any number of ways, politics *was* group activity, and democracy emerged from the diverse play of interests. The more technocratically minded Chicago group was not willing to go as far. They, too, recognized the increasing diversity of modern life and began to perceive organic and racialist accounts of political difference as "traditional" and "authoritarian" and to cast about for alternatives. But rather than following the pluralists in embracing contingency and flux, they looked instead to science and method in order to anchor (fallible) human rationality. That is, for this group, recognizing the diversity of interests structuring political life did not mean, "giv[ing] up on the effort to organize culture around science." If anything, this effort became more urgent. Historical forces could no longer simply be parsed for their underlying rationality—they had to be tamed, controlled, and directed. If the political knowledge necessary to such a task was subjective, it would have to be grounded in procedures that might guarantee its validity.[10]

Merriam gave perhaps the most elaborate account of what he hoped political science could achieve in his 1925 book, *New Aspects of Politics*.[11] In many ways, the book echoed perennial calls for a scientific turn in the discipline, emphasizing empiricism and doubling down on the appeal to science as an anchor for political judgment. But it differed in important ways as well. In earlier decades, to do "empirical" political science had generally meant to reject a given set of abstractions ("natural law," for example, or Hegelian teleology); "science," correspondingly, had meant primarily rigorous historical–institutional analysis, some version of evolutionary theory, and/or gestures toward "ethnology." For Merriam and the group of students and colleagues that he cultivated, however, empiricism was increasingly to invoke a present-oriented study of behavior and process, with a view toward "control." Science, above all, was to imply measurement, and, whenever possible, the use of statistical or other instruments to produce "objective," verifiable results. Viewed in this light, the Chicago group's "methodological refinement" arises in response to changed ideas about historical change and political community, as well as about the strategies by which one might understand and communicate knowledge about political life.[12]

Pluralism, Science, and Interwar Challenges to Democratic Theory

As we shall see later in this chapter, the forces driving historical change and the relationships among groups and individuals were the subject of intense investigation and controversy in psychology, biology, and anthropology—investigations to which members of the Chicago School and their associates were highly attentive. However, before exploring the ways in which some of these figures looked to race theory for solutions to the problems facing political science, it may be worth delving a bit deeper into what they perceived those problems to be. By the time *New Aspects of Politics* came out, the APSA's membership had grown dramatically (reaching 1,300 in 1920). Attendance at its annual meetings doubled to about 300 and, with a sharp rise in the number of political science doctorates awarded and teaching posts available, came to be dominated by professors rather than the mix of academics, lawyers, diplomats, journalists, and others who had populated the early organization. The geography of political scholarship shifted as well, with Harvard and the Universities of Chicago, Wisconsin, Iowa, Illinois, and California joining (and, in Chicago's case, surpassing) Columbia and Johns Hopkins as the main producers of credentialed political scientists.[13]

New size and breadth presented challenges to theoretical coherence. As Columbia's Gordon Dewey put it later in the decade, U.S. political science in the 1920s found itself in an "amorphous condition." Where "once by general agreement political scientists concerned themselves solely with the state," by then "not merely the methods to be followed, but [political science's] objectives, even the matters with which it should deal" had become "subjects of controversy."

New Aspects of Politics declared emphatically for those hoping to move beyond the study of government and its animating spirit and, in Dewey's words, "dig deeper."[14] In particular, Merriam's book stressed that students of politics had to turn to the "material, the measurable, and the comparable," at the expense of the "traditional and authoritarian." Merriam assured readers that this did not mean he was "suggesting that we ask our older friends [history and law] to go." Unfortunately, though, historically oriented science "tended to glorify tradition" and Americans in the 1920s were entering a "new" world. As a result, those old friends would have to "sit around the table" with the other social sciences as well as with psychology, statistics, biology, geography, and anthropology. Only then could politics as "the art of the traditional" "advance" to "politics as the science of constructive, intelligent social control."[15]

Here and often in his work, Merriam did not distinguish in any clear way between "politics" and "political science."[16] This conflation reflected his biography. While Merriam spent almost his entire working life as University of Chicago faculty, he also maintained the family tradition of involvement in local politics. By the time *New Aspects of Politics* appeared, he had already served an eight-year stint as alderman and twice run credible campaigns for mayor of Chicago. (Julius Rosenwald was one of the wealthy, reform-minded backers who supported him; Harold Ickes was his campaign manager.) A disappointing 1920 mayoral primary against a machine politician led Merriam to give up his electoral ambitions in some disillusion. But he maintained his commitment to public life, transferring it from democratic to scientific politics.[17]

In any event, the tasks of politics and its science were identical: nothing less than to "release" the "constructive possibilities in human nature" through "the organization of human intelligence" and "scientific adjustments of individuals and groups."[18] The Orwellian ring to the latter and to Merriam's use of "social control" is not entirely misleading, but it does require some unpacking. The "adjustment" and "control" he called for was often *of* political and technological forces *by* an educated, organized, democratic public. The problem was that the actually existing public, such as it was, was clearly unfit for the job.[19] This did not lead him to abandon the faith entirely, however. As he saw it, if the right kind of citizenry was lacking, it would fall to "politics" (in both senses) to create one.[20]

The stakes seemed high. The war and its aftermath had dealt blows to Progressive Era optimism about the course of modern life. For Merriam and many of his colleagues, technology, industry, and mass communication were advancing exponentially, and, unless knowledge kept pace, those "titanic forces" would fall into the hands of "jungle governors" animated by "ignorance and prejudice." Existing explanations of historical development and world order were suspect, "often overlaid with race prejudice or with national influence or propaganda of an absurdly transparent type." Much political analysis and commentary was nothing more than "opinion . . . , appeal to the tomtom and tradition"—jungle science for jungle politics. Social science for a new world would have to take its inspiration from the laboratory, dealing in "uncolored facts."[21]

Merriam's intervention was meant to reconcile centrifugal forces threatening to rend the growing discipline. As he saw it, the disorder of modern life was leading some among its ranks to call for the "passing of politics." "It is said," he wrote, that we "must . . . turn our backs on state and government, boycott politics, and endeavor to reconstruct new types of institutions other than those we call political."[22] Among his referents here were recent stirrings of "revolt" against "the monistic state and its disciplinary handmaidens" in the name of "pluralism."[23] In the Cold War context, pluralism would become a dominant, normative image of American liberal democracy in U.S. political science and beyond. This earlier iteration had a more critical edge.

As early as 1908, Arthur Bentley's *Process of Government* had advanced a group-centered view of politics in the United States. However the book was imperfectly understood when it came out, its thesis requiring at least a decade to "gain respectability."[24] When it came, the catalyst for renewed interest in Bentley was a young, British socialist, Harold J. Laski.

In later life, Laski would move toward more conventional Marxism. (He became an important Labour Party leader until he was eventually sidelined by moderates.) In the early decades of the twentieth century, however, his socialism was Jamesian and antistatist. Along with like-minded scholars, many of them European, Laski denied that there was any one, all-encompassing people for the state to embody or reflect.[25] Solidarity between individuals was expressed in a multifarious group life, formed in the diversity of experience. The state was simply one group among many and required, "like every other association" to "prove itself by what it achieves." In this view, rather than representing *the* organized form of *the* community, the state was simply a form of association meant to fill certain functions, with no special claim on citizens' loyalty beyond how well it performed socially useful duties. Other groups—such as churches, labor unions, and professional associations—were subject to the same test, and equally legitimate if they passed.[26]

While U.S. political scientists were highly attentive to Laski's pluralism, few wholeheartedly embraced its normative elements. Pluralism often appeared in the literature (pejoratively) as a brand of guild socialism, anarcho-syndicalism, or worse. In *New Aspects of Politics*, Merriam portrayed pluralism as emerging from a long tradition of "anarchists and antistatists of various types." William Yandell Elliott suggested that while Laski paid lip service to the role of other associations such as churches, these were really just "stalking horses for the unions of the world of labor." For Elliott, Laski belonged on a continuum with Georges Sorel ("the syndicalist priest of the myth-cult of violent revolution through the general strike") and Italian Fascism.[27]

But Laski's politics were not the only problem. His theory also threatened to leave political science without an object. If political life was just another form of group life, what was to keep political science from melting into sociology, psychology, or some other, more general account of "behavior?" As we have seen, the discipline had by this point rejected much of the theoretical edifice that Burgess had erected around "the state." However, reactions to the challenge posed by Laski and pluralism highlight the extent to which central assumptions of state theory had lingered. We have seen that Wilson and others associated with both the early APSA and the *JRD* continued to rely on something quite like "the state"—and still rooted in a racial unity—to authorize their accounts of American democratic legitimacy, prescriptions for democratic reform, and visions of international order. The challenge of pluralism caused some scholars to recur once again to the idea of a stable, moral community behind and lending its character to government.

Of these scholars, Elliott most staunchly defended the sovereign state against the assault of pluralism. To his mind, pluralism offered no guiding ethic for political life. To the extent that it described the actual state of politics, it was not something to be celebrated but rather a "pathological symptom" of "unsettled times" that threatened to rend "the majesty of law" into "a thing of shreds and patches." Elliott's answer was to insist on the state–government distinction, holding that, however flawed in practice, the federal state created by the Constitution embodied a "common moral ideal" that was the real subject of American democracy and object of a science of American politics. To deny this was to offer "no escape from anarchy."[28] Ellen Ellis of Mount Holyoke College, one of a handful of women whose work began to appear in the *APSR* in the 1920s, agreed that to allow the state no special status was to court "something approaching chaos."[29]

The "chaos" and "anarchy" that threatened were intellectual as well as political. For Ellis, political science was at a "crossroads," its "chief strongholds . . . under fire from" and in danger of being "absorbed" by "neighboring fields." Elliott sounded similar warnings, as did even some more sympathetic to pluralism or otherwise critical of state-centric accounts of politics. William B. Munro, for example, used his parting address as president of APSA to advise his colleagues to keep "clear of the sociologists and social psychologists who, if they could have their way, would only get us deeper into the morass of meaningless terminology."[30]

George E. G. Catlin, then a young, British expatriate and rising star at Cornell University, attempted to solve this problem by offering a new, unifying principle for the study of politics. He acknowledged that the "age-long advertisement of the so-called social sciences has been: Wanted, a unit."[31] For him, "the state" in its old sense was too clearly a fiction, and the "will to dominate" that he identified as the basis of politics existed both inside and outside government and its institutions. He suggested that the discipline's "unit" could be "peculiarly political" behavior "patterns."[32] However, even some who saw merit in Catlin's desire to broaden the scope of political science worried that this might be shaky ground for a discipline, to say nothing of a democratic polity. (As Gordon Dewey wrote of Catlin's proposition, "In proportion as principles become inclusive, they become tenuous."[33])

Merriam, characteristically, looked to have it both ways. Unlike Elliott and Ellis, who sought to maintain a special status for the discipline by insisting that "the state" was "essentially real," Merriam was content to define political science by its purposes.[34] These encompassed the intellectual and practical tasks required for political "adjustment." That is, if pluralism described the actual state of affairs, it would be the business of political science to figure out how to knit that fractured polity together into something that could at least function as a democratic public.[35] Along with Lasswell, Merriam would sometimes refer to this as "social therapy." From this vantage point, other sciences appeared less as irredentists to be held off and more as useful allies offering tools and perspectives that would allow the would-be therapist to render a diagnosis and test his remedies.

Merriam and Lasswell's reception of pluralism was fairly typical and would become even more widely shared by the end of the 1920s. That is, they were wary of pluralism's normative thrust—if Elliott was right about Laski, his pluralism gave off a whiff of class struggle, which was not a framework that most American political scientists were willing to embrace. Nonetheless, U.S. political scientists increasingly came to accept pluralism as a realistic description of modern political life.

This recognition raised practical and intellectual problems. For political scientists like Burgess, Paul Reinsch, George Blakeslee, Henry Jones Ford, and others, difference had been largely racialized. So, for example, an early career Woodrow Wilson could write, "To know the public mind of this country, one must know the mind, not of Americans of the older stocks only, but also of Irishmen, of Germans, of negroes. In order to get a footing for new doctrine, one must influence minds cast in every mould of race, minds inheriting every bias of environment, warped by the histories of a score of different nations, warmed or chilled, closed or expanded by almost every climate of the globe."[36]

For some, this racialization of difference was so thorough that even class differences could be framed in racial terms, as when Burgess explained socialistic demands as emanating from "those elements of the population" brought in by non-Teutonic immigration. Pluralistic reality, however, suggested that much more fine-grained distinctions would be necessary to really "know the public." Moreover, the inherited, nineteenth-century conceptions of race that had shaped many of political science's core concepts were woefully imprecise. Levels of "civilization" and "geniuses" for self-government did not readily lend themselves to measurement. Fortunately, as one of Merriam's collaborators put it, those very categories were being critically reexamined in "the work of a group of American anthropologists led by Professor Franz Boas [and using] a truly inductive method."[37]

Franz Boas and Antiracist Science

While political science was becoming increasingly differentiated, theoretical disagreements rarely left much blood on the floor. Certainly harsh words were printed, and left-liberal figures such as Charles Beard and Arthur Bentley's influence suffered because of their politics. (Beard's 1913 *An Economic Interpretation of the Constitution* "unleashed a political storm . . . that has few if any parallels in our history." President Taft publicly denounced it and Warren Harding, at the time a newspaper publisher, attacked it in an article titled "Scavengers, Hyena-Like, Desecrate the Graves of the Dead Patriots We Revere."[38] Beard eventually resigned from Columbia in a fight prompted by his opposition to the war.) But more often than not, disagreement remained cordial. Bentley (who in any event was a journalist, not a professor) was more marginalized than attacked, and Beard was welcomed back into the fold in 1927, becoming the APSA's president despite several years of isolation on his Connecticut farm and his increasingly sharp criticism of the newly influential trend toward scientism in the study of politics. It is possible that this prevailing collegiality reflects that in the discipline's formative years the material stakes of theoretical combat remained comparatively low. (While individual scholars or programs had patrons—George Blakeslee was supported by the World Peace Foundation's Edwin Ginn, for example—organized, competitive financial support for political research had not yet emerged.) Ideological, class, and ethnic solidarities were doubtless also at work. While there were exceptions, young radicals still found more congenial homes in other disciplines. Moreover, while political science's regional base in the northeast had diversified, the discipline "maintained a heavily Anglo-Saxon gentility."[39]

What were still understood as the natural sciences of man were a different story. Much of the acrimony in that area was due to the emergence since the turn of the century of a challenge to scientific racism from Boas and his students in anthropology. The reaction against this challenge was largely led by figures holding university, museum, or foundation posts and affiliated with what Jonathan Spiro has called the "interlocking directorate of scientific racism"—a tangle of organizations with overlapping membership, including the American Eugenics Society, the Eugenics Research Association, and the Galton Society, as well as conservation groups such as Madison Grant's Save-the-Redwoods League.[40]

Born to a "free-thinking" German Jewish family in 1858, and trained in physics and geography in Kiel, Germany, Boas came to anthropology through an interest in the "relationship between the life of a people and environment." That interest—along with a sense that he would be able to have more influence outside Germany—brought him to North America for fieldwork among native people in British Columbia in the mid-1880s.[41] After several years and some struggling to find his professional footing, Boas settled in his wife's native New York. His efforts finally yielded a suitable position in the U.S. academy when he was appointed the first professor of anthropology at Columbia in 1899.[42] All along, however, he courted controversy.

Boas's work seems to have been driven by a core, ethical commitment—by his own account shaped by the "ideals of the revolution of 1848"—to the interests of the "oppressed and mistreated."[43] This included a deep resistance to claims of racial supremacy championed by hard-liners in the science establishment. The students he attracted often shared these commitments. As a result, tensions between Boasians and racial determinists began early and simmered for a long time.

That conflict reached a boiling point at the close of World War I. The immediate cause was a 1919 letter that Boas published in *The Nation*, in which he denounced a set of (unnamed) anthropologists who had conducted covert intelligence work in Mexico during the war. In a strongly worded statement that also took aim at "familiar discrepancies" between President Wilson's "words and the actual facts," Boas argued that such conduct put "patriotism over everyday common decency" and in so doing violated the "very essence" of scientific life: "the service of truth." Moreover, such violations of professional ethics would hinder international scientific exchange by giving governments reason to suspect foreign scholars of espionage.[44]

In the uproar that followed, Boas was censured by the American Anthropological Association (AAA), stripped of his seat on its governing council, and pressured into resigning from the NRC.[45] By the next year, conflict between factions would get so heated that anthropologist Robert Lowie would lament that he could "hardly remember" a professional meeting "when every mother's son of us who stood for the [Boasian] Right" wasn't urged to attend, "armed to the hilt against the enemy."[46] Certainly, this was a high point of postwar reaction, and Boas was a German Jew who had been an outspoken critic of the war, so his loyalties were automatically suspect.[47] But the swift and organized reaction to the letter was not only about jingoism and the closing of professional ranks. The larger context was a "scientific reaction against cultural anthropology," pitting powerful and committed racial determinists (Lowie's "enemy") against the Boasians, whose work on the status and meaning of racial categories both sides understood to have far-reaching intellectual, social, and political implications.[48]

The nineteenth-century understanding of "culture" was, in its very structure, a claim to racial supremacy. It referred to the accumulated knowledge, artistic accomplishment, and technical prowess of mankind—the gradual *transcendence* of custom, tradition, and the nonrational, rather than the sum of those things. It was progressive and singular—possessed to different degrees by different groups, depending on the level of evolutionary progress they had achieved. It corresponded to the organic, essentialist conception of race that prevailed as well in late nineteenth- and early twentieth-century political science. In this view, humanity was divided into natural groupings, each with its own typical set of characteristics and potentials; Northern Europeans and their descendants possessed the most culture; Africans and other "primitives" remained mired in custom and superstition, held back by the deficits of their (vaguely specified) racial "type."

Whatever its determinants, cultural development in nineteenth-century anthropology appeared very much as the product and property of straightforwardly distinguishable groups. Progress, in turn, was understood to happen in a uniform order—matriarchal families were replaced by patriarchal ones, communal forms of property by private, and so on.[49] While this framework allowed for limited civilizational "borrowing," it held that innovations mostly occurred independently, on parallel tracks of evolutionary progress toward more complex, hierarchical, differentiated, and technically sophisticated societies. The work of Boas and his students cast this orderly picture into doubt.

From the beginning, Boas's scientific work chipped away at the racial-evolutionary framework. For example, he observed that among the native people of North America's northwest coast, cultural, linguistic, and racial traits did not co-vary—among groups of presumably similar racial "stock," some spoke the same language but had different folklore, others shared folklore but not linguistic similarities, and so on—and geographical influences mapped on to none. Similarly, kinship forms were equally variable and sometimes coexisted within groups in confusing ways that did not conform to Victorian "stage" theories of development. At the same time, Boas's analyses of this confusion of language, folklore, and kinship structures did yield a pattern: Groups that lived nearer to one another, or had higher degrees of contact historically, were more similar; for more mutually isolated groups the correlation was reversed. That is, the variation Boas observed failed to conform to the static racial/developmental/evolutionary schema that had largely dominated the social sciences to that point but was intelligible in terms of contact and influence—the accidents of history.

Moreover, while Boas continued to use Victorian racial terminology for much of his early career, work with his research group in what we would now call physical anthropology undermined formalistic racial categories themselves. For example, a study of "half-breed Indians" in 1894 gave lie to claims that miscegenation led to feeble offspring. Most dramatically, a series of anthropometric studies of immigrants and their children, most famously a 1908, Dillingham Commission–funded study on head forms, found that physical attributes—including the much discussed size and shape of the skull—responded over the course of a single generation to environmental change.[50] This challenged a fundamental premise of physical anthropology at the time (which relied heavily on varieties of what Stephen Jay Gould has called "skull measuring"): the idea that racial "types" could be identified, and that characteristic mental traits could be linked to the physical features of each type.[51] As Boas wrote in his report for the commission, while "heretofore we had the right to assume that human types are stable, all the evidence is now in favor of a great plasticity of human types, and that permanence of types in new surroundings appears rather as the exception than as the rule."[52] That is, heredity wasn't destiny, and the differences that were supposed to mark the boundaries between races and the limits of their respective capacities had as much to do with nutrition and other conditions affecting growth as anything else.

These insights—that peoples' lifeways were shaped by history and contact and that formalistic categorization of racial types was unsustainable—implied that no cultural (or political) concatenation could be the product of the essential "genius" of a particular people, nor could one be said to be farther along a particular evolutionary continuum than another. Rather, in Boas's emerging perspective, just as bodies were shaped by the environments in which they grew, behavior and perception alike were shaped by the "body of custom and traditional material that was transmitted from one generation to the next" and from one group to another.[53]

No longer progressive and (sort of) universal, culture came to appear as a particular tradition shared by members of groups and subject to influences from outside. As such, it was simultaneously common to all—applying to both "civilized" and "primitive man"—and plural; one could now speak of distinct cultures. This move opened two radical possibilities: that the social could be disentangled from the biological and that one could speak of cultural difference but not of cultural superiority.

These insights presented a direct challenge to eugenics and the political projects related to it (including most immediately the push for immigration restriction). Leading eugenicists sought actively to contain that challenge. One effort in this direction resulted in the formation of the Galton Society, spearheaded by Charles B. Davenport and housed within the American Museum of Natural History. Davenport was the founder of the prestigious Department of Experimental Biology and the Eugenics Record Office, both at Cold Spring Harbor on Long Island. He was also "the most prominent racist among American scientists" at the time. He had started his career in zoology and morphology but had developed an interest in human evolution, collecting family histories and seeking to identify statistical regularities in the occurrence of physical and behavioral traits. An obsession with "degeneration" led him to become one of the world's foremost early proponents of "negative" eugenics, including forced sterilization and institutionalization of the "unfit," and a tireless promoter of eugenics doctrine in popular culture and in the science establishment. The Galton Society was to be a node for this activism. In a 1918 letter outlining his plans to Henry Fairfield Osborn, the American Natural History Museum's president, Davenport explained that the society was meant to be "an anthropological society . . . self-selected and . . . very limited in numbers, . . . and also confined to native Americans, who are anthropologically, socially and politically sound, no Bolsheviki need apply."[54]

The Galton Society produced little in the way of scientific research, but the patrician social network it represented was powerful. Along with Davenport, founding members included Osborn (a geologist), Madison Grant, Lothrop Stoddard, the psychologist and intelligence-testing expert Robert M. Yerkes—and, as it happens, Charles Merriam's older brother, John C. Merriam.

The older Merriam brother was a University of California paleontologist. When the Galton Society was founded, he had recently helped Madison Grant establish the Save-the-Redwoods League, which sought at once to preserve the noble Redwood trees of the Pacific coast and the purity of the noble Nordic people. Soon to be appointed president of the Carnegie Institute of Washington and chair of the National Research Council, he took an active interest in blunting the Boasians' influence. This was to involve confining NRC largesse to his fellow racial determinists, as well as involvement in a series of proxy wars, such as the contretemps in the AAA (Merriam in particular was instrumental in forcing Boas's resignation from the NRC during the controversy over Boas's letter) and a contest for control over the *Journal of Physical Anthropology*.

In a number of respects, this was a rearguard action. By 1923, Boasians had reasserted control of the anthropology group. The NRC remained a redoubt of hereditarianism through the decade, but by the run-up to World War II, and with some help from the Depression (which had made poverty seem rather less hereditary) and the Nazis (who were making eugenics seem rather less American), the modern culture concept would become paradigmatic for U.S. social science. In the early 1920s, however, the biologically determinist "enemy" (as Lowie had termed them) still dominated the heights of respectability.[55]

It is not clear to what extent the younger Merriam was specifically attentive to his brother's dealings with Boas. It is certainly true that while Charles does not seem to have had any overt, ideological commitment to white supremacy, he was much closer to the "enemy" than to the (Boasian) "Right" in personal and sociological terms. However, the Boasians replaced evolutionary schema with a more open-ended set of possibilities for social change and challenged the "authoritarian," organic category of race, creating space for alternative conceptions of difference. This move held appeal for the scientific program Charles Merriam and his colleagues sought to promote for the study of politics. Moreover, as Boasian anthropology diffused out of the charged orbit of anthropology and biology, its critical edge did not always travel with it. Scholars who did not share the Boasians' politics in some cases readily absorbed aspects of their framework without following them to their more radical conclusions. Charles Merriam, along with several of his colleagues, seems to have fallen into this category. As a result, people on both sides of the determinism wars could be found in and around the circles that Merriam did so much to mobilize. Likewise, perspectives from both "camps" were taken up by scholars in Merriam's milieu, with little concern for what today appear clearly as glaring and irreconcilable contradictions between them.

"Recent" Political Theory and Boasian Anthropology

The milieu in question included a dizzying number of collaborations, associations, and institutions that Merriam initiated, fostered, or otherwise participated in during the 1920s. Foremost among these were the University of Chicago's political science department and Local Community Research Council, an APSA Committee on Political Research, a series of National Conferences on the Science of Politics, annual Social Science Research Council (SSRC)–run Hanover Conferences on the Social Sciences, and of course the SSRC itself, which Merriam was primarily responsible for founding. One of Merriam's frequent partners in these efforts was Harry Elmer Barnes, a sociologist, historian, and political theorist then teaching at Clark University.

Barnes was a similar figure to Merriam in many respects, sharing Merriam's penchant for discipline building *and* his conviction that disciplinary borders were largely artificial. It is not surprising, then, that one of the first instances of extended attention to Boas and his students' work for political science should come from the two of them, in the form of *A History of Political Theories, Recent Times,* a *Festschrift* they co-edited in honor of William A. Dunning.[56] Subtitled *Essays on Contemporary Developments in Political Theory*[57] and intended to serve as a textbook for political science courses,[58] the book was meant as a sort of sequel to Dunning's three-volume *History of Political Theories.*[59] Those books had surveyed Western political thought from ancient Greece through the theories of Herbert Spencer and also served as the model for Merriam's dissertation (and first book). Commissioned essays by Dunning's former students and associates would bring the story up to the present and outline a program for the fundamental development of political science into the future. Notably, one of the essays was by the anthropologist and "brilliant Boasian maverick" Alexander Goldenweiser.[60] An additional six of the book's thirteen chapters devoted significant attention to the Boasian critique of racial anthropology.

History of Political Theories was political science's entry into a rash of thick volumes addressing the scope and methods of the various social sciences that would appear in the space of a few years, many by leaders in other fields whose interests aligned to an extent with Merriam's. Barnes himself was one of the editors of *The History and Prospects of the Social Sciences.*[61] Other examples include *Recent Developments in the Social Sciences,*[62] as well as more specialized collections like Thomas Vernor Smith and Leonard D. White's *Chicago: An Experiment in Social Science Research.*[63] The culmination of this trend was the 1930 publication of the pathbreaking *Encyclopedia of the Social Sciences.*[64]

By their very inclusiveness, all of these works instantiated an interest in integrating the various spheres of human knowledge, and their editors' comments generally presented this task as an urgent response to a perceived increase in the complexity (and recently demonstrated destructive capacity) of modern, industrial civilization. All the same, the books betrayed concerns about the status of the individual fields, similar to those plaguing some quarters of political science. This desire for both integration and professional differentiation is visible in Barnes's introduction to *The History and Prospects of the Social Sciences*. In that essay, Barnes looked to "earnest and prolonged collaboration of natural and social scientists" to "bring about" "better and saner types of conduct . . . by giving the individual a better set of . . . guiding criteria." Crucially, these scientists were to be "each a specialist, and all dominated by the aim of social betterment."[65]

For its part, Merriam and Barnes's *History of Political Theories* included contributions from people holding positions not only in political science, sociology, law, and philosophy but also in anthropology and psychology, still generally classed as natural sciences. In part, this reflects the diverse careers of Dunning's many students and colleagues as well as the still-incomplete nature of professional specialization by this time. (Whatever their affiliation, most of the scholars represented in *History of Political Theories* published articles in the *APSR* and *PSQ*; the political scientists, for their part, wrote for a wide range of journals, including those identified with sociology, history, philosophy, economics, law, and statistics.) But it was also linked to the purpose of the editors. For Barnes, this purpose was nothing less than to "rejuvenate" the subject of "political rights" and "divest" it of "metaphysical origins and implications."[66] Merriam amplified this point in his contribution, characteristically titled "Recent Tendencies in Political Thought,"[67] in which he applauded the beginnings of a revival and "restudy" of the "Aristotelian doctrine" of man's political nature "more and more upon the ground of fundamental impulses." In this vision, echoed throughout the volume, political science, in order to claim its own place and achieve relevance in the modern world, needed fundamental knowledge about human behavior. Paradoxically, perhaps, that knowledge was to come at least at the outset from other disciplines. Sociology, anthropology, and psychology in particular seemed poised to reveal such basic truths.[68]

The Merriam and Barnes volume turned to the "critical anthropologists" primarily for their attack on teleological and evolutionary theories of sociopolitical development. This was the subject of Goldenweiser's "Anthropological Theories of Political Origins." Along with Alfred Kroeber,

Robert Lowie, and Edward Sapir, Goldenweiser had been among the first of Boas's students to achieve independent stature in the discipline. When he wrote the essay, Goldenweiser was among a number of refugees from Columbia's wartime nationalism who were teaching at the New School for Social Research.[69] The thrust of his essay was simply that formulaic accounts of social evolution could "no longer be entertained."

The larger purpose of the essay was an assault on the "undue recourse to hypothetical argument" in extant "theories of social and political evolution."[70] The burgeoning ethnographic record showed few examples of the successions (matriarchal to patriarchal families, for example) predicted by the theory, and many counterexamples. On the subject of "primitive political organization," Goldenweiser argued that while politics, or rather the "integrating" tendency of political "consciousness," is "universal and as old as society itself,"[71] the "modern state" is something else altogether, characterized by a coordination in one institution or set of institutions of the "legal, religious, economic and other cultural functions" that are generally dispersed in "primitive society" among various nonstate organs (such as religious societies or clans). As a result, the shape and workings of the modern state emerged from contingent historical circumstance, such as war, territorial expansion, and economic change. Each "modern historic state" was to be studied not in terms of a racial *telos* or defining essence but on its own terms, and in its particular context.[72]

The contingency and historical specificity of modern political arrangements is emphasized again in the next two essays in the volume, in which, respectively, Franklin Thomas gives extended consideration to Boas student Robert Lowie's critique of geographical determinism and Franklin Hamilton Hankins attacks Nordicism (together these three essays conclude the book), again emphasizing the dangers of assuming uniform causes for similar historical phenomena. Charles Elmer Gehlke and Herbert Schneider similarly link what Barnes characterized as the Boasian "destruction" of linear evolutionism to a foreshortened time horizon for political analysis.[73]

Despite Merriam's protestations about political science's "older friends," then, the work of Boas and his students in this volume at least seems to be mobilized firmly against the brands of historicism that still lingered in political science and toward more open-ended accounts of political life. Such disavowals of historicism were not new, of course, but the editors and contributors affirmed that previous attempts to free the discipline from historicism's grip remained incomplete.

They did not offer a fully realized alternative. However, they had clear ideas as to where such a thing might be found, and, despite their partial embrace of the Boasian critique, the innate characteristics of individuals and groups were always central. Indeed, the essays that address race and evolutionism are the only ones in the volume to claim to offer methodological or foundational claims for political science as a whole.[74] Their thrust was captured by Barnes, for whom "the state, of modern political terminology" was a "very late and recent" phenomenon. It was a "product, creation, and creature" not of developing human nature but "of society." The scientific study of society and its constituent elements, then, was an "indispensable prolegomena" to a science of politics.[75]

Similarly, the Boasian critique of race formalism was welcome in that it replaced the "authoritarian" idea of "types" with a more fluid conception of variations that could be studied "using a truly inductive method." However, most of the commentary on Boas in the Merriam and Barnes volume failed to engage with his work on the environmental determinants of biological difference. That is, the ideas that culture (including political arrangements and tendencies) was not race-bound and that racial categories themselves were in some sense artificial broke through. But the more radical critique of biological determinism itself went mostly unremarked.

This relative inattention to the deeper challenge to the idea of racial difference contained in the Boasian program is no doubt connected to the cautious, evolving nature of that program itself. Boas himself had a commitment to equal human dignity that predated his anthropological work, and that animated his lifelong intellectual and public engagement. He was closely allied with W. E. B. Du Bois and the fledgling National Association for the Advancement of Colored People (NAACP) early on. Consistently during his long life, Boas mentored and advocated for African American and Native American scholars, spoke out against both fascism and Red-baiting, and, as we have seen, withstood harsh attacks for his stance against racist and politically conservative elements of the science establishment. Similarly, many of his students were leftists or left-liberals whose research often took direct aim at the scientific supports for racist justifications of hierarchy. However, Boas's thoroughgoing materialism meant that his critique of biological determinism evolved over time and was often couched in cautious, scientific terms. As George Stocking writes, "Boas wrote as a skeptic of received belief rather than as staunch advocate of racial equipotentiality. . . . His criticism . . . expressed itself within the categories of orthodox belief."[76] What his work showed, positively, was that the physical (and, by extension, presumably mental) characteristics of individuals within any given race varied widely. That is, his work portrayed differences between groups as quantitative, not qualitative; "racial types" were replaced by arrays of "overlapping frequency curves."[77] Combined as this was in many of the Boasians' work with cultural relativism and an emphasis on the effects of environment on behavior and growth alike, this suggested strongly that inequalities observed in society stemmed from historical and environmental factors rather than fundamental group difference.

Again, however, not all elements of this synthesis were always fore-grounded, nor did they translate equally as they migrated outward from anthropology. Moreover, even some who did perceive the full import of the Boasian critique of racial anthropology chose to embrace only some aspects of it. The final article of the Merriam and Barnes volume is an especially vivid example. In it, Franklin Hankins at once launched a glee-fully intemperate attack on racial theories of politics *and* announced that the "cure" for "race dogmatism" was not a commitment to egalitarianism but rather, "an ounce of eugenics."[78] That is, Hankins embraced most of the substance of Boas's critique of social evolutionism, while rejecting its social implications and casting his lot instead with Boas's intellectual and political enemies.

Hankins's perspective attracted wide notice and praise. Reviews of the book as a whole were positive, commenting especially on its calls for theo-retical innovation and its critique of racialism. To the reviewer for the *American Journal of International Law*, the book represented a "treasure-house" of all that was "current" in political theory.[79] In the *International Journal of Ethics*, Chicago philosophy professor Thomas Vernor Smith noted that, in a change "for the better," "political theory has become social-ized."[80] Likewise, for Raymond Gettell in the *American Historical Review*, the volume was "strongest where Dunning was weakest"; that is, in recog-nizing the "change in point of view resulting from the contributions of anthropology, sociology, and social psychology."[81] Writing in the *APSR*, Elliott, unsurprisingly, qualified an otherwise friendly review with the com-plaint that the book's "tone" was "too largely sociological." The lone, mainly negative notice appeared in the *Philosophical Review*, where Mat-toon M. Curtis of Western Reserve University commented, "Insofar as poli-tics has leaned on sociology, it has become weak and incoherent, forgetting logic, ethics, and aesthetics alike."[82]

Even Curtis, however, was favorable toward the book's treatment of race, praising Hankins's and Goldenweiser's attacks on racial theories of political origins and Thomas's critique of simplistic, racialized anthropogeography. Other notices echoed the sentiments, as when the reviewer for the *American Journal of Sociology* called Hankins's essay the "greatest single pleasure of the book," commenting that "Professor Hankins's refutal of the Aryan and Teutonic myths has a gusto which ought to lay these specters to rest for good."[83]

Hankins's "Race as a Factor in Political Theory" was indeed a blistering attack on those "myths."[84] Hankins allowed that Aryanism and its variants had become "somewhat *passé* in informed circles" since the turn of the century. All the same, he asserted that "naïve," "popular" conceptions of race belonging to "an age preceding the discoveries of modern anthropology and ethnology" continued to exert a "powerful," if often unacknowledged, influence on political scholarship.[85]

Hankins was a prominent pacifist and reformer who had recently left his post as head of Clark's Department of Political and Social Science for a job at Smith College. He treated Dunning respectfully. But a rogues' gallery of other nineteenth- and early twentieth-century highbrow racists came in for a pummeling. Burgess (then eighty years old) was subjected (again) to particular, personalized scorn. In Hankins's account, Burgess and his teachers, "acting in harmony with that type of pseudo-science which was considered good political policy in certain German university circles," had combined "the race mysticism of Gobineau" with Fichte and Hegel's "even more mystical philosophy of state." (Herbert Baxter Adams was lumped with Burgess as embracing "quite as extreme" a version of Teutonism.) For Hankins, Burgess's "Nordic mythologizing" was scientifically bankrupt and politically irresponsible, encouraging wanton colonial brutality and playing to the "psychological features" of "popular tradition and race egotism" that had contributed to the outbreak of the first World War. Other targets included Houston Stewart Chamberlain; Madison Grant; Lothrop Stoddard; the craniologist Paul Broca; the eugenicists Francis Galton, Georges Vacher de Lapouge, and Clinton Stoddard Burr; the psychologists William McDougall, Carl Brigham, and Robert Yerkes; and a host of other writers whose contributions to various strands of white supremacist theorizing have faded more completely into well-deserved obscurity.[86]

In fact, Hankins went beyond theories of Nordic supremacy to attack the very idea that races were organic collectivities, going so far as to characterize the Aryan race as "imaginary" and recourse to it in political or social theory as relying on nothing more scientific than "intuitive discernment of spiritual affinity." He disdained the imperative that "aspiring and subject nationalities" (such as the Poles, Albanians, Lithuanians, "and what not") get "an opportunity to work out their destinies as they pleased" and to make "the full impress of their special aptitudes." Indeed, almost as an aside, Hankins made the very social-constructionist–sounding argument that the perception of racial unity was a consequence, not a cause, of political integration.[87]

However, while the emphasis of this essay was on "race mysticism," Hankins was equally dismissive of "certain of the American anthropologists" and their "dreadful and deluding modification of eighteenth-century egalitarianism, that the races are all equal." That is, Hankins's critique of racialism was not categorical. Each figure was taken to task to the degree that his work relied on outdated ideas of racial inequality, rather than on more modern ones. Hankins's concluding passage, in which he prescribes an "ounce of eugenics," merits quoting at length:

> We are thus inclined to make this slight concession to the race dogmatists, that there is doubtless some difference between races in special powers and aptitudes in different directions. Just what and how extensive these differences are is largely a matter of future determination. As regards the European races, these differences, for the races as wholes, are small in terms of averages and if they exist at all are less than the differences between certain nationality groups in this country. But vastly more important than any possible differences between the average capacities of the European races are the individual differences among members of the same race. An ounce of eugenics is worth a pound of race dogmatism so far as the future political security of the country is concerned.

The problem, for Hankins, was that too many commentators were content to "muddle up the whole issue" of inequality with race, when it was in fact one of individual (biological) differences, particularly with regard to the European races (whose differences were "small in terms of averages"). However, where "the white and negro" or contemporary Northern and Southern European immigrants to America were concerned, for Hankins "there [could], on the other hand, be no longer doubt of differences in average mental capacity."[88]

The "average" in the preceding sentence is important, and it points to one of the key features of the new conception of difference that was beginning to inform political scholarship in these circles. For Hankins, political scientists needed to consider *both* "average" inequalities *and* "the wide variation of abilities in each group" as well as the "overlapping . . . throughout most of the range of variation." This echoed a number of urgent calls elsewhere in the book to attend to "individual" variation and indeed more generally to replace "traditional and authoritarian" measures of populations ("races and nations") with "material," "measurable," and "comparable" ones. In practice, this meant replacing both the "mystical" and "legalistic" (i.e. categorical) formulations of race theory that had influenced earlier generations of political scientists *and* the (also "mystical" and categorical) "egalitarianism" attributed to Boas's circle.[89]

The idea that the nature and meaning of racial differences remained an open, and urgent, question was again clearly enunciated by a 1925 report issued by the APSA's "Second National Conference on the Science of Politics." This group (which included Charles Merriam, had been convened at his urging, and was chaired by a former student of his) affirmed that most treatments of "such questions as the influence of Nordic or Mediterranean nationalities on American civilization" belonged to a "period of speculation and historical inquiry." A science of politics wouldn't reject such a proposition but would require it to be broken "gradually into groups of more specific questions that may be studied with the quantitative controls of scientific method."[90]

A reconstructed political science was still to concern itself with difference, including racial difference. But it was to be a modern, American, liberal account, based on "the facts" of individual differences and their patterning within groups.[91] This image of populations had appeared in Boas's work. But it appeared far more strikingly in the results of Robert M. Yerkes's Army intelligence testing program.

Finding New Premises: Race Science, Philanthropy, and the Institutional Establishment of Political Science

Frank Hankins was not the only contributor to the Dunning *Festschrift* to express interest in eugenics or to reject any settled commitment to human equipotentiality. As much as Charles Merriam cautioned that eugenicists' wilder claims were probably overblown, he still frequently cited eugenics as a possible technique of intelligent "political control."[1] Moreover, if Merriam had reservations about inherent racial differences, it wasn't so much that he rejected or even doubted their existence—he simply remained agnostic as to what and how significant they might be. All the same, he occasionally endorsed considerably less tempered assessments of eugenics. For example, he was particularly enthusiastic about an essay in the *Festschrift* by Dartmouth's Malcolm Willey—Merriam called it "excellent" and among the most fundamental to "political theory in the narrower sense" that he and his co-editor Harry Elmer Barnes had included.[2] In that essay, Willey argued that the findings of modern science "utterly blast[ed] the hopes of the older equality theorists," leaving us to put our faith in "a democratic-aristocracy" produced at least in part by "a program of intelligent mating."[3]

Of the various elements of the research and political programs related to eugenics, Merriam himself was most attracted to "differential psychology," which had seen its greatest success with the mass administration of intelligence tests to army personnel during the war. That program, administered by research psychologists and using cutting-edge techniques, had found that "native whites" had the highest intelligence and "negroes" the lowest;

the foreign-born fell somewhere between the two. All this was perfectly in accordance with scientific and popular expectations and was fodder for proponents of immigration restriction, Jim Crow, and the push for forced sterilization laws that would be adopted by thirty states as of the late 1920s. A fourth finding was more surprising, to both testers and the public, and also seemed to require a response from political science: the average American draftee, the testers found, had a "mental age" of just thirteen. This bombshell provoked wide public debate and led some to conclude that what many elites had long believed was finally right there in black and white: the people were simply far too stupid to rule in any meaningful sense.

The publication of these results led to many expressions of consternation within and outside political science as to the basic viability of the American system of government. At the same time, the results and the new technologies they deployed occasioned great excitement among intellectuals, many of whom found the "IQ version of intelligence . . . nearly irresistible."[4] Science-minded political scientists such as Merriam were no exception. They may have found cause for concern in some of the tests' results, but the tests themselves presented intriguing possibilities for both knowledge and social control. Most promisingly, the tests seemed to demonstrate that fundamental human traits could be measured and ranked.

These new techniques for measuring and sorting the population promised a way to replace traditional accounts of group difference with new ones rooted in the "material," "measurable," and "comparable." In this frame, you no longer had to recur to an Anglo-Saxon "genius for liberty" or the racial character of some monolithic entity like "the negro" or another subject people. Rather, it was becoming possible to imagine groups in the liberal, individualized form of statistical arrays—overlapping frequency curves of fundamental traits, still hierarchically arranged, but only in terms of their respective "averages," and with room for individual outliers—rather than the "authoritarian" forms of types and essences.

As with Boasian anthropology, the Dunning *Festschrift* offers a useful snapshot of opinion on the matter of the intelligence and its tests. Willey and Hankins alike accepted the need for a dramatic revision of democracy. Merriam and other contributors were more judicious. But there was wide agreement that what Charles Elmer Gehlke referred to as the "variability of mental capacity" within the population was an urgent question for a science of politics.[5] For Harry Barnes, for example, understanding "innate mental differences" was the "all-important problem" that outstripped even those related to "economic and social power and capacity." Mental testing would give social scientists the tools to solve it.[6]

Of course, the interest in the tests within this circle reflected a much wider trend. And not everyone was equally impressed. Several years later, in an article lamenting the "overemphasis" on "collection and observation of data" in the political science of his time, Charles Beard would single out intelligence testing for criticism. He allowed that testing might have limited occupational use, but he remained mostly dismissive of the "gentlemen who are busy testing this electric fluid" while unable to specify exactly "what they are talking about."[7] Thomas Vernor Smith specifically targeted Barnes on this score; Smith thought that Barnes had "like so many other modern students . . . suffered prematurely . . . at the hands of differential psychology" and the suggestion that "methodology alone" could direct social science without the guidance of "equalitarian sympathy."[8]

Enthusiasm for the new technologies of intelligence seems to have mapped roughly on to the emerging divide among scholars of politics between the influential group around Merriam and others more skeptical of the idea of remaking the discipline on a natural-science model, such as Smith, William Yandell Elliott, Charles Beard, and Edward Corwin.[9] The former included the students, colleagues, and collaborators discussed in the previous chapter, as well as pioneers in the field of opinion research, such as Floyd Allport, and others clustered around the APSA Committee on Political Research. Ross points out that this cohort probably never commanded an absolute majority in the discipline, but they were an entrepreneurial lot. As a group, they harnessed institutional power, the prestige of science, and the "moral authority of purists" to good effect, laying much of the groundwork for the interdisciplinary, methodologically minded, science-oriented turn that the discipline would take in the postwar years.[10]

Unlike many of those involved with the army tests, this group does not appear to have been primarily drawn to intelligence testing by a desire to justify racial hierarchy or exclusionary policies. While, for some, "proofs" of Anglo-Saxon upper-class superiority might have been a bonus, the greater draw was the intellectual and methodological possibilities that mental testing seemed to open. For Merriam and others, the tests modeled new ways for thinking about difference and suggested an angle on the longstanding problem of accommodating America's egalitarian ideals with its hierarchies.

What's more, Merriam in particular saw that links to the "social biology" establishment could have tangible benefits in the areas of institution building and research funding. This led him to cultivate intellectual and institutional connections at the National Research Council and in the foundation world, as well as with colleagues in psychology, biology, and the emerging field of opinion research. As we shall see, he vigorously exploited those connections to build up social and political science research at Chicago and within the American Political Science Association and the Social Science Research Council, in the process effectively creating new institutional forms that would do much to cement the course that U.S. political science would take for much of the twentieth century.

"Entirely at a Loss"

"We are interested in the field of politics, and when we try to approach that field I think all of us are entirely at a loss at the present time." This lament came from University of Michigan political scientist Robert T. Crane in early 1923. His concern was that "political science has . . . been simply studying government," which seemed to him to amount to "very little." The "most hopeful prospect," he mused, "seems to be along the psychological line." However, there were still only "few of us who have any idea what that really means" or "how we can approach the question, unless it is through the help of the psychologist."[11]

Crane's comment was addressed to a multidisciplinary group of scholars, foundation officials, and science administrators gathered in the offices of the NRC. Crane was there as part of a group organized by the fledgling SSRC, which Merriam had only recently begun to organize.[12] Their stated purpose was to discuss social science research on "human migration." Crane's broader mandate from Merriam was to deepen lines of communication between the social sciences and the NRC, with an eye to seeing the SSRC absorbed into the science body. While Crane's confession does not seem like the best pitch for that purpose, it was nothing other political scientists weren't also saying publicly. In a report on the first National Conference on the Science of Politics held the previous year, A. B. Hall asserted that the discipline had yet to enter "the realm of reality and fact."[13] A year later, he was kinder but no less firm, affirming that those "who have attended the Conferences on the Science of Politics can have no doubts as to the genuine eagerness" of the profession to advance scientific methods. However, they lacked even the rudiments of "technique and method."[14]

In any event, Crane had reason to believe that the social scientists' overtures would get a friendly hearing at the NRC meeting. The chair of the NRC at the time was none other than Merriam's brother John; another ally, Mary van Kleeck, was the Russell Sage Foundation official bankrolling the meeting. So, it was less a pitch than an attempt to underscore the urgency of closer ties with the disciplines already represented in the NRC, such as biology, psychology, and anthropology (still largely classified as a natural science).

While Crane did not specify what sort of help he expected from psychology, the context offers clues. The specific program into which the SSRC sought entrée was one the NRC was putting together on "Scientific Problems of Human Migration." Its chair was Robert Mearns Yerkes, the psychologist who had been in charge of the army intelligence-testing program.

Yerkes was on board with the inclusion of the SSRC, but he had his own extra-intellectual agenda as well. Conducted over the course of the war, the intelligence program had examined about 1,750,000 men, with the goal of rationalizing personnel decisions. It had also created unprecedented opportunities to refine the testing instruments themselves and to direct material resources to psychometric research. But funding dried up after the war, leaving Yerkes in need of ways to continue his work in peacetime.[15]

The NRC's Migration Committee was one answer. The personnel problems of war mobilization had been the justification for investment in psychological research. Those were now moot, but with the aftermath of the war seeing calls for still more draconian restrictions, immigration problems looked like a good substitute. As Yerkes put it in his 1922 proposal to the Russell Sage Foundation for the establishment of such a committee, it seemed "evident" that "America's policy of restriction of immigration" was to "be reconsidered in the near future." This called for "the further perfecting of psychological tests which would yield information never before adequately collected on racial characteristics" and "enabl[e] the United States to know through facts and not through mere impressions what effect upon a nation will result from migration."[16]

It wasn't hard to predict what the NRC committee might recommend on this score—Yerkes had strong ties to the eugenics establishment and his very public interpretation of the results of the army tests had been unflattering to non-Nordic immigrants, to put it mildly. Other researchers on the committee were almost all hard-line racial determinists, many already publicly committed to immigration restriction. So while the Migration Committee eventually sponsored research on a smattering of other topics as well, Crane would have been aware that the focus was on "differential psychology," with a specific focus on mental differences between racial groups that were presumed (1) to exist and (2) to have important policy implications that would involve limiting the life chances of some groups to the benefit of others. In that context, it seems clear that whatever Crane meant by the "field of politics" beyond mere "government," he imagined that technologies for measuring people's putatively natural, inborn traits and capacities was the most promising way to "approach" it. Merriam enthusiastically shared this belief and forged a strong partnership with Yerkes aimed at realizing the possibilities of such an effort.

Yerkes did not start out as an intelligence researcher. In fact, his true and lifelong passion was primate behavior.[17] But he was having more success in funding and publicizing his intelligence research, the crowning achievement of which was the army program. Dreamed up by Yerkes and somewhat grudgingly accepted by the U.S. Army (the U.S. Navy rebuffed Yerkes's advances), that effort ultimately did little to transform military practices. Even though the army eventually routinized some mental testing, official resistance to "mental meddlers" questioning officers' judgment meant that the army never fully embraced Yerkes's vision. However, the program demonstrated that government agencies might be willing to sponsor social-control–oriented research. Beyond the testing program itself, for example, the army established a school of military psychology at Fort Oglethorpe in Georgia that employed and trained large numbers of testers. Moreover, the vote of confidence signaled by the army's investment in testing had significant knock-on effects. Yerkes himself was inundated with requests for the tests and was given $25,000 of Rockefeller money to establish a school-based testing program. Private consulting firms, too, began to make significant investments in psychometrics research and to employ psychological experts.[18]

This success must have been heady, given that this brand of intelligence research was still in its infancy. Early nineteenth-century "mental philosophy" had stressed the variety of human "talents" and privileged effort and character over inborn nature.[19] Amid the intensifying debate over slavery in the mid-nineteenth century, however, many elites no longer found this view congenial, turning instead to the more deterministic science of "craniometry."

Using skull size and form as a proxy for intelligence, craniometrists assigned to each racial group hierarchically ranked qualities (skull shapes) and quantities (skull volume), which were meant to define a typical or pure racial "type." However, in the new century the skull measurers and their racial types in turn lost ground, this time to psychologists and their norm-referenced curves. The psychologists returned to the "mind rather than the body" but not to viewing intelligence in qualitative terms. Rather, they conjured a concrete, quantifiable version of intelligence, made visible by "its own technology, the mental test."[20]

Initial efforts in this direction had begun in the 1880s, aided by William James's and G. Stanley Hall's efforts to promote laboratory-based, experimental research psychology. This made for a favorable climate when, in 1910, Henry H. Goddard of the Vineland Training School for Feeble-Minded Boys and Girls in New Jersey introduced the French Binet-Simon scale to the American psychological community. Intended for use in evaluating schoolchildren, this was a method for assigning students a "mental age" (the age at which the median student would achieve a given score). Mental testing gained wide interest among psychologists when, in 1916, Lewis Terman published an Americanized version of the scale as the Stanford-Binet and coined the term "Intelligence Quotient," or "IQ," for a ratio of mental to chronological age.

However, this new perspective only exploded into the wider public consciousness with the army tests. In addition to introducing a substantial group of American men to the tests (as subjects), the program received wide publicity after the war. Information became available in 1920 in Yerkes and Clarence Stone Yoakum's brief *Army Mental Tests*, and more comprehensively the following year in an 890-page National Academy of Sciences report that Yerkes edited. These statements certainly generated interest from both lay and scientific observers, but the program reached a much bigger audience—and generated new controversy—with the 1922 appearance of *A Study of American Intelligence* by Yerkes's junior colleague, Carl C. Brigham.

Yerkes, an enthusiastic publicist for Brigham's book, contributed an introduction affirming that (much as skeptical War Department officials had suspected) the testers had broader ambitions than just contributing to the war effort. As Yerkes put it, "For our purposes in this country, the army mental tests give us an opportunity for a national inventory of our own mental capacity, and the mental capacity of those we have invited to live with us."[21] The book made a splash among scientists, in the popular press, and in the halls of Congress (where it was discussed in hearings of the House Committee on Immigration and Naturalization that led to a new, racially restrictionist immigration policy two years later).

As noted above, Brigham reported stark racial disparities, with a striking eight-and-a-half-year gap in "mental age" between "native," white officers, and the "negro draft," which averaged a childish 10.5 years.[22] But the real source of alarm was the low average (13) achieved by the "white draft" (foreign and "native" alike). To explain this trend, Brigham broke down the scores of the foreign-born by test-takers' national origin. Average scores of immigrants from England, Scotland, and Holland exceeded that of native-born American whites. However, those from the countries providing the greatest numbers of new immigrants were below that number. Germany and Denmark were closest to the "native" American white average; Italy and Poland were at the bottom of the distribution.[23] The lesson he drew was clear: democracy was imperiled by a doltish mass of citizens and the situation was worsening by the day as low-quality immigrants streamed in.

Two findings were not as easily squared with testers' expectations. The first was that African Americans from southern states scored below their northern counterparts. This prompted a rare (and very partial) concession to an environmental explanation from Brigham, who attributed part of the "superior intelligence measurements of the northern negro" to "the greater amount of educational opportunity, which does affect, to some extent, scores on our present intelligence tests."[24] However, he continued to maintain that racial and innate factors were determinative, explaining the remainder of the differential by a putative "greater amount of admixture of white blood" as well as "the operation of economic and social forces, such as higher wages . . . and a less complete social ostracism, tending to draw the more intelligent negro to the North."[25]

A second troublesome data point was that immigrants who had been in the United States longer scored higher than those more recently arrived. Brigham spent more time on this problem but concluded that the difference between "older" and "newer" immigrants represented a "real difference of intelligence" rather than "an artifact of the method of examination"—a question the earlier National Academy of Sciences report had left open. For Brigham, that is, this unexpected finding did not indicate a problem with the tests (e.g. that they might be testing familiarity with cultural norms rather than innate ability), nor did it challenge the notion that intelligence was inborn and fixed. Rather, it was that the immigrants themselves were of different quality, with fewer coming from England, Germany, Scotland, Sweden, and Ireland and more from Austria, Russia, and Italy.[26]

Brigham did conclude, however, that the "race factor," while real, did not explain all the differences among immigrants. Rather, intra-racial differences also had a substantial hereditary component that the tests could measure and map on to class differences: "the decline in intelligence" of more recent compared to earlier immigrants was "due to two factors, the change in the races migrating to this country and to the additional factor of the sending of lower and lower representatives of each race."[27] To support this hypothesis, Brigham cited "the observation, repeatedly confirmed by experiment [by Lewis Terman and others], that children from the professional, semi-professional and higher business classes have, on the whole, an hereditary endowment superior to that of children from the semi-skilled and unskilled laboring classes."[28]

Brigham concluded his study, unsurprisingly, with warnings against miscegenation and calls for selective immigration restriction and further, unspecified "legal steps . . . which would ensure a continuously progressive upward evolution." This was hardly a new tune—a host of racial doomsayers and eugenicists, including Madison Grant, Charles W. Gould, and Georges Vacher de Lapouge (all of whom Brigham cited), had been singing it to beguiled audiences of elites for quite some time. But the sheer volume of scientific data generated by the tests made it that much more compelling.[29]

While the book and intelligence testing in general both generated wide notice, not everyone was bowled over by the scientific bells and whistles. Controversy arose in particular over the racial and class interpretations of the test results, as well as over the supposed proof that the average white American man had the mental capacity of a barely pubescent teen. Indeed, Charles Merriam was among those publicly urging caution. In *New Aspects of Politics*, he commented that many of those making "dogmatic assertions regarding the bearing of differential psychology on democracy" were "neither students of government nor of psychology." He also allowed that intelligence might be a "product of environment" rather than "unalterably fixed at birth," and he treated as an open question how "the differentials in intelligence" might bear on "the kind of capacity" necessary for "political cooperation and organization in governmental association."[30]

He expressed similar reservations in private, as in a 1922 letter to William C. Bagley, a prominent critic of the tests and of "educational determinism" more generally. Merriam told Bagley, "What you are saying needs to be said on a good many occasions, and rather forcibly," going on to comment that "the lines of reasoning followed by some of the psychological group" might be more of a "threat to democracy" than any supposed excess of mentally deficient citizens.

However, Merriam was never one to throw the baby out with the bathwater. He may have cautioned against "the danger . . . that half-truths or unverified hypotheses" might "be used for class purposes,"[31] but he was optimistic that the right kind of technology could indeed offer access to the substance of merit or of the basic, politically relevant traits of individuals and populations. And he frequently expressed the hope that political science could employ such technology in the project of "social control."

In fact, he shared this nuanced position on mental testing with his friend Walter Lippmann, who among his many other roles was probably the best-known public critic of the racist and otherwise immoderate conclusions many were drawing from the results of the army program. In a protracted debate with Lewis Terman in the *New Republic*, Lippmann cast significant doubt on the validity of the entire enterprise. However, toward the end of that debate Lippmann proposed "A Future for the Tests," in which, once their "pretensions" to being true "measurements of intelligence" were "defeated" and it was recognized that they were "simply a somewhat more abstract kind of examination," their "real usefulness" would become clear and they could "be adapted to the purposes in view, whether it be to indicate the feeble-minded for segregation, or to classify children in school, or to select recruits from the army for officers' training camps, or to pick bank clerks."[32]

Lippmann underscored this position in a 1923 letter to Merriam, complaining, "Why [Yerkes] should think I am opposed to mental measurements is more than I can imagine. Is it necessary to confuse criticism of an interpretation with opposition to a method?" While Lippmann was scornful of the rush to hasty interpretation of the army tests and skeptical that something as amorphous as "intelligence" could be perfectly captured by them, he was entirely open to the idea that mental testing could supply valid, politically useful information about the public. In Lippmann's words, he, like Merriam, saw great promise in "an examination of the relation between political science and the sciences which are now attempting to supply us with our premises."[33]

In Search of Premises

Merriam's correspondence reveals that, despite his reservations, he agreed that technological access to such "premises" might be a thing of the near future. He wrote repeatedly to prominent psychometricians (most of them affiliated with the Migration Committee), including Yerkes and Harold C. Bingham, as well as the pioneering opinion researcher L. L. Thurstone, about the possibility of developing tests for "leadership," aggressiveness, and other political traits, and frequently reminded them to keep him abreast of any promising developments in that area.[34] (Merriam protégé Harold F. Gosnell publicly expressed similar hopes, writing in a 1923 article titled "Some Practical Applications of Psychology in Government" that "perfection of tests of emotional, volitional, and moral traits would be a great aid to the public administration" as would the development by psychologists of possible "qualification tests" for electors and others charged with public duties.")[35]

Merriam got some encouragement in this endeavor, particularly from Yerkes and Thurstone. Yerkes, for example, wrote to Merriam in January 1923 about impending "important developments" with respect to work sponsored by the Institute for Government Research on "character rating or measurement" and the Migration Committee's work on "development of methods of measuring human characteristics."[36] But in terms of concrete findings or actual testing programs, little came of it. Merriam and Gosnell each tried to apply the psychological "attitude" in their books of the early 1920s. Technical and practical constraints, however, meant they were forced to content themselves with making gestures in the direction of "hard," psychological assessment to accompany their rigorous institutional analyses. (One only slightly disappointed *APSR* reviewer wrote of both Merriam's 1923 *The American Party System* and Gosnell's 1924 *Boss Platt and His New York Machine* that, despite the authors' pretensions to the contrary, the books' conclusions depended "primarily on exhaustive analysis of political forces and political organization rather than upon 'psycho-biological' analysis.")[37]

Indeed, in the end, the promise of "psycho-biological analysis" remained unfulfilled. Nobody developed any reliable, massively deployable instruments for identifying the traits of what Merriam called "efficient citizenship" or by which "obstacles" to its development could be "located . . . diagnosed," and "measurably trained and controlled."[38] Merriam even reported difficulty in beginning to identify what those traits might be. When Yerkes, responding to Merriam's request for tests for "efficient citizenship," asked for a more specific list of traits, Merriam responded, "I worked on this subject through the summer and fall with one of my classes, but thus far have not come to anything like a definite conclusion." He remained hopeful that a "little more fumbling around" might yield some "common judgment of traits of good, bad, and indifferent citizens," but there is no evidence in his correspondence that he judged later efforts to have been any more conclusive.[39] Nor, clearly, was the Migration Committee able to put the question of immigration on a "secure, objective basis."

The committee had directed more than $140,000 of foundation money—most of it eventually from the Laura Spelman Rockefeller Memorial (LSRM) fund, under the leadership of Beardsley Ruml—to scientific studies of physical and mental differences between racialized groups. Topics included the influence of language barriers on intelligence tests; group and individual differences in neurological and physiological responses; methods for testing nonintellectual traits; race differences in mechanical ability, "pathology," and even right- or left-handedness; anatomical effects of "race crossing"; and the "Comparative . . . Mental Traits of Negroes and Whites"; among several others.[40]

Nonetheless, like Merriam's quest for a test for responsible citizenship, on its own terms the committee was a failure. Its (few) public reports and (numerous) funding requests and internal memos, as well as the correspondence between its members and discussion at its meetings, had presented the committee's object as nothing less than fundamental methodological work that would make it possible to gather more nuanced and authoritative data about racial traits and the consequences of race contact than had hitherto been possible.[41] But results appear to have been meager, lacking in new technologies or insights and difficult to synthesize because of methodological and interpretive inconsistencies between projects. Already by 1926, Ruml was privately cautioning that "it would be a mistake to print a public report from the Committee" because its work "could not help being misunderstood, and the lack of cohesiveness as between the various projects would, I feel, be subject to a good deal of unfavorable comment by persons who were not informed more intimately than any report could be counted upon to make them."[42] The group began to wind down its work at this point, and was quietly shuttered in 1928, without much to show in terms of fundamental scientific advance. This was a blow to Yerkes, who repeatedly referred to his experience on the Migration Committee as a great disappointment, despite remaining committed to its basic premises throughout his career.[43]

All the same, the immigration restriction that the committee had been engineered to legitimate was enacted (in the form of the 1924 Johnson-Reed Immigration Act, which severely limited southern European and non-white immigration to the United States). The committee itself began work too late to credit it with having much effect on that development.[44] However, there is no doubt it helped reserve funds for the hard-line determinists who were competing at the time with Boas and other culturally minded scholars for power within institutions like the NRC, major research museums, and the American Anthropological Association. For historian Elazar Barkan, this meant "delaying" for much of the 1920s "the oncoming dominance of the cultural school" and its environmental analysis of group difference.[45] It also provided a boost for psychometrics researchers who, even when the eugenics movement began to wane, found demand for their skills in educational and occupational testing.[46]

Another failed, yet still productive project related to the Migration Committee involved the status of the social sciences. Merriam first floated the idea for what eventually became the SSRC to colleagues on the APSA's Committee on Political Research. Finding support, Merriam approached leaders of other major social science associations about joining together in a "Social Research Council," which, by the end of 1923, had become the SSRC, with Merriam at the helm.

This was a consequential innovation. Dorothy Ross sees it as "a major catalyst for the focus of social science on scientific method." For Martin Bulmer, the advent of the SSRC's activities was among the most important of a set of "fundamental changes in social science research [that] marked the beginning of a modern phase in its organization." This included crucial and early support for what became known as the "behavioral sciences"— precisely the liberal, interdisciplinary, scientistic approach to social and political research that Merriam and others were beginning to imagine in this period.[47]

These changes could be seen in the conceptualization of research itself; the relationship between academic research and foundations (and the viability of both, with funds flowing to the former and credibility to the latter); the balance of power within and among various academic centers (to the great benefit of the University of Chicago, for example); and, somewhat later, the relationship between social scientists and the state (when Merriam and other SSRC-affiliated scholars staffed Herbert Hoover's Committee on Social Trends and then Franklin Delano Roosevelt's National Resources Planning Board, for example). That is, the SSRC eventually worked to dramatically raise the visibility and prestige of the social sciences—and therefore of the notion of "the social" as a legitimate object of inquiry—and was a major element in the social and intellectual configuration "that led one political scientist to grandly describe the twentieth century as 'the century of the social sciences.' "[48]

However, autonomy for "the social" was not the original plan. A series of resolutions at planning meetings in early 1923 indicated that the "general opinion was that it would be highly desirable to enter the National Research Council," as opposed to joining the American Council of Learned Societies (ACLS) or remaining independent.[49] The advantages of such an arrangement would include prestige, already established sources of funding, and possibilities for cooperation with the natural sciences along the lines of Merriam's proposed collaboration on new forms of mental testing.[50] In the end, the SSRC's overtures to the Migration Committee failed to get the social sciences into the NRC. However, they had the enormously consequential effect of bringing Charles Merriam together with Beardsley Ruml.

Ruml would eventually become the chairman of the board of Macy's and the director and later chairman of the New York Federal Reserve Bank. He was active in New Deal planning, participated in the Bretton Woods Conference, and came up with the withholding, pay-as-you-go system for income taxes that was adopted by Congress in 1943. But when he was asked in 1921 to join the Laura Spelman Rockefeller Memorial as director he was a 26-year-old University of Chicago-trained psychology PhD and rising star in applied psychology. For all his youth he had worked with most of the luminaries in the field and had experience and high-level contacts in academia, the military, and business. He trained first at Dartmouth under the industrial psychologist Walter Van Dyke Bingham. Later, at Chicago for his doctorate, he worked with James Angell, a psychologist who also supervised John Watson, the pioneer of behavioral psychology. Subsequently, Ruml worked briefly for the Carnegie Institute of Technology before following Angell to the War Department, where both were involved in army mental testing.[51] After the war, Ruml moved to Philadelphia, briefly helping to found the nation's first industrial psychology consulting firm, then returned to another of the proliferating Carnegie agencies as assistant to

Angell, who by then was president of the Carnegie Corporation of New York.[52] During this time, Ruml managed to produce a fair amount of scholarly research, including original work in statistical correlation, a coauthored book on mental testing of schoolchildren, and journal articles on occupational and intelligence testing.

When Ruml joined them, the Rockefeller foundations and particularly the Laura Spelman Rockefeller Memorial were oriented toward the ethically oriented (and predominantly female-identified) model of social welfare work.[53] Ruml's chief innovation was to redirect the LSRM's nearly $74 million endowment to the pursuit of "objective" knowledge as a means to achieving social change. In practical terms, this meant vast new sums not only for universities themselves (which were already getting significant resources from foundations and the robber barons who endowed them) but now for specific research programs and (mostly male) researchers who were certified by expert bodies and new, ostensibly rigorous disciplinary norms. But the fund's move away from the Progressive Era service model did not mean abandoning its upper-class zeal to reform and reconstruct everyone else. Rather, for the officials charged with dispensing Rockefeller largesse, Ruml included, social-welfare work and academic research would combine to form an "informal, loosely defined human engineering effort."[54]

Ruml was obviously a figure of real importance for anyone aiming to foster large-scale, capital-intensive research in areas of social and political relevance, and his connections to Yerkes, John Merriam, and others would have put him in Charles Merriam's sights early. Add to this intellectual and temperamental affinities—the two shared an enthusiasm for the possibilities of social change through technocratic management, and both were big, charismatic personalities who liked to make big plans—and their association seems almost inevitable.

But, in fact, at the outset Ruml was not especially impressed with what the social sciences had to offer. As he put it in a memo to his new employers, the social science available in 1922 was "abstract and remote, of little help" to the would-be "social engineer . . . in the solution of his problems." As a result, Merriam's initial overtures to Ruml were met coolly. Ruml's correspondence at the end of 1922 and the beginning of 1923 shows him to be skeptical about the younger of the two Merriam brothers and the various plans Charles was championing at the University of Chicago. When Merriam requested funding for a new "Local Community Research Committee" at Chicago, the LSRM did offer some funding but only on the strength of the involvement of another former protégé of Ruml's old boss, Angell. Early funding requests for Merriam's research on "citizenship" were bounced back to the new Chicago committee.[55] Ruml was also initially a bit disparaging in internal memos about Merriam's plans for a "Social Research Council," commenting in July 1923, "I have not talked personally with any of the people who propose the formation of this council but . . . it is a much less distinguished group than that which sponsored . . . [the American Council of Learned Societies] . . . and in general it seems to me a less promising movement."[56]

However, within a year the tide had turned: by early 1924, LSRM money was flowing freely to both social science research at Chicago and the SSRC, and Ruml and Merriam were beginning a close professional and personal association that would span the rest of the older man's career. In the end, Ruml, and Rockefeller philanthropy more generally, were to become the principal patrons of Merriam's institutionalizing work and his and his students' research; in the 1930s, Merriam would even direct the Spelman Foundation of New York, which was established to continue the LSRM's work on a smaller scale after the LSRM was disbanded. It is not entirely clear what turned Ruml in Merriam's favor. But the Migration Committee was where the two men came together, and they did so around the desire to produce, in Ruml's words, "substantiated and widely accepted generalizations as to human capacities and motives and as to the behavior of human beings as individuals and groups."[57]

It was at the very first full Migration Committee meeting that Yerkes and others suggested involving social scientists in the committee's work, specifically "the political science and historical group" being organized by "Dr. Merriam's brother."[58] This suggestion hardly came out of the blue, however. Charles Merriam had for a period of time been closely attentive to the work of the NRC, even advising its efforts to reorganize as a peacetime body. Of course he was also connected to the NRC through his brother, whom he very much admired and who repeatedly expressed interest in the possibilities of Charles's work for "bring[ing] into relation to political studies the evidence available from the related fields which have heretofore been considered a legitimate part of scientific research."[59]

The same figures in connection with their work on the Migration Committee repeatedly brought Charles Merriam to Ruml's attention.[60] By that fall, Merriam and Ruml were co-conspirators, and their correspondence makes it clear that the two men shared the goal of folding the SSRC into the NRC with Yerkes, John Merriam, and others involved in planning the social science body.[61] (Charles commented to Ruml that he was "greatly taken with the idea," later noting that Yerkes was taking their proposal to various figures in the NRC's governing body, the National Academy of Sciences [NAS], and commenting that, "I sincerely hope that Dr. Yerkes has been able to make some progress in the direction we should like to go."[62])

It became clear from an early stage that the NAS wasn't especially eager to embrace the social sciences, so Merriam and Ruml and their allies in the Migration Committee tried a number of tacks. One was to create a "joint committee on methods" that would bring together representatives of the new council with the NRC.[63] Another was to keep pushing for formal joint representation of the two councils on the Migration Committee, something that was repeatedly proposed until it became clear in 1924 that it would not go through. Failing that, the SSRC settled on a strategy of setting up parallel and cooperating committees that might demonstrate the value of collaboration. This, too, was a disappointment. The most notable results produced by a "sociological conference group," which worked in parallel to the NRC Migration Committee, concerned the relationship of migration patterns to the business cycle, the labor supply, and trends in industrial mechanization. These were perfectly respectable projects, to be sure, but not at all the sort of fundamental linkages between the social and natural sciences that Merriam originally had in mind.

Still, the conference group's formation had the significant side effect of putting the fledgling "SRC" for the first time in front of the full Rockefeller board, when the original Migration Committee funding request was considered and approved at the board's April 1923 meeting.[64] Moreover, by the end of all this, Ruml was committed to Merriam's project, and Rockefeller money made Merriam's new, independent council viable. Over a seven-year collaboration, the LSRM and SSRC together doled out $41 million in support of favored work and institutions in social science and social work.[65] The relationship was not just a boon to the social scientists. The SSRC provided valuable service to the LSRM, acting as a vetting agency for its funding programs and providing political cover—studies were not "Rockefeller funded" but sponsored by a body of independent experts. Indeed, it was often difficult to tell precisely where programs originated. To give just a few examples: Ruml and Merriam essentially planned the SSRC fellowship program together, and the second major SSRC initiative following collaboration with the Migration Committee was a committee on international communication that Ruml had proposed.[66] On a smaller scale, a study by the (non-Boasian) anthropologist Manuel Gamio of the communities supplying Mexican migration to the United States was essentially planned and so enthusiastically promoted by one Rockefeller official (with active support from both John Merriam and Ruml) before its adoption that some embarrassment and a flurry of apologetic letters ensued. (The project still went through as envisioned.)[67] Merriam and Ruml's was a working partnership with substantial agreement on the ends to be pursued and the means by which they might be achieved. And it was centered on a vision for technocratic social intervention informed by a deep understanding of the public's capacities, tendencies, and limitations.

During the period that the SSRC was being organized, Ruml and Merriam explored their shared interest in such "psycho-biological" determinants of politics through a number of initiatives in addition to the Migration Committee. Beginning in 1923, Ruml provided the funding for the National Conferences on the Science of Politics. Merriam organized a popular section on politics and psychology that hosted several speakers with ties to the Migration Committee. It provided a visible pulpit for Merriam to preach his conviction that, present defects aside, particularly in the fields of mental and occupational testing, "genuine progress in the study of politics [was] likely to be made" from a "continuation" of "significant advances . . . toward more scientific study of traits of human nature underlying political action, and of the processes that in reality constitute government."[68] A few years later, the Science of Politics conferences were folded into the APSA meetings, their place taken by the more inclusive Hanover Conferences on the Social Sciences, under SSRC auspices. Also jointly planned by Merriam and Ruml, and underwritten with Rockefeller money, these conferences provided a still more interdisciplinary setting in which Merriam could pursue these connections and encourage the sort of research he favored—the first conference, for example, included a session on "Professor Merriam's [proposal for] study of differential and social traits of races or other groups."[69]

All the same, for Merriam at least, race was less a central concern than a heuristic—his interest lay primarily with those "other groups." That is, if the characteristics of racial groups could be measured and compared, why could the same techniques not be applied to discover the outlines of other, less obvious groupings within society? So, for example, through NRC official Vernon Kellogg, Merriam came to champion the work of an Australian "psychopathologist" named George Elton Mayo who was working on the links between neurosis and industrial and political agitation. Together, Merriam and Kellogg commended Mayo to Ruml, who was to become Mayo's close friend and patron, securing funding for a temporary position for Mayo at the University of Pennsylvania and later helping him to find a permanent job at Harvard.[70] Merriam and Ruml also worked together to arrange for Lasswell to work with Mayo, first at Harvard and later during a research trip to Germany, "on tests . . . designed to develop if possible a physiological or psychopathological basis of varying types of citizens."[71] The idea, according to Merriam, was to determine whether the relation of "different types of personality responses . . . with reference to civic affairs" to "temperament, physical makeup, personal experience, and kindred factors" might be "directly discoverable by the application of more modern scientific methods to the problem."[72]

Lasswell's expectations for these combined efforts were expansive—he wrote to Merriam in 1926 that "an exposure of the biological factors which condition response [to political stimuli] will . . . open a whole new field of reference points for research and restatement of politics."[73] Once again, the results were somewhat less dramatic than all that—a volume by Mayo and Lasswell on civic personalities was planned but never written, and a 1927 memorandum on the research commented that it "was not expected that Mr. Lasswell would discover specific relationships between civic types and physiological and psychiatric traits but significant progress was made in the development of a method for this purpose."[74] However, the project not only stimulated Lasswell's interest in psychopathology and politics, it also gave him his first experience conducting psychoanalytic interviews and tests, which he was allowed to do at the Boston Psychopathic Hospital during his sojourn with Mayo.[75] This experience contributed directly to Lasswell's 1930 *Psychopathology and Politics*, a seminal text that did much to launch the field of political psychology.[76]

Merriam and Gosnell's work on "leadership" constituted analogous, though less technically ambitious efforts, which also received Rockefeller money, this time through a research committee that the LSRM supported at the University of Chicago.[77] As noted, these, too, fell short of expectation. However, Gosnell would go on to much more groundbreaking studies (some with Merriam's help, and all with Rockefeller support) that made novel use of survey research and statistical analysis to distinguish the characteristics of voters from those of nonvoters and of immigrants who naturalized from those who didn't.[78] In 1928, Gosnell began research on "the negro in politics"[79] that resulted in a 1935 book, *Negro Politicians,* one of the first book-length treatments of black politics in the United States by a white political scientist.[80]

That Chicago committee (the Local Community Research Council, or LCRC) was also the vehicle for achieving one of Merriam's long-standing institutional goals. While he was not able to persuade the university administration or the Rockefellers to fund an independent Institute of Politics, he was key to the LCRC's eventual success in getting Ruml's support for the construction of the Social Science Building at the University of Chicago.[81] (At his speech at the building's dedication in 1929, Merriam commented, "When I look at the Building, I see 'B' [for Beardsley] written upon it from every angle"; in 1931, Ruml even moved to Chicago for a brief period to serve as dean of the Social Sciences Division housed there.[82])

Merriam was intimately involved in planning the building, and his vision of interdisciplinarity—and specifically of the need for collaboration between political scientists and others who studied human behavior from a naturalistic perspective—is clearly visible in the plans for the building. Facilities included a number of card-sorting-machine and statistical-data rooms, and a "psychological-psychiatric laboratory." Moreover, faculty members were not housed by discipline but rather in clusters related to subject matter—Gosnell was paired with the sociologist William Ogburn, and Lasswell's office adjoined that of the pioneering intelligence and attitude researcher L. L. Thurstone.[83]

This does not begin to exhaust the dense intellectual, personal, and institutional web to which Merriam was central and that so profoundly shaped his own discipline and the social sciences generally in this period. As I see it, however, this slice of that history is revealing of the political imaginary that animated Merriam's scientific project. The technologies for a specifically political realization of this imaginary did not take the form Merriam had hoped—rather than tests that would reveal or confirm hidden, specific, inherent, political characteristics, what emerged instead were measures of attitudes, or correlations between less occult attributes such as class and race with behaviors or attitudes such as voting or partisanship. Nonetheless, the nexus of the Laura Spelman Rockefeller Memorial, the various APSA committees and meetings, the SSRC, the NRC, and the University of Chicago constitutes a site where a new image of human difference began to come into focus and where a political science oriented around it began to be imaginable.

The point of this discussion is not that these efforts were somehow tainted by association with the frankly racist science promoted by Yerkes, Brigham, and John C. Merriam. Rather, I am suggesting that race research, and particularly eugenics and mental testing, modeled a new way of thinking about difference as deeply individual, patterned within groups, and originating somewhere deeper than and precedent to political life. Scientists committed to racial determinism were not the only ones to deploy such models at this time, of course, but they did so in compelling ways. Moreover, as much as their work was turned to the service of racist projects—as by the Nazis; in colonial genocides; and in immigration restriction, compulsory sterilization, and the institutionalization of the "unfit" in the United States and elsewhere—it could also be recruited to liberal, meritocratic ones. As John Carson notes, for example, a number of Jewish and African American intellectuals welcomed intelligence testing, particularly in education, precisely because it seemed to promise some measure of vindication to their own elites.[84]

More important, it could also be detached from race even more completely—or, rather, one could imagine that many kinds of difference operated on the same model as racial difference. So, for example, the same report on the National Conference on the Science of Politics that advocated "breaking down" the question of how racial strains "influenced" American civilization "into . . . more specific questions" to "be studied with the quantitative controls of scientific method" suggested that psychology, and particularly those quarters of psychology focused on "biometrics," held the key to understanding various kinds of difference.[85]

In his introduction to the conference report, chair A. B. Hall highlighted an "almost spontaneous unanimity with which the directors [of the various sections] reached the conclusion that every round table needed the presence of both a psychologist and a statistician." Political scientists with "working knowledge of psychology's contribution to the technique of mental measurement" in particular would be equipped to approach the "problem of public opinion, mass psychology, the role of suggestion in political propaganda—in fact, the whole field of what might be called the psychology of political behavior."[86]

It is hard to disagree with the directors that the most innovative ideas produced at the conference related strongly to the work of the psychometricians. Despite the conference's emphasis on new techniques, much of the work discussed in the report was fairly conventional, having to do with gathering information on civil service commissions, municipal finance, party and legislative procedures, and international affairs. Most came with some gestures toward methodological innovations, but, as with a subcommittee interested in the relative efficiency of cities, in most cases they were forced to admit those would be "less simple" to come by than they might have hoped.[87]

More genuinely innovative and actionable were proposals for "experimental measurement of nationality, race, sex, schooling, age, economic status, occupation, religion, and other factors as determinants" of opinion, susceptibility to propaganda (and to different forms of propaganda) or to emotional versus rational appeals. Other proposals included measurements for within-population distributions of opinion and differences in group and individual responses to get-out-the-vote techniques.[88]

Here we see that Merriam's most deterministic fantasies—the idea that people were somehow hardwired to have a certain kind of politics and that political science could turn knowledge about that hardwiring to a project of "social control" or "social therapy"—gave way in practice to the more mundane, and now deeply familiar, idea that the task of political science was to determine how various kinds of difference might shape political behavior. But on both registers the differences in question were essentially pre-political. Where once, racial difference and political difference had been largely conflated, now the differences that mattered appeared to emerge from other, more basic realms.

Epilogue

I opened this book with a discussion of "genes and politics" research—twenty-first century attempts by political scientists and behavioral geneticists to find the sources of our political ideas and behavior in our genes. My point was that this work retooled themes that were present in U.S. political science at its origins. Today, we look for genes for voting. At the close of the nineteenth century, it was germs of self-government. However, readers might by this point find a more precise parallel in Charles Merriam, Harold Lasswell, Beardsley Ruml, and others' early, and most deterministic, hopes for a science of politics. Like the attempt to pin our ideology to our DNA, the idea of psychometric or other tests to reveal people's capacities for leadership or "efficient" citizenship, or any neurotic tendencies to radicalism, represented the hope that political scientists might see past the confusing surface of politics, down to its primal substrate.

Each of those projects, like many of the others described in this book, turns for purchase on political life to revelations about the workings of human nature produced in other, supposedly more basic, fields. The rhetorical move each makes is to say, in effect, that while others may be content to deal in airy speculation, *we* root *our* accounts of politics in the hard facts of nature (as revealed by history, evolutionary theory, psychology, or genetics, for example). Each also re-describes political difference in ascriptive terms. The deepest sources of political conflict, they imply, are not to be sought in ideology, class, capitalism, or indeed any other feature of sociopolitical life, but rather in the participants' very constitutions—the kinds of people we are.

All the same, the scientistic turn of the 1920s shares a kind of technological imagination with today's "empirical biopolitics" that was not visible in earlier political scholarship. Like genomics today, in the 1920s intelligence tests and the statistical apparatus within which they were embedded (and by which populations could be mapped and displayed) seemed to offer impersonal, technical ways to, as Malcolm Willey had hoped, fit the "abstraction" of democracy to its "actual life conditions" and give observers "a firmer basis for their inductions . . . upon the solid ground of objective fact."[1] For political science, this "basis" would no longer be the dynamic field of teleological or evolutionary change from which politics and political development emerged but rather arrays of data about individual and group traits. Moreover, the empirical focus could move from the organic collective to the multifarious population.

As the last chapter shows, this push did not yield precisely the results for which many had initially hoped. Still, the emergence of this new technological imagination seems to me a significant development for the scientistic project in political science as well as for the fate of "race" within that project. I have already suggested that, despite the accompanying disappointments, political science's encounter with race science in the 1920s was enormously productive for the discipline in a few senses. That encounter provided a framework with which to unravel constrictive ideas of national community. It also suggested alternative visions, which in turn animated fruitful research programs. Finally and perhaps most significantly, it brought together people and resources that worked to set the course of political science, and indeed of the behavioral sciences, in profound ways. What I will submit here, however briefly, is that these developments may in other ways have worked to limit our ability to make sense of the racial dynamics of American life.

Most of the work I discuss in this book was explicitly committed to one vision or another of a definite racial order. This ranged from frank white supremacy and even exterminationism á la John Burgess and others to the more optimistic takes on the possibilities of racial uplift articulated in the pages of the *Journal of Race Development* and elsewhere. In the case of Charles Merriam and many of the science-minded political researchers in his orbit, these commitments are harder to pin down. Certainly people in this milieu often endorsed the idea that racial differences were inherent and that African Americans and other racialized groups were probably or certainly inferior to Anglo-Saxons in at least some ways. At the same time, I have noted that many of them seem not to have been especially committed to white supremacist ideology as a political stance. Or rather, while they did not mount any kind of sustained challenge to white supremacy, neither did this set of political scientists aim to shore it up in the obsessive manner of hard-line eugenicists and race psychologists (among others). (As we have seen, Merriam in particular sometimes cautioned against race scientists' rush to judgment, and his student, Harold Gosnell, was the first prominent, white political scientist to write seriously about African American politics.)

My point is not to excuse this group as somewhat less racist than other early twentieth-century American elites—a low bar in any event. Rather, I want to highlight what seems to be novel in this moment. As I see it, for this group psychometric testing and race research represented above all a hope of technical access to merit and other traits. Armed with such knowledge, political science might be better able to predict (and possibly even to direct) people's behavior. That is, race science appealed not so much as proof positive of white superiority but as a possible means to satisfy long-standing, internal demands for empiricism, rigor, and real-world applicability within political science. Moreover, it was also suited to—and indeed was implicated in the construction of—a new institutional landscape.

Political scientists had long contrasted their own (empirical, scientific) work to others' speculative fancy. However, in most instances discussed in this book, those contrasts were drawn within a fairly homogeneous community and mostly directed at outsiders, straw men, or elders whose influence was already waning.[2] By contrast in the 1920s the community of political scholarship had grown, and fractured to the extent that "even the matters with which it should deal" had become "subjects of controversy." This meant that those who wished to "dig deeper" (as Gordon Dewey put it at the time) faced challenges from within the profession, a situation that created new dilemmas.[3]

To make matters more complicated, the push for a scientific renovation of the study of politics was also connected to a larger, interdisciplinary project and to specific efforts at engaging new kinds of extra-university support. The National Research Council was reorganizing to mobilize science for the state on a peacetime basis, and private foundations were beginning to move away from a social-service model. This made it possible to imagine that academic social research could be inserted into a network of private funders and government agencies, much as the natural sciences already were. As Beardsley Ruml's initial reaction to the idea of a "Social Research Council" and the National Academy of Sciences' resistance to the social sciences both indicated, however, this would take some doing.

That is, whatever prestige leading political scientists may have had within their own networks, it would not suffice to immediately convince skeptical outsiders to invest in their work. If they were going to be successful in existing networks, and create new ones, political science and the social sciences more broadly needed ways to establish authority outside their own communities. In particular, they would have to satisfy bureaucrats' and foundation boards' demands for impersonal measures of the value of the work they were asked to support.

This was not a new aspiration. Statistical data carried great weight in the context of the paramount Progressive Era values of "continuity and regularity, functionality and rationality, administration and management," and political scientists had long hoped that enough hard data would help them catch the ear of "the perplexed legislator in time of his need."[4] Moreover, as historicism lost its cachet after the turn of the century, the need for adequate, quantitative data on the present and recent past became a consistent and urgent theme. Lack of uniformity, coverage, and professionalism in government statistical reporting was frequently lamented in the pages of the *American Political Science Review*, and various schemes for generating alternative and complementary sources of data were consistently proposed, and some instituted, during the early decades of the twentieth century.

The type of data that race scientists were generating, however, went beyond previous efforts in that it seemed to probe beneath the surface level of vital and other government statistics to reveal the deeper causes of political behavior. Psychometrics in particular purported to be elaborating techniques for gathering scientific information about the population, its tendencies and its potential. Those methods offered to reveal a fine-grained array of human differences that were at once consonant with the pluralistic view of political life that was gaining currency at that time *and* with the technocratic, managerial, reform ambitions that Merriam and others largely carried over from progressivism. In conjunction with the insights of Boasian anthropology, this seemed to point political science toward a way to relinquish the monolithic categories of state theory and its descendants without giving up at least the possibility that some form of functional, democratic unity might someday be produced via scientific methods of "social control."

Crucially, a version of psychometrics tailored to their purposes might allow political scientists to arrive at generalizations about the political world using technical means—a set of rule-bound procedures that, theoretically at least, would deliver the same results regardless of the investigator. Theodore Porter identifies this aspiration as the attempt to achieve "mechanical objectivity." In contrast to "disciplinary objectivity," in which truth arises from consensus within a defined community with common standards, "mechanical objectivity" is meant to produce agreement under conditions of mistrust. Technology mediates between the knower and the known; expertise is "mechanized," "objectified," and "grounded in specific techniques." Under these conditions, "mere judgment, with all its gaps and idiosyncrasies, seems almost to disappear."[5] Intelligence testing had earned psychologists unprecedented levels of financial support and entrée into the realms of state decision-making.[6] For a group of political scientists committed to the enlightened reconstruction of politics, the naturalistic, quantitative approach to human difference articulated in race research promised findings that might similarly travel across disciplinary lines and into the halls of power.

External pressures to produce reliable, plausibly nonideological political knowledge returned with a vengeance during World War II and especially during the Cold War. Beginning with wartime mobilization, and increasing in the postwar era, American social scientists received unprecedented levels of funding from new sources, including the National Science Foundation, the Ford Foundation Behavioral Sciences Program, and other foundations, as well as military and intelligence agencies. In this context, it became more important than ever to counter suspicions that political scientists' work was merely dressed-up partisanship.

These patrons did at points support efforts to resist the scientistic tide.[7] However, as Mark Solovey shows, such instances were the exception. The rule was "informal cooperation" between funders that "supported striking commonalities" in favor of social science that met criteria for quantitative rigor and (at least apparent) value-neutrality. In practice, this meant scholarship that eschewed any suggestion of Marxism and, often, celebrated a kind of liberal nationalism.[8] In political science, these pressures worked to the great benefit of behavioralism, the lineal descendant (in both intellectual and personnel terms) of the proponents of scientism in the interwar period. It also benefited the by-then clearly allied pluralist account of U.S. politics as the free, liberal interplay of largely self-constituting groups.[9] Many elements of this emerging perspective were synthesized in David Easton's 1953 proposal that the proper object of political science was "political systems" consisting of "inputs," "feedback," and "outputs."[10]

That is, key features of the vision of politics and the structure of patron–social science relations that began to take shape in the 1920s—in large measure through leading political scientists' engagement with race science—recurred and were extended into the political science mainstream at midcentury and beyond. I do not mean to overstate continuities or causality here. Postwar, behavioralist political science differed substantially from the output of the scholars I discuss in this book, not least in the sophistication of its methods. Moreover, in the ideological climate of the Cold War, funders, government agencies, and political scientists alike valued a stance of political detachment—or "separation of fact and value"—far more than Merriam and his cohort ever had. Nor do I want to suggest that the encounter between political science and race science in the 1920s somehow *caused* a quantitative, scientistic bent to become hegemonic in the discipline in subsequent decades. Indeed that encounter might best be conceptualized as an *effect* of the same internal pressures and external demands that made quantitative, naturalistic research attractive to many social scientists in this period.

Nonetheless, as John Dryzek argues, behavioralism—with its methodological individualism and focus on technique—was less a qualitative shift than a "radicalization" and an extension of "existing tendencies"—tendencies that began to take shape in the 1920s and that stand in sharp contrast to the racialized, evolutionary organicism of the discipline's founding decades.[11] Those tendencies bear the mark of their origins in at least two clear ways. First, while transformations in racial thought in the 1920s could not have been sufficient to cause Merriam and other science-minded political scientists to begin to reimagine politics in the 1920s, they may yet have been necessary for that to happen in the way that it did. Racial thinking was central to the ideas of political community that Merriam and his cohort inherited. Updating that ideal would require them to either maintain or somehow reimagine the racial organicism at its core. We have seen that some political scientists in this period preferred to hold on to an idea of the national state as "essentially real."[12] Others were willing to relinquish the whole thing in favor of a pluralist vision. But Merriam and the technocratic, liberal tendency he represented sought to chart a middle course. For them, the Boasian critique of racial evolutionism and the racialized sciences of intelligence and eugenics together seemed to offer new ways to think about "the people" that could account at once for the multiplicity that pluralists identified *and* still offer the possibility of meaningful integration or "social control."

Second, the Social Science Research Council and the model it elaborated for both interdisciplinary research and patron–social scientist relationships were important sites for the promotion of the behavioral sciences. As Solovey has shown, the SSRC was also a key staging ground in the early postwar years for the argument that the social sciences could and should be as apolitical as the natural sciences. (Or, rather, as apolitical as the natural sciences were imagined to be.)[13] However, the negotiations around the council's origins show that this was not a new attempt. The desire to position the social sciences as an adjunct to or even as a branch of the natural sciences was a long-standing one that animated the council's origins in consequential ways, particularly through the collaboration between Charles Merriam and Beardsley Ruml. And those two men came together around the shared idea that the findings and methods of eugenicists and immigration restrictionists might unlock the secrets connecting political behavior to deeper, more basic processes of nature or social existence.

All the same, while I do see antecedents of later and even current practices being elaborated in the 1920s, the idea here is not to brand behavioralist political science and the research programs that emerged from it as racist by virtue of some ancestral link to scientific racism. (And of course some elements of midcentury political science, such as the idea of political culture, develop out of the Boasian tradition.)[14] Nor is it to identify and recuperate some other, more virtuous current of political science that lost out at one moment or another. Postwar political scientists' racial commitments were their own and were tied to their own moment. And even if I could identify such an alternative current, I am not sure what would be gained in the effort. However, I do think this story has significant implications. Certainly it should inform our understanding of political science's place in a larger history of social scientific engagement with race. More broadly though, it is useful for thinking about the possibilities and limitations of political science's attempts to address the racial dynamics of American life today.

At the very least, this account should put a dent in what I have come to think of as "political science exceptionalism." Thanks to a wealth of careful studies by historians and practitioner-historians alike, we are learning how anthropology, sociology, criminology, and other social sciences both responded to and helped to construct American racial ideology.[15] It is my hope that this book, alongside recent work focusing on international relations specifically, will help to embed political science into this emerging account of the co-production of "race" and the social sciences in the United States.[16]

I hope also that it will help to place political science into a larger set of processes that have shaped both U.S. racial hierarchy and efforts to combat it. One major product of the social scientific construction of race in America in the twentieth century is the "race-relations paradigm," or what historian Leah Gordon calls "racial individualism."[17] When Robert Park and his colleagues in Chicago sociology made the term "race relations" a staple of sociological language in the early decades of the twentieth century, it referred to a cultural evolutionary process. Chicago sociologists described a "race-relations cycle" that emerged from sociohistorical conditions but still operated according to a naturalistic logic of its own.[18] As it developed in the postwar era, however, race-relations scholarship increasingly framed the subordinate position of African Americans and other racialized minorities as fundamentally a problem of individuals' racism. This, famously, was the "American Dilemma" so searingly outlined in Gunnar Myrdal's two-volume, 1944 exploration of race in America.[19] The volumes themselves are full of data pointing to the many social-structural determinants of racial oppression. Nonetheless, for most readers, the takeaway was that unethical or irrational attitudes that persisted alongside America's egalitarian ideals (particularly among poor whites) were the primary cause of America's "race problem." This was the framework that launched a thousand "conversations on race" and similar "therapeutic" interventions. Scholarship in this vein was (and remains) heavily behavioristic, focused on questions of racial attitudes and the psychology of prejudice. Moreover, civil rights efforts that accept this frame often emphasize the importance of "rights-based individualism . . . and anti-prejudice education" over demands for structural reform or redistribution.[20]

We have seen that many commentators charge U.S. political science with a similarly depoliticized view of race. From Mack Jones and Alex Willingham observing in 1970 that the discipline largely excluded racial questions from "fundamental political questions about the nature of society"[21] to Rogers Smith's reflection on the "puzzling place" of race in U.S. political science more than three decades later, much of the force of these critiques centers on the disciplinary production of what Charles Mills has called an "epistemology of ignorance."[22] As Smith puts it, political science has largely proceeded as if "race" were pre-political, "generated at root by biology and/ or economics and/or culture and/or history and/or often unconscious or at least informal social psychological processes and social activities"—problems, maybe, but not political science's.[23]

Another way of putting this is that the dominant currents in postwar political science, to the extent that they addressed race at all, did so firmly within a race-relations frame. The history discussed in this book suggests, however, that this paradigm was not just bestowed on political scientists, fully formed, by sociology, psychology, or some other field. Rather, political scientists participated actively in its construction, rethinking their discipline's racial commitments and in the process beginning to elaborate a political imaginary in which "race" was, essentially, an independent variable—something that impinged on political life from some other, more basic realm.

What this obscures, however, is how the social, psychological, and cultural characteristics that appear to shape political reality may in important ways be artifacts of political processes. This is the critique Smith advances in his article identifying the 1920s as the moment when race drops out of political science. As he puts it, understanding race as pre-political contributes to political scientists' failure "to explore fully the role of politics in creating racial identities and racial conflicts" and, by extension, "the role of racial politics in shaping many political patterns, identities, institutions, and developments that do not appear to have much to do with race."[24]

Efforts to correct for this failure—to uncover "how the ideological and material elements of race are produced, negotiated, and altered in and through politics" and how "race has structured . . . political institutions, political discourse, and public policy"—are numerous and ongoing.[25] Examples include explorations by scholars in and outside political science of how patterns of residential and labor-market segregation as well as attitudes about the welfare state and affirmative action emerged from New Deal– and Great Society–era policy decisions; how urban development policies in the twentieth century have taken up social scientific ideas about race, and have in turn shaped local racial political alignments; how ethnic and racial categories change over time and are negotiated through political and bureaucratic practices; how legal, political, and racial doctrines shape one another; and so on.[26] Nonetheless, as Michael Dawson and Cathy Cohen observe, even as the mainstream of political science increasingly addresses the political lives of racialized groups and the dynamics of racial exclusion, the focus is still overwhelmingly on "individual manifestations of political differences" that correlate unproblematically with "visible and self-identified racial differences."[27] That is, a definite gap still remains between what we know about the co-production of identity and politics and mainstream political science's engagement with those topics.

A consistent theme throughout this book has been that "race" is in many senses a language for thinking about the contingency of history and the efficacy of politics as a site for directing its course. In her account of the origins of U.S. social science, Dorothy Ross identifies a central impulse to "naturalize the historical world," wrapped up with a positivist view of science that sustains American exceptionalism while at the same time absolving social scientists from recognizing their commitment to it.[28] This impulse to naturalize history and society is nowhere more apparent than in attempts to racialize those things. At their most extreme, these projects have sought to establish racial hierarchy and separation as an iron law of nature. At other points, a naturalized vision of the social world suggests a point of entry for technocratic management but still within proscriptive limits—evolutionary time, say, or the points at which "nature" seems to resist the blandishments of "nurture."

These dynamics are most clearly visible in the strongly deterministic accounts of political life discussed in this book. However, as the critiques above indicate, they recur in more diffuse ways when "race" is exiled to the domain of "attitudes" or "prejudice" and their effects. At best, the methodological individualism of much political scholarship fails to capture the structural and power dynamics of racial oppression. At worst, in declining to interrogate the sources of observed discrepancies and patterns of behavior among and between racialized groups, such treatments effectively loan "race" (or "prejudice" or "discrimination") a kind of ontological force.

They also, ironically enough, minimize the social weight given to politics itself. In such accounts, most of the important action occurs elsewhere—in social, economic, or psychological processes, for example. The world of politics appears as an arena of interaction or a set of rules or structures. However, if we view politics primarily as what happens inside a space conditioned by institutional features and outside "inputs" we are not prompted to ask how it may actually generate a lot of the variables that we are taking as exogenous, or how political knowledge (such as political science's) fits into those processes. Politics is consigned to a sort of superstructural status, reflecting but not generating the factors that shape social life more broadly. This is a wasted opportunity. If we can attend more closely to the ways in which political life has shaped the identities we have, we may be better positioned to think about how we might mobilize it to transform them and to build new solidarities.

Notes

Introduction

1. Notably, the authors present their findings as an intervention *against* excessively deterministic, "existing models" in behavioral genetics that "assume that culture is merely a passenger on a genetic foundation." Peter K. Hatemi, Lindon Eaves, and Rose McDermott, "It's the End of Ideology as We Know It," *Journal of Theoretical Politics* 24, no. 3 (2012): 345, 347.

2. The only acknowledgment of the resonance with Foucault that I have found in this literature is Laurette T. Liesen and Mary Barbara Walsh, "The Competing Meanings of 'Biopolitics' in Political Science: Biological and Postmodern Approaches to Politics," *Politics and the Life Sciences* 31, no. 1/2 (2012).

3. As it happens, the "manifesto" of this tendency is by Albert Somit, "Toward a More Biologically-Oriented Political Science: Ethology and Psychopharmacology," *Midwest Journal of Political Science* 12, no. 4 (1968); Somit is the coauthor with Joseph Tanenhaus of a seminal entry into the historiography of political science, *The Development of American Political Science* (New York: Irvington Publishers, 1982). Empirical "biopolitics" was first highlighted at a 1975 conference in Paris sponsored by the International Political Science Association (IPSA) and by an accompanying book the following year, *Biology and Politics: Recent Explorations* (Paris: Mouton, 1976). In 1980, the Scaife Foundation bankrolled a Center for Biopolitics (later, the Program for Biosocial Research) at Northern Illinois University. A journal (*Politics and the Life Sciences*) and an Association for Politics and the Life Sciences (APLS) followed in 1982. The APLS was briefly a section of the American Political Science Association but was unable to maintain the required number of members.

4. John R. Alford, Carolyn L. Funk, and John R. Hibbing, "Are Political Orientations Genetically Transmitted?" *American Political Science Review* 99, no. 2 (2005).

5. Studies identifying "candidate genes" for such traits include, John R. Alford, Carolyn L. Funk, and John R. Hibbing, "Beyond Liberals and Conservatives to Political Genotypes and Phenotypes," *Perspectives on Politics* 6, no. 2 (2008); Peter K. Hatemi, Nathan A. Gillespie, Lindon J. Eaves, Brion S. Maher, Bradley T. Webb, Andrew C. Heath, Sarah E. Medland, et al., "A Genome-Wide Analysis of Liberal and Conservative Political Attitudes," *Journal of Politics* 73, no. 1 (2011); Kristen D. Deppe et al.,

"Candidate Genes and Voter Turnout: Further Evidence on the Role of 5-HTTLPR," *American Political Science Review* 107, no. 2 (2013); Carolyn L. Funk, Kevin B. Smith, John R. Alford, Matthew V. Hibbing, Nicholas R. Eaton, Robert K. Krueger, Lindon J. Eaves et al.,"Genetic and Environmental Transmission of Political Orientations," *Political Psychology* 36, no. 4 (2013); William D. Anderson and Cliff H. Summers, "Neuroendocrine Mechanisms, Stress Coping Strategies, and Social Dominance: Comparative Lessons About Leadership Potential," *Annals of the American Academy of Political and Social Science* 614 (2007); Peter K. Hatemi, Sarah E. Medland, and Lindon J. Eaves, "Genetic Sources of the Gender Gap?" *Journal of Politics* 71, no. 1 (2009); Robert Klemmensen et al., "The Genetics of Political Participation, Civic Duty, and Political Efficacy Across Cultures: Denmark and the United States," *Journal of Theoretical Politics* 24, no. 3 (2012); John Hibbing and Kevin Smith, "We Are What We Vote," *New Scientist* 226, no. 3015 (2015); and Peter K. Hatemi et al., "Fear as a Disposition and an Emotional State: A Genetic and Environmental Approach to Out-Group Political Preferences," *American Journal of Political Science* 57, no. 2 (2013). On "Machiavellianism," see Peter K. Hatemi, Kevin Smith, John R. Alford, Nicholas G. Martin, and John R. Hibbing, "The Genetic and Environmental Foundations of Political, Psychological, Social, and Economic Behaviors: A Panel Study of Twins and Families," *Twin Research and Human Genetics* 18, no. 3 (2015). A related literature looks to patterns of neurological or physiological response to predict similar traits, e.g., Rose McDermott, "Mutual Interests: The Case for Increasing Dialogue Between Political Science and Neuroscience," *Political Research Quarterly* 62, no. 3 (2009); John R. Hibbing, Kevin B. Smith, and John R. Alford, "Differences in Negativity Bias Underlie Variations in Political Ideology," *Behavioral and Brain Sciences* 37, no. 3 (2014); and Woo-Young Ahn, Kenneth T. Kishida, Xiaosi Gu, Terry Lohrenz, Ann Harvey, John R. Alford, Kevin B. Smith, et al., "Nonpolitical Images Evoke Neural Predictors of Political Ideology," *Current Biology* 24, no. 22 (2014).

6. Ira H. Carmen, "Genetic Configurations of Political Phenomena: New Theories, New Methods," *Annals of the American Academy of Political and Social Science* 614, no. 1 (2007).

7. Lee Sigelman, "Report of the Editor of the *American Political Science Review*, 2004–2005," *PS: Political Science and Politics* 39, no. 1 (2006).

8. Some media coverage of "genes and politics" research has been breathless—in 2012, *New York* magazine ran a piece titled, "Born This Way: The New Weird Science of Hardwired Political Identity"—but much has been more balanced. Much of the most credulous media coverage was pegged to a 2010 study that the University of California, San Diego's public relations department announced with a press release titled, "Researchers Find a 'Liberal Gene.'" (Jaime E. Settle, Christopher T. Dawes, Nicholas A. Christakis, and James H. Fowler, "Friendships Moderate an Association Between a Dopamine Gene Variant and Political Ideology," *Journal of Politics* 72, no. 4 [2010].) Response from more conventional politics researchers has been interested, but measuredly so. This is surely related to the simple fact that few political scientists have the expertise to engage with it or much inclination to retrain in genetics or send

their students off to do so. As a result, the political science mainstream mostly goes about its business seemingly unaware of its paradigms' imminent supersession.

9. For example, Evan Charney and William English, "Candidate Genes and Political Behavior," *American Political Science Review* 106, no. 1 (2012).

10. After thirty years as a science columnist, Wade left the *New York Times* amid controversy over a 2014 book in which he offered "a full-throated defense of 'scientific racism'" was rapturously received by a number of white supremacist outlets. He remains a *New York Times* contributor. Steve Rendall, "Highly Placed Media Racists," *FAIR: Fairness and Accuracy in Reporting*, 2014. http://fair.org/uncategorized/highly -placed-media-racists/. On racially specific medicine, see Adolph Reed Jr., "Making Sense of Race, I: The Biology of Human Variation, and the Problem of Medical and Public Health Research," *Journal of Race and Policy* 1 (2005).

11. Charles B. Davenport, *Heredity in Relation to Eugenics* (New York: Henry Holt, 1911), 80, 54; Charles Davenport, *Naval Officers: Their Heredity and Development* (Washington DC: Carnegie Institute of Washington, 1919), 25.

12. Troy Duster, *Backdoor to Eugenics* (1990) (New York: Routledge, 2003). For useful overviews of these developments and the concerns they raise, see Sheldon Krimsky and Kathleen Sloan, eds., *Race and the Genetic Revolution: Science, Myth, and Culture* (New York: Columbia University Press, 2011); and W. Carson Byrd and Matthew W. Hughey, eds., *Race, Racial Inequality, and Biological Determinism in the Genetic and Genomic Era*, vol. 661, *Annals of the American Academy of Political & Social Science* (2015).

13. Jaime E. Settle et al., "Friendships Moderate an Association between a Dopamine Gene Variant and Political Ideology," *Journal of Politics* 72, no. 4 (2010); Michael W. Gruszczynski et al., "The Physiology of Political Participation," *Political Behavior* 35, no. 1 (2013).

14. The word *gene* was only coined to describe units of heredity in 1909.

15. John W. Burgess, *Political Science and Comparative Constitutional Law* (Boston: Ginn and Co., 1890), 48.

16. James Farr, John S. Dryzek, and Stephen T. Leonard, eds., *Political Science in History: Research Programs and Political Traditions* (New York: Cambridge University Press, 1995), 13.

17. On international relations, see especially Robert Vitalis, *White World Order: Black Power Politics: The Birth of American International Relations* (Ithaca, NY: Cornell University Press, 2015); Robert Vitalis, "The Graceful and Generous Liberal Gesture: Making Racism Invisible in American International Relations," *Millennium: Journal of International Studies* 29, no. 2 (2000); Robert Vitalis, "The Noble American Science of Imperial Relations and Its Laws of Race Development," *Comparative Studies in Society and History* 52, no. 4 (2010); David Long and Brian C. Schmidt, eds., *Imperialism and Internationalism in the Discipline of International Relations* (Albany, NY: SUNY Press, 2003); Brian C. Schmidt, "Political Science and the American Empire: A Disciplinary History of the 'Politics' Section and the Discourse of Imperialism and Colonialism,"

International Politics 45 (2008); Alexander Anievas, Nivi Manchanda, and Robbie Shilliam, eds., *Race and Racism in International Relations: Confronting the Global Colour Line* (New York: Routledge, 2015). For a similar perspective regarding international relations in the U.K., see Duncan Bell, "Beyond the Sovereign State: Isopolitan Citizenship, Race and Anglo-American Union," *Political Studies* 62, no. 2 (2013).

18. Henry Jones Ford, *The Natural History of the State: An Introduction to Political Science* (Princeton, NJ: Princeton University Press, 1915).

19. Franklin Hamilton Hankins, "Race as a Factor in Political Theory," in *A History of Political Theories, Recent Times: Essays on Contemporary Developments in Political Theory*, ed. Charles E. Merriam and Harry Elmer Barnes (New York: MacMillan Company, 1924), 540.

20. John G. Gunnell, *Imagining the American Polity: Political Science and the Discourse of Democracy* (University Park: Pennsylvania State University Press, 2004), 255 (emphasis in the original).

21. References to this literature are found throughout this work. Key synthetic histories include Gunnell, *Imagining the American Polity*; Dorothy Ross, *The Origins of American Social Science* (New York: Cambridge University Press, 1991); Farr, Dryzek, and Leonard, *Political Science in History*; and Richard Adcock, *Liberalism and the Emergence of American Political Science: A Transatlantic Tale* (New York: Oxford University Press, 2014).

22. On anthropology, see George Stocking Jr., *Race, Culture, and Evolution: Essays in the History of Anthropology* (1968) (Chicago: University of Chicago Press, 1982); Lee Baker, *From Savage to Negro: Anthropology and the Construction of Race, 1896–1954* (Berkeley: University of California Press, 1998). On sociology, Stephen Steinberg, *Race Relations: A Critique* (Palo Alto, CA: Stanford University Press, 2007); Davarian Baldwin, "Black Belts and Ivory Towers: The Place of Race in U.S. Social Thought, 1892–1948," *Critical Sociology* 30, no. 2 (March 2004); Alice O'Connor, *Poverty Knowledge: Social Science, Social Policy, and the Poor in Twentieth-Century U.S. History* (Princeton, NJ: Princeton University Press, 2002); Leah Gordon, *From Power to Prejudice: The Rise of Racial Individualism in Midcentury America* (Chicago: University of Chicago Press, 2015). On criminology, see Kahlil Gibran Muhammad, *The Condemnation of Blackness: Race, Crime, and the Making of Modern Urban America* (Cambridge, MA: Harvard University Press, 2011); Jeannette Covington, "Racial Classification in Criminology: The Reproduction of Racialized Crime," *Sociological Forum* 10, no. 4 (1995). On economics, see Thomas C. Leonard, "Eugenics and Economics in the Progressive Era," *Journal of Economic Perspectives* 19, no. 4 (Fall 2005); on psychology, see Graham Richards, *Race, Racism, and Psychology: Toward a Reflective History* (New York: Routledge, 1997); for a perspective on the co-construction of race and the social sciences more broadly, see Howard Winant, "Race, Ethnicity, and Social Science," *Ethnic and Racial Studies* 38, no. 13 (2015).

23. Dorothy Ross, "'Are We a Nation?': The Conjuncture of Nationhood and Race in the United States, 1850–1876," *Modern Intellectual History* 2, no. 3 (2005), is

an important exploration of how ethnonationalism shaped pre-professional political science in the Civil War era. I have also published previous work on this topic, including in the article on which Chapter 1 is based: Jessica Blatt, "John W. Burgess, the Racial State, and the Making of the American Science of Politics," *Ethnic and Racial Studies* 37, no. 6 (2014). Also recently, Robert Vitalis includes a discussion of Burgess and his generation in *Black Power Politics, White World* Order (Ithaca, NY: Cornell University Press, 2015); as do Paula D. McClain, Gloria Y. A. Ayee, Taniesha N. Means, Alicia M. Reyes-Barriéntz, and Nura A. Sedique in "Race, Power, and Knowledge: Tracing the Roots of Exclusion in the Development of Political Science in the United States," *Politics, Groups, and Identities* 4, no. 3 (2016).

24. Bernard Crick, *The American Science of Politics* (Berkeley: University of California Press, 1959), vi, 234. Subsequent accounts that make similar critical claims include David M. Ricci, *The Tragedy of Political Science: Politics, Scholarship and Democracy* (New Haven, CT: Yale University Press, 1984), and Raymond Seidelman with the assistance of Edward Harpham, *Disenchanted Realists: Political Science and the American Crisis* (Albany: State University of New York Press, 1985).

25. Ross, *The Origins of American Social Science*, 471.

26. Gunnell, *Imagining the American Polity*, 3; Adcock, *Liberalism and the Emergence of American Political Science*, 6.

27. Ido Oren, *Our Enemies and US: America's Rivalries and the Making of Political Science* (Ithaca, NY: Cornell University Press, 2002.)

28. In this way, my project intersects with efforts by scholars of American political development to understand how illiberal ideology has shaped American political thought and institutions. See Rogers M. Smith, *Civic Ideals: Conflicting Visions of Citizenship in U.S. History* (New Haven, CT: Yale University Press, 1997). On the complicated interrelation of liberal and racial ideas, see especially Stephen Skowronek, "The Reassociation of Ideas and Purposes: Racism, Liberalism, and the American Political Tradition," *American Political Science Review* 100, no. 3 (2006).

29. Rogers M. Smith, "The Puzzling Place of Race in American Political Science," *PS: Political Science and Politics* 37, no. 1 (2004): 41.

30. Mack H. Jones and Alex Willingham, "The White Custodians of the Black Experience: A Reply to Rudwick and Meier," *Social Science Quarterly* 51, no. 1 (1970): 32.

31. Matthew Holden, *Moral Engagement and Combat Scholarship* (MacLean, VA: Court Square Institute, 1983); Hanes Walton Jr., *Invisible Politics: Black Political Behavior* (Albany: State University of New York Press, 1985).

32. Ernest J. Wilson, "Why Political Scientists Don't Study Black Politics, but Historians and Sociologists Do," *PS: Political Science & Politics* 18, no. 3 (1985).

33. Ernest J. Wilson and Lorrie Frasure, "Still at the Margins: The Persistence of Neglect of African American Issues in Political Science," in *African American Perspectives on Political Science*, ed. Wilbur Rich (Philadelphia. PA: Temple University Press, 2007); Paula D. McClain and John A. Garcia, "Expanding Disciplinary Boundaries: Black, Latino and Minority Group Politics in Political Science," in *Political Science:*

The State of the Discipline, ed. A. W. Finifter (Washington, DC: American Political Science Association, 1993); "Report of the Task Force on Political Science in the 21st Century" (Washington, DC: American Political Science Association, 2011).

34. Smith, "The Puzzling Place of Race," 41.

35. "Political Science in the 21st Century," 1.

36. In this, it joins the recent international relations historiography referenced above.

37. Stocking, *Race, Culture, and Evolution,* 265, 232.

Chapter 1

1. Both Presidents Roosevelt were impressed by Burgess's constitutional law courses, R. Gordon Hoxie, *A History of the Faculty of Political Science, Columbia University* (New York: Columbia University Press, 1955), 81; and Theodore Roosevelt wrote to Burgess in 1910 to praise his former teacher's great "influence in my life" (quoted in James Bradley, *The Imperial Cruise: A Secret History of Empire and War* [New York: Little, Brown, 2009], 114). The admiration was not entirely mutual. While Burgess was impressed with Roosevelt as a student, and appreciatively occupied the Theodore Roosevelt chair at the University of Berlin in the early 1900s, he was unhappy with his student's political career. He described the latter in his memoir as follows: "He bustled around noisily, even boisterously, and finally in a little battle which we old soldiers of the Civil War considered only a skirmish, he won the laurel crown which made him governor of New York and then President of the United States." John W. Burgess, *Reminiscences of an American Scholar* (New York: Columbia University Press, 1934), 317.

2. John G. Gunnell, *Imagining the American Polity: Political Science and the Discourse of Democracy* (University Park: Pennsylvania State University Press, 2004), 73. Like Gunnell's, most major accounts of U.S. political science acknowledge Burgess as the father of a modern, university-based discipline, though some extend this history to the Civil War–era writer and publicist Francis Lieber. According to Albert Somit and Joseph Tanenhaus, the school Burgess founded was "the formative institution in the development of the discipline, [the] program . . . that other universities consciously emulated or deliberately deviated from in setting up their own graduate work in political science"; *The Development of American Political Science* (New York, Irvington Publishers, 1967), 21. Additional works emphasizing Burgess's formative place in the discipline include Dorothy Ross, *The Origins of American Social Science* (New York: Cambridge University Press, 1991) and Daniel T. Rodgers, *Contested Truths: Keywords in American Politics Since Independence* (Boston: Basic Books, 1987), 145–46.

3. The Academy of Political Science, primarily an alumni organization for graduates of Burgess's School of Political Science at Columbia University, began publishing *Political Science Quarterly* in 1886.

4. Eric Foner, "The Supreme Court and the History of Reconstruction—and Vice-Versa," *Columbia Law Review* 112, no. 7 (2012): 1585; John W. Burgess, *Reconstruction*

and the Constitution (New York: Charles Scribner's Sons, 1902), 249. *Birth of a Nation* is an adaptation of Thomas Dixon, *The Clansman: A Historical Romance of the Ku-Klux Klan* (New York: Doubleday, 1904). Dixon (along with Woodrow Wilson, who famously showed *The Birth of a Nation* in the White House) in fact studied with Burgess's counterpart at Johns Hopkins, Herbert Baxter Adams. See Melvyn Stokes, *D. W. Griffith's* The Birth of a Nation: *A History of "the Most Controversial Motion Picture of All Time"* (Oxford: Oxford University Press, 2008), 32.

5. Burgess, *Reconstruction and the Constitution*, 263, 52.

6. John W. Burgess, "The Ideal of the American Commonwealth," *Political Science Quarterly* 10, no. 3 (1895): 406.

7. John W. Burgess, "How May the United States Govern Its Extra-Continental Territory?" *Political Science Quarterly* 14, no. 1 (1899): 1; John W. Burgess, *Political Science and Comparative Constitutional Law*, vol. 1 (Boston: Ginn, 1890), 46.

8. John W. Burgess, "The American University: When Shall It Be? Where Shall It Be? What Shall It Be?" (1884) in *Reminiscences of an American Scholar* (New York: Columbia University Press, 1934), 75; John W. Burgess, *The Middle Period (1817–1858)* (New York: Charles Scribner's Sons, 1897), 267 (emphasis in the original).

9. Burgess, *Reconstruction and the Constitution*, ix.

10. On Burgess's Reconstruction scholarship, see, e.g., John David Smith and J. Vincent Lowery, eds., *The Dunning School: Historians, Race, and the Meaning of Reconstruction* (Lexington: University Press of Kentucky, 2013). On racism and debates over U.S. imperialism, see Eric T. Love, *Race Over Empire: Racism and U.S. Imperialism, 1865–1900* (Chapel Hill: University of North Carolina Press, 2004); Bradley, *The Imperial Cruise*; and John M. Hobson, *The Eurocentric Conception of World Politics: Western International Theory, 1760–2010* (Cambridge: Cambridge University Press, 2012).

11. Burgess, *Reminiscences of an American Scholar*, 29.

12. One could also argue that Burgess's racial attitudes have received plenty of notice. As of this writing, a Google scholar search for "John W. Burgess" and "racism" yields more than ten pages of results, mostly focused on his Reconstruction historiography. Notably, Burgess's work, particularly his 1902 *Reconstruction and the Constitution*, still circulates on white supremacist (or "alt-right") websites. However, the Tennessee Political Science Association and a few Southern colleges (including the University of Memphis, Cumberland University, and Knox College; Burgess taught for a brief, unhappy stint at Knox) still give out "John W. Burgess" awards.

13. Later renamed the Rensselaer Polytechnic Institute.

14. Richard Hofstader and C. DeWitt Hardy, *The Development and Scope of Higher Education in the United States* (New York: Columbia University Press, 1952).

15. Others Lieber influenced included Theodore Dwight Woolsey, Woolsey's student Andrew White, and Herbert Baxter Adams. For a general discussion of this cohort, see Ross, *The Origins of American Social Science*, 66–77. Lieber himself emigrated to the United States in 1827 and taught history, political science, and law at Columbia from 1857 until his death in 1872. Ross explores the racial ideas of Lieber

and his contemporaries in " 'Are We a Nation?': The Conjuncture of Nationhood and Race in the United States, 1850–1876," *Modern Intellectual History* 2, no. 3 (2005).

16. Thomas L. Haskell, *The Emergence of Professional Social Science: The American Social Science Association and the Nineteenth-Century Crisis of Authority* (Baltimore: Johns Hopkins University Press, 2000); and Ross, *The Origins of American Social Science*. See also George Frederickson, *The Inner Civil War: Northern Intellectuals and the Crisis of the Union* (Urbana: University of Illinois Press, 1993), viii, on how the experiences of the Civil War shaped the efforts of a "demoralized gentry without a clearly defined social role" 15t17o refashion itself as a "self-confident, modernizing elite."

17. Stephen Skowronek, *Building a New American State: The Expansion of American Administrative Capacities 1877–1920* (New York: Cambridge University Press, 1982).

18. Burgess, *The Middle Period (1817–1858)*, x.

19. Rodgers, *Contested Truths*, 145–46.

20. John W. Burgess, *Reconciliation of Government with Liberty* (New York: Charles Scribner's Sons, 1915), i.

21. The school, now known as the Institut d'Études Politiques de Paris or "Sciences Po," has since been integrated into the French public system. Noting that it attracted the hostility of the French government, Burgess nonetheless approved of the private model, judging it "a most admirable institution for keeping the French Republic sane and promoting its development along conservative lines"; Burgess, *Reminiscences of an American Scholar*, 193. He sought to replicate it for U.S. graduate education, considering a government-run university not "consonant with the genius of American institutions." In his view, the "American university must . . . be a private institution, supported by private donations, and directed by an association of private persons." Moreover, while the courts might appropriately hold it to "the fulfillment of its trusts . . . any supervision by legislature or executive should be most decidedly repelled" in favor of the management of "a company of respectable gentlemen" of "public spirit"; Burgess, "The American University," 357–58, 60.

22. John Louis Recchiuti, *Civic Engagement: Social Science and Progressive-Era Reform in New York City* (Philadelphia: University of Pennsylvania Press, 2007), 30, 160.

23. William E. Nelson, *The Roots of American Bureaucracy, 1830–1900*, (Cambridge, MA: Harvard University Press, 1982), 90.

24. For a general discussion of this theme, see Rogers Smith, *Civic Ideals: Conflicting Visions of Citizenship in U.S. History* (New Haven, CT: Yale University Press, 1997).

25. See Smith and Lowery, *The Dunning School*.

26. Bryce was another close acquaintance of Theodore Roosevelt. See Marilyn Lake and Henry Reynolds, *Drawing the Global Colour Line: White Men's Countries and the International Challenge of Racial Equality* (New York: Cambridge University Press, 2008), 58–59.

27. Quoted in Joseph D. Reid Jr. and Michael M. Kurth, "The Rise and Fall of Political Patronage Machines," in *Strategic Factors in Nineteenth Century American Economic History: A Volume to Honor Robert W. Fogel*, ed. Claudia Goldin and Hugh Rockoff (Chicago: University of Chicago Press, 1992), 428.

28. Burgess, *Political Science and Comparative Constitutional Law*, vol. 1, 45, 4, 37.

29. Quoted in Hoxie, *A History of the Faculty of Political Science*, 11–12, 15.

30. Louis Menand, *The Metaphysical Club: A Story of Ideas in America* (New York: Farrar, Straus and Giroux, 2001), x.

31. Burgess, *The Middle Period (1817–1858)*, vii–viii.

32. Burgess, *Reminiscences of an American Scholar*, 22–25.

33. Ibid., 28–29.

34. Ibid., 52, 54.

35. Jurgen Herbst, *The German Historical School in American Scholarship: A Study in the Transfer of Culture* (Ithaca, NY: Cornell University Press, 1965), 8–13.

36. Burgess, *Reminiscences of an American Scholar*, 131.

37. Ibid., 96, 136. Mac-Mahon had led the suppression of the Communards under Thiers.

38. Ibid., 86.

39. Ibid., 161, 168.

40. Ibid., 162, 137, 163.

41. Ibid., 176, 163. Burgess shared the ambition of creating a science of law with Christopher Columbus Langdell, who similarly sought to insulate law from the vagaries of democratic politics. See Paul D. Carrington, "Hail! Langdell!," *Law & Social Inquiry* 20 no. 3 (1995).

42. The school was later organized into several departments, encompassing much of what we now think of as the social sciences. Hoxie, *A History of the Faculty of Political Science*, 24.

43. Rodgers, *Contested Truths*, 157.

44. Burgess, *The Middle Period (1817–1858)*, 246.

45. Robert Knox, *The Races of Men: A Fragment* (Philadelphia, PA: Lea and Blanchard, 1850).

46. James Bryce, *The American Commonwealth*, 1893, vol. 2 (New York: MacMillan, 1915), 459.

47. Burgess, *The Middle Period (1817–1858)*, 40–42. Edward Baptist notes that post-Reconstruction historiography universally treated slavery as incompatible with capitalism. In Baptist's view, this narrative of slavery as premodern persists in modern scholarship, serving to render the instiution as an aberration, fundamentally separate from the great social and industrial forces fuelling American progress. Edward Baptist, *The Half Has Never Been Told: Slavery and the Making of American Capitalism* (New York: Basic Books, 2014), xx.

48. Burgess, *The Middle Period (1817–1858)*, 42, 246.

49. Ibid., 267.

50. Burgess, *Reconstruction and the Constitution*, viii, 252.

51. Burgess, *Reminiscences of an American Scholar*, 86, vii–viii.

52. Dunning considered himself a political theorist—his proudest achievement was what he estimated to be an "epoch-making," three-volume survey of political thought from Socrates to Spencer: William A. Dunning, *A History of Political Theories, Ancient and Medieval* (New York: MacMillan, 1902); William A. Dunning, *A History of Political Theories, from Luther to Montesquieu* (New York: MacMillan, 1905); William A. Dunning, *A History of Political Theories, from Rousseau to Spencer* (New York: MacMillan, 1922). During his lifetime, he was recognized as much for his political science as for his historical work. He served as president of both the American Historical Association (1913) and the American Political Science Association (1921). His obituary in the *New York Times* cited as his primary claim to fame an appearance as an expert on political theories in Henry Ford's libel suit against the *Chicago Tribune*; Philip R. Muller, "Look Back Without Anger: A Reappraisal of William A. Dunning," *Journal of American History* 61, no. 2 (1974): 325. However, more recently he has come to be recalled primarily as the leading figure of the now-infamous "Dunning School" of Reconstruction historiography; see Eric Foner, "Reconstruction Revisited," *Reviews in American History* 10, no. 4 (1982); and Smith and Lowery, *The Dunning School*.

53. Students in this group included Walter Fleming, James Wilford Garner, Frederic Bancroft, Edwin C. Woolley, and Joseph Grégoire de Roulhac Hamilton. Quotes are drawn from David Miller DeWitt, "Review of *Civil War and Reconstruction in Alabama* by Walter L. Fleming," *Political Science Quarterly* 21, no. 3 (1906): 539.

54. See, for example, William A. Dunning, *Essays on the Civil War and Reconstruction and Related Topics* (1897) (New York: MacMillan, 1904); William A. Dunning, *Reconstruction, Political and Economic, 1865–1877* (New York: Harper and Brothers Publishers, 1907).

55. James Bryce, "The Relations of History and Geography," *Contemporary Review* 49 (1886): 442.

56. Bryce hoped to apply these lessons not only to America but to Britain's imperial possessions as well; Lake and Reynolds, *Drawing the Global Colour Line*, chap. 2. He worked particularly closely with J. X. Merriman, then governor of the Cape Colony in what would later become South Africa, advising him on the lessons of the American South for the administration of Africans by white men.

57. On British Anglo-Saxonist political theory, see Duncan Bell, "Beyond the Sovereign State: Isopolitan Citizenship, Race and Anglo-American Union," *Political Studies* 62, no. 2 (2013).

58. John W. Burgess, *Political Science and Comparative Constitutional Law*, vol. 2 (Boston: Ginn, 1891), 34.

59. Ross, "Are We a Nation?"

60. Burgess studied statistics and ethnology under Johann Eduard Wappäus at Göttingen, an early pioneer in the professionalization of statistics and their application

to ethnology in Germany, and a prominent advocate of German colonial expansion. Burgess found much of this work "dull." However, he "reaped the greatest profit out of [Wappäus's] ethnological statistics" and claimed that he "could not have completed the chapters on "the nation" in *Political Science and Comparative Constitutional Law,* without his notes from Wappäus's lectures; Burgess, *Reminiscences of an American Scholar,* 103–4.

61. Burgess, *Political Science and Comparative Constitutional Law,* vol. 1, 59, 1, 4.

62. Bluford Adams, "World Conquerors or a Dying People: Racial Theory, Regional Anxiety, and the Brahmin Anglo-Saxonists," *Journal of the Gilded Age and Progressive Era* 8, no. 2 (2009): 190.

63. While the distinction was still fuzzy, and both worked on the border of history and political science, Burgess is remembered as a political scientist and Adams as a historian.

64. Herbst, *The German Historical School,* 108–11. Leopold von Ranke (1795–1886) was a hugely influential German historian who promoted an empirical, scientific approach to history writing that emphasized the use of primary sources.

65. George W. Stocking Jr., *Race, Culture, and Evolution: Essays in the History of Anthropology* (1968) (Chicago: University of Chicago Press, 1982), 112.

66. Ross captures the mix of historical narratives discernible in Burgess's work, writing, "Burgess' Whig story of Teutonic freedom was inserted first into a Hegelian story of history as the realization of freedom in the State, and then dissected according to the evolutionary, comparative method." Dorothy Ross, "Anglo-American Political Science," in *Modern Political Science: Anglo-American Exchanges Since 1880,* ed. Robert Adcock, Mark Bevis, and Shannon C. Stimson (Princeton, NJ: Princeton University Press, 2007), 23.

67. Herbert B. Adams, *The German Origins of New England Towns* (Baltimore: Johns Hopkins University Press, 1882); Herbert B. Adams, *Saxon Tithing-Men in America* (Baltimore: Johns Hopkins University Press, 1883); Herbert B. Adams, *Norman Constables in America* (Baltimore: Johns Hopkins University Press, 1883).

68. Adams, *The German Origins of New England Towns,* 8.

69. Herbert B. Adams, *Methods of Historical Study* (Baltimore: Johns Hopkins University Press, 1884), 455.

70. Burgess, *Reconciliation of Government with Liberty;* Burgess, *Reminiscences of an American Scholar,* 255.

71. Burgess, Reminiscences of an American Scholar, 252. Burgess did not as a rule capitalize "state," so I do not either. Where he did, however, I have maintained it.

72. Burgess, "The Ideal of the American Commonwealth," 407.

73. Burgess, *Reconciliation of Government with Liberty,* i.

74. Burgess, *Political Science and Comparative Constitutional Law,* vol. 1, 70.

75. Burgess, *Political Science and Comparative Constitutional Law,* vol. 2, 365.

76. The Declaration of Independence does not figure in Burgess's heroic account of the founding.

77. Charles E. Merriam, *A History of American Political Theories* (New York: Mac-Millan, 1903), 306.

78. Peter Novick, *That Noble Dream: The "Objectivity Question" and the American Historical Profession* (New York: Cambridge University Press, 1988), 48.

79. A. B. Hall et al., "Reports of the Second National Conference on the Science of Politics," *American Political Science Review* 19, no. 1 (1925): 113.

80. Elisha Mulford, *The Nation: The Foundation of Civil Order and Political Life in the United States* (New York: Hurd and Houghton, 1870), 72, 11.

81. Burgess, *Political Science and Comparative Constitutional Law*, vol. 1, 1, 48.

82. Ibid., 3, 39.

83. Burgess, "The Ideal of the American Commonwealth," 420.

84. Burgess, *Reminiscences of an American Scholar*, 253.

85. For example, Burgess complained that the Supreme Court's resolution of the *Slaughterhouse* cases (1873) constituted an unwarranted expansion of state police powers relative to property rights. Burgess, *Political Science and Comparative Constitutional Law*, vol. 1, 222–23.

86. Burgess, "The Ideal of the American Commonwealth," 425.

87. Ibid., 407, 410–12.

88. Daniel Rodgers observes that Burgess's interpretation of such powers was "as broad as anything Jeremy Bentham had imagined"; Rodgers, *Contested Truths*, 155. However, he does not note the racial entailments of Burgess's interpretation.

89. Burgess, *Political Science and Comparative Constitutional Law*, vol. 1, 40–43.

90. Quoted in Mary O. Furner, *Advocacy and Objectivity: A Crisis in the Professionalization of American Social Science, 1865–1905* (New Brunswick, NJ: Transaction Publishers, 2011), 71.

91. E. R. A. Seligman, "Richmond Mayo Smith 1854–1901," in *Memoirs of the National Academy of Sciences* (Washington, DC: Government Printing Office, 1924), 75.

92. Richmond Mayo-Smith, "Control of Immigration III," *Political Science Quarterly* 3, no. 3 (1888): 410–11, 13.

93. Ibid., 413.

94. Burgess, *Political Science and Comparative Constitutional Law*, vol. 1, 45.

95. Burgess, *Reminiscences of an American Scholar*, 317.

96. Burgess, "How May the United States Govern Its Extra-Continental Territory?," 1–2.

97. Burgess, *Reminiscences of an American Scholar*, 315–16.

98. Burgess, *Political Science and Comparative Constitutional Law*, vol. 1, vi.

Chapter 2

1. Woodrow Wilson, *Congressional Government: A Study in American Politics* (1885) (Mineola, NY: Dover Editions, 2006).

2. Woodrow Wilson, Review of *Political Science and Comparative Constitutional Law* by John W. Burgess, *Atlantic Monthly* 67 (1891), 694–98.

3. Leo Stanton Rowe, "The Problem of Political Science," *Annals of the American Academy of Political and Social Science* 10 (1897): 17.

4. Wilson, Review of *Political Science and Comparative Constitutional Law*, 694.

5. Woodrow Wilson, *The State: Elements of Historical and Practical Politics* (1889) (Boston: D. C. Heath & Company, 1911), 1–11, 627. For a discussion of the valence of "the state" for Wilson, see John G. Gunnell, *Imagining the American Polity: Political Science and the Discourse of Democracy* (University Park,: Pennsylvania State University Press, 2004) 79–81.

6. Wilson, Review of *Political Science and Comparative Constitutional Law*, 698.

7. For example, "Government is merely the executive organ of society, the organ through which its habit acts, through which its will becomes operative." Wilson, *The State*, 576. Notably, this book may represent Wilson at his most capital-P Progressive. In it, he endorses regulation of monopolies and a host of labor reforms more forcefully than he would later in his career.

8. Woodrow Wilson, "Bryce's American Commonwealth," *Political Science Quarterly* 4, no. 1 (1889): 165.

9. James Bryce, *The American Commonwealth*, vol. 2 (1893) (New York: MacMillan, 1915), 515.

10. Wilson, *The State*, xxxv.

11. By the turn of the century, advanced political science training was available at a handful of institutions, with the University of Wisconsin and the newly established University of Chicago joining Columbia and Johns Hopkins in producing the most doctorates. Albert Somit and Joseph Tanenhaus, *The Development of American Political Science* (New York: Irvington Publishers, 1982), 40–41.

12. The two associations' memberships overlapped substantially; early APSA presidents who also led the AHA at one point in their careers included Wilson himself, Simeon Baldwin, Albert Bushnell Hart, William Dunning, and Charles Beard. The American Economic Association (AEA) was another of what APSA president Albert Shaw called "our allied associations." Albert Shaw, "Presidential Address: Third Annual Meeting of the American Political Science Association," *American Political Science Review* 1, no. 2 (1907): 177.

13. Wilson, *Congressional Government*, 52.

14. W. W. Willoughby, "The American Political Science Association," *Political Science Quarterly* 19, no. 1 (1904): 109.

15. While faculty from Columbia and Johns Hopkins led the first executive board of the APSA, also represented were Iowa College; the Universities of Chicago, Pennsylvania, Texas, Michigan, Wisconsin, California, and Minnesota; and nonprofessors, such as a former ambassador to Germany, a journal editor, and a representative of the Library of Congress. Willoughby, "The American Political Science Association," 110.

16. Frank Goodnow, "The Work of the American Political Science Association," *Proceedings of the American Political Science Association* 1, no. 1 (1904): 41–42, 38.

17. As John G. Gunnell has shown, the word *state* likewise appeared more and more in political scientists' work as a simple synonym for "government." Gunnell, *Imagining the American Polity*.

18. On the emergence of "ethnicity," see Werner Sollors, ed., *The Invention of Ethnicity* (Oxford: Oxford University Press, 1989); and Victoria Hattam, *In the Shadow of Race: Jews, Latinos, and Immigrant Politics in the United States* (Chicago: University of Chicago Press, 2007).

19. Michael McGerr, *A Fierce Discontent: The Rise and Fall of the Progressive Movement in America, 1870–1920* (New York: Free Press, 2003), xv.; Rogers Smith, *Civic Ideals: Conflicting Visions of Citizenship in U.S. History* (New Haven, CT: Yale University Press, 1997), 411–12.

20. By 1900, nearly 40 percent of the U.S. population lived in cities, up from just over one quarter of the population in 1870, and just more than one-third of the U.S population was born elsewhere. Campbell J. Gibson and Emily Lennon, "Historical Census Statistics on the Foreign-Born Population of the United States: 1850–1990" (Washington, DC: U.S. Bureau of the Census, Population Division, 1999).

21. Beverly Gage, *The Day Wall Street Exploded: A Story of America in Its First Age of Terror* (New York: Oxford University Press, 2009), 3.

22. Herbert Croly, *The Promise of American Life* (New York: MacMillan Company, 1909), 5.

23. Goodnow, "The Work of the American Political Science Association," 41.

24. Shaw, "Presidential Address," 181.

25. Woodrow Wilson, "The Study of Administration," *Political Science Quarterly* 2, no. 2 (1887): 200 (emphasis in the original).

26. Harold M. Bowman, "Proceedings of the American Political Science Association," *Political Science Quarterly* 20, no. 4 (1905): 725.

27. Goodnow, "The Work of the American Political Science Association," 42. Six years later, Francis Coker would characterize "organismic theories of the state" as "nineteenth century interpretations." Francis Coker, *Organismic Theories of the State: Nineteenth Century Interpretations of the State as Organism or as Person* (New York: Columbia University, 1910).

28. Goodnow is something of an exception, emerging as a prominent left progressive by 1910. However, until then he "gave little indication of popular sympathies." Dorothy Ross, *The Origins of American Social Science* (New York: Cambridge University Press, 1991), 259.

29. Ross, *The Origins of American Social Science*, 257; see also Mary O. Furner, Review of *The Emergence of Professional Social Science: The American Social Science Association and the Nineteenth-Century Crisis of Authority* by Thomas L. Haskell, *American Journal of Sociology* 85, no. 5 (1980); Thomas L Haskell, *The Emergence of*

Professional Social Science: The American Social Science Association and the Nineteenth-Century Crisis of Authority (Baltimore: Johns Hopkins University Press, 2000).

30. On the discipline's political center and cross-generational harmony in that respect, see Ross, *The Origins of American Social Science*, 257–61. One important exception was the U.S. annexation of the Philippines and other tropical "dependencies." While Burgess approved of colonialism in principle, he was, as we have seen, a fervent opponent of U.S. colonial adventures. APSA's leadership, by contrast, largely embraced U.S. imperialism (see Chapter 3).

31. Shaw, "Presidential Address," 182–86.

32. Stephen Skowronek, "The Reassociation of Ideas and Purposes: Racism, Liberalism, and the American Political Tradition," *American Political Science Review* 100, no. 3 (2006).

33. Woodrow Wilson, *Division and Reunion: 1829–1889* (New York: Longman's, Green, and Company, 1893), 273, 268.

34. John W. Burgess, "The Ideal of the American Commonwealth," *Political Science Quarterly* 10, no. 3 (1895).

35. Wilson, *Congressional Government*, 42–43.

36. Woodrow Wilson, *Constitutional Government in the United States* (New York: Columbia University Press, 1908), 60.

37. John W. Burgess, *Political Science and Comparative Constitutional Law*, vol. 2 (Boston: Ginn, 1891), 365.

38. There were, of course, many important African American scholars and intellectuals writing about American politics and international relations at the time. But with few exceptions (see Chapter 4), they were not doing so in political science journals. No American university conferred a doctorate in political science on an African American until 1934, when Ralph Bunche earned his at Harvard.

39. William C. Langdon, "The Case of the Negro," *Political Science Quarterly* 6, no. 1 (1891): 31.

40. David Miller DeWitt, "Review of *Civil War and Reconstruction in Alabama* by Walter L. Fleming," *Political Science Quarterly* 21, no. 3 (1906): 536.

41. Gilbert T. Stephenson, "Racial Distinctions in Southern Law," *American Political Science Review* 1, no. 1 (1906): 60.

42. Frederic Bancroft, Review of *The Negro in Maryland* by Jeffrey R. Brackett, Review of *Notes on the Progress of the Colored People of Maryland Since the War* by Jeffrey R. Brackett, Review of *The Plantation Negro as a Freeman* by Philip A. Bruce, and Review of *The Negro Question* by George W. Cable, *Political Science Quarterly* 5, no. 4 (1890): 688–92.

43. William Starr Myers, Review of *Legislative and Judicial History of the Fifteenth Amendment* by John Mabry Mathews, *American Political Science Review* 3, no. 4 (1909): 627.

44. Walter L. Fleming, "Immigration to the Southern States," *Political Science Quarterly* 20, no. 2 (1905): 279.

45. J. Martin, S. C. Mitchell, and Henry E. Shepherd, "Discussion," *Proceedings of the American Political Science Association* 2 (1905): 169.

46. Langdon, "The Case of the Negro," 40–41.

47. Gary N. Calkins, Review of *Race Traits and Tendencies of the American Negro* by Frederick L. Hoffman, *Political Science Quarterly* 11, no. 4 (1896): 754.

48. Frank R. Hathaway, Review of *Studies in Statistics: Social, Political, and Medical* by George Blundell Longstaff, *Political Science Quarterly* 6 (1891): 745.

49. James Bryce, "Thoughts on the Negro Problem," *North American Review* 153, no. 421 (1891): 642.

50. Of more than fifty articles and talks touching on the subjects. I omitted from this review the *Annals of the American Academy of Political and Social Sciences* (AAAPSS), which began publication in 1890, because of its looser connection to political science as a discipline; in fact, the *AAAPSS* explicitly resisted the sort of disciplinary specialization and vocational distinctions (above all, between the theorist and the reformer) that leading political scientists were pursuing. If I had included it, I would have found greater sympathy for Reconstruction, not least in the writings of contributor W. E. B. Du Bois. Interestingly and by way of contrast, up to and through the passage of the Nineteenth Amendment, political scientists paid scant attention to the question of female suffrage. On the rare occasions they did, they seemed to find it neither urgently required by justice nor particularly alarming.

51. James M. McPherson, *The Abolitionist Legacy: From Reconstruction to the NAACP* (Princeton, NJ: Princeton University Press, 1995), 336.

52. Wilson, *Division and Reunion*; William A. Dunning, *Essays on the Civil War and Reconstruction and Related Topics* (1897) (New York: MacMillan Company, 1904); Alfred H. Stone, Review of *The Southern South* by Albert Bushnell Hart, *American Political Science Review* 4, no. 4 (1910): 613.

53. Albert B. Hart, "The Realities of Negro Suffrage," *Proceedings of the American Political Science Association* 2 (1905): 157.

54. John C. Rose, "Suffrage Conditions in the South: The Constitutional Point of View," *Proceedings of the American Political Science Association* 2 (1905): 166.

55. John C. Rose, "Negro Suffrage: The Constitutional Point of View," *American Political Science Review* 1, no. 1 (1906); Stephenson, "Racial Distinctions in Southern Law."

56. Rose, "Negro Suffrage," 35, 43.

57. Martin, Mitchell, and Shepherd, "Discussion," 166.

58. Stephenson, "Racial Distinctions in Southern Law."

59. Gilbert T. Stephenson, "The Separation of the Races in Public Conveyances," *American Political Science Review* 9, no. 2 (1909), 189, 203. The case was *West Chester & Philadelphia R.R. Co. v. Miles* 55 Pa. 209 (1896). It is worth noting that Stephenson dates the Supreme Court's affirmation of segregation laws to an 1891 Supreme Court decision five years before the much more famous *Plessy v. Ferguson*. For an illuminating discussion of the conventionality of the *Plessy* decision, see Charles A.

Lofgren, *The Plessy Case: A Legal-Historical Interpretation* (Oxford: Oxford University Press, 1988).

60. Daniel Agnew, quoted in Stephenson, "The Separation of the Races in Public Conveyances," 203. Stephenson quotes a full page of Agnew's decision—I have presented just a representative extract here.

61. According to Tuskegee Institute data from the 1950s, every state in the union had at least one confirmed report of a lynching between 1882 and 1951. Jessie P. Guzman, ed., *The Negro Year Book* (New York: Wm. H. Wise and Company, 1952), 276–78.

62. The section appeared under varying titles, including "The Race Problem," "Lynch Law," "Lynch Law and Race Feuds" (or "Riots"), or "The Race Problem and Lynching." The first Niagara Falls conference (a precursor to the founding of the National Association for the Advancement of Colored People [NAACP]) was reported under the latter heading in 1905.

63. William A. Dunning, "Record of Political Events," *Political Science Quarterly* 9, no. 2 (1894).

64. William A. Dunning, "Record of Political Events," *Political Science Quarterly* 11, no. 4 (1896).

65. Woodrow Wilson, *A History of the American People*, 5 vols. (New York: Harper and Brothers, 1902), 58, 61–62 (emphasis added).

66. Henry C. Lodge, "Lynch Law and Unrestricted Immigration," *North American Review* 152, no. 414 (1891): 612.

67. Martin, Mitchell, and Shepherd, "Discussion," 169–70. Interestingly, lynching is discussed in these terms as well in the *Annals of the American Academy of Political and Social Science*. That is, it is often deplored and often blamed on the (lamentable) impossibility of governing disparate races under a uniform system of law.

68. Alvin Johnson, Review of *Lynch Law* by James E. Cutler, *Political Science Quarterly* 21, no. 1 (1906): 140. Johnson, trained at Columbia, was at the time the assistant editor of *PSQ*. He would go on to become an editor of the *New Republic* and the *Encyclopedia of the Social Sciences* (1930) as well as the founding leader of the New School for Social Research.

69. Albert B. Hart, *The Southern South* (New York: D. Appleton and Company, 1910), 208–17.

70. Johnson, Review of *Lynch Law*, 140.

71. These included the Philippines, Hawaii, Puerto Rico, Cuba, Guam, and Wake Island.

72. Henry Jones Ford, *The Rise and Growth of American Politics: A Sketch of Constitutional Development* (1898) (New York: Da Capo Press, 1967).

73. Paul S. Reinsch, "Colonial Autonomy, with Special Reference to the Government of the Philippine Islands," in *Proceedings of the American Political Science Association* 1 (Chicago: American Political Science Association, 1904), 119.

Chapter 3

1. W. E. B. Du Bois, *The Souls of Black Folk* (Chicago: A. C. McClurg, 1903), vii.

2. Adolph L. Reed Jr., *Stirrings in the Jug: Black Politics in the Post-Segregation Era* (Minneapolis: University of Minnesota Press, 1999), 72.

3. W. E. B. Du Bois, "To the Nations of the World," lecture given at the first Pan-African Conference in 1900, in Alexander Walters, *My Life and Work* (New York: Fleming H. Revell, 1917), 258, http://docsouth.unc.edu/neh/walters/walters.html# walt257.

4. Du Bois's relationship to the racial thought of his contemporaries is penetratingly explored in Adolph L. Reed Jr., *W. E. B. Du Bois and American Political Thought: Fabianism and the Color Line* (New York: Oxford University Press, 1997).

5. See Carlos Figueroa, "Quakerism and Racialism in Early Twentieth-Century U.S. Politics," in *Faith and Race in American Political Life*, ed. Robin Dale Jacobson and Nancy D. Wadsworth (Charlottesville: University of Virginia Press, 2012).

6. Paul A. Kramer, *The Blood of Government: Race, Empire, the United States, and the Philippines* (Chapel Hill: University of North Carolina Press, 2006), 169. Roosevelt, speaking at the inauguration of the Arlington National Cemetery in 1902, was referring specifically to the colonial war then raging in the Philippines. Note also that the Roosevelt-style imperialists and the more reform-minded tendencies were not at all cleanly distinct from one another. For example, earlier in his career Roosevelt attended some of the Lake Mohonk conferences sponsored by the Quaker organization "Friends of the Indians"; e.g., "Lake Mohonk and Our Dependent Peoples," *Friends Intelligencer* (1906), 621.

7. Peter Bowler, "Darwinism and Modernism: Genetics, Palaeontology, and the Challenge to Progressivism, 1880–1930," in *Modernist Impulses in the Human Sciences 1870–1930*, ed. Dorothy Poss (Baltimore: Johns Hopkins University Press, 1994).

8. Postwar international relations theory is remembered as being dominated by "realists" who emphasized power and conflict between national states in an anarchic international realm over "idealist" or "liberal" emphases on cooperation and law. Robert Vitalis, *White World Order, Black Power Politics: The Birth of American International Relations* (Ithaca, NY: Cornell University Press, 2015). Lothrop Stoddard, *The Rising Tide of Color Against White World Supremacy* (New York: Charles Scribner's Sons, 1920), v–vii.

9. Peter H. Odegard, "Review of *Into the Darkness* by Lothrop Stoddard," *Annals of the American Academy of Political and Social Science* 213 (1941): 201–2.

10. Lothrop Stoddard, *Into the Darkness: A Sympathetic Report from Hitler's Wartime Reich* (1940) (Newport Beach, CA: Noontide Press, 2000).

11. Stoddard's work, and especially its racialism, came in for criticism, to be sure; see Chapter 5. But it was not beyond the pale of serious consideration, and it continued to appear or get the occasional respectful notice in well-regarded political science journals into the 1930s; e.g., "Pan-Turanism," *American Political Science Review* 11,

no. 1 (1917); J. B. Moore, "Review of *The French Revolution in San Domingo* by T. Lothrop Stoddard," *Political Science Quarterly* 31, no. 1 (1916); J. R. C., Review of *Clashing Tides of Colour* by Lothrop Stoddard, *International Affairs* 14, no. 4 (1935). Only in the 1940s did Stoddard come consistently to be treated as a racist ideologue and an apologist for fascism; e.g., Odegard, "Review of *Into the Darkness.*" For a fascinating account of political science's changing estimation of fascism (and consequent redefinition of democracy), see Ido Oren, *Our Enemies and US: America's Rivalries and the Making of American Political Science* (Ithaca, NY: Cornell University Press, 2003).

12. For revisionist critiques of this trope in addition to Vitalis's, see Brian C. Schmidt and David Long, eds., *Imperialism and Internationalism in the Discipline of International Relations* (Albany: State University of New York Press, 2005). An alternative revisionist account is provided by Ole Wæver, "The Speech Act of Realism: The Move That Made IR," in *The Invention of International Relations Theory*, ed. Nicolas Guilhot (New York: Columbia University Press, 2011).

13. Vitalis, *White World Order, Black Power Politics*, 120. On the delimitation of international relations as a distinct field, see Nicolas Guilhot, ed. *The Invention of International Relations Theory: Realism, the Rockefeller Foundation, and the 1954 Conference on Theory* (New York: Columbia University Press, 2011).

14. Or, more properly, on new, less progressionist interpretations of Darwinism then emerging. See Peter J. Bowler, "Darwinism and Modernism."

15. Henry C. Morris, Theodore Marburg, and W. W. Willoughby, "Discussion," *Proceedings of the American Political Science Association* 1 (1904): 143.

16. Henry Jones Ford, *The Rise and Growth of American Politics: A Sketch of Constitutional Development* (1898) (New York: Da Capo Press, 1967), 378–79.

17. Henry Jones Ford, "The Scope of Political Science," *Proceedings of the American Political Science Association* 2 (1905): 201.

18. Ford, *The Rise and Growth of American Politics*, 334, 88.

19. Edward S. Crowin, "Henry Jones Ford," *American Political Science Review* 19, no. 4 (1925), 814. Ford prefigured Wilson's later turn, seizing on a reinvigorated presidency as the remedy for party irresponsibility and the vehicle for a more thorough popular sovereignty. Wilson similarly echoed Ford in 1908, commenting that the founders' "Whig" theory had been unconsciously "Newtonian" in positing a single set of laws for the workings of politics and the relations of institutions, and that a "Darwinian" approach would offer a more suitable framework for understanding how politics was "modified by its environment"; Woodrow Wilson, *Constitutional Government in the United States* (New York: Columbia University Press, 1908), 57.

20. Ford, *The Rise and Growth of American Politics*, 199–203; Henry Jones Ford, *The Natural History of the State: An Introduction to Political Science* (Princeton, NJ: Princeton University Press, 1915).

21. Ford, *The Rise and Growth of American Politics*, 199–206.

22. Ford argued that such a system would allow Congress to serve "as the agency of the moral inhibition which should attend the exercise of the [democratic] will," thus lending "ease and placidity" to U.S. party politics; Ford, *The Rise and Growth of American Politics*, 370.

23. Stuart C. Miller, "Compadre Colonialism," *Wilson Quarterly* 10, no. 3 (1986): 94.

24. Theresa Marie Ventura, "American Empire, Agrarian Reform and the Problem of Tropical Nature in the Philippines, 1898–1916," (PhD diss., Columbia University, 2009), 12.

25. This first wave of American teachers was known collectively as the Thomasites for the *Thomas*, the army ship that brought close to 500 of them. Jonathan Zimmerman, *Innocents Abroad: American Teachers in the American Century* (Cambridge, MA: Harvard University Press, 2009).

26. In Miller, "Compadre Colonialism," 94–95.

27. William J. Bryan, "The Paralyzing Influence of Imperialism," (speech, Democratic National Convention, Kansas City MO, 1900).

28. Morris, Marburg, and Willoughby, "Discussion," 140.

29. Brian C. Schmidt, "Political Science and the American Empire: A Disciplinary History of the 'Politics' Section and the Discourse of Imperialism and Colonialism," *International Politics* 45 (2008): 48, 51.

30. Alleyne Ireland, "On the Need for a Scientific Study of Colonial Administration," *Proceedings of the American Political Science Association* 3 (1906): 210–11. Ireland was a journalist and prominent authority on colonial affairs who would later emerge as a major proponent of eugenics. See also Henry Jones Ford, "The Ethics of Empire," *Political Science Quarterly* 22, no. 3 (1907): 503.

31. Paul S. Reinsch, "The Negro Race and European Civilization," *American Journal of Sociology* 11, no. 2 (1905): 117.

32. Brian C. Schmidt, "Paul S. Reinsch and the Study of Imperialism and Internationalism," in Long and Schmidt, *Imperialism and Internationalism*, 55.

33. Paul Reinsch, *Colonial Administration* (New York: MacMillan Company, 1905), 9–10.

34. In Vitalis, *White World Order, Black Power Politics*, 11.

35. As to the "ethics" of his title, Ford argued that imperial expansion on the part of the great powers was justifiable in the name of "self-preservation." Ford, "The Ethics of Empire," 499–500, 505.

36. Reinsch, *Colonial Administration*, 6.

37. Ireland, "On the Need for a Scientific Study of Colonial Administration," 211, 217.

38. Ibid., 221.

39. Schmidt, "Political Science and the American Empire," 61.

40. Ventura, "American Empire, Agrarian Reform."

41. Reinsch, *Colonial Administration*, 9–8; quoted in Schmidt, "Paul S. Reinsch and the Study of Imperialism and Internationalism," 58.

42. Reinsch, *Colonial Administration*, 7–8.

43. Ireland, "On the Need for a Scientific Study of Colonial Administration," 215–16.

44. Winston Crouch, *A History of the Department of Political Science: University of California, Los Angeles, 1920–1987* (unpublished paper, Department of Political Science, University of California, Los Angeles, 1987).

45. Bernard Moses, "Colonial Policy with Reference to the Philippines," *Proceedings of the American Political Science Association* 1 (1904): 98. (As it happened, Moses was not present at the meeting; the paper he submitted nonetheless appears in full in the first volume of the *Proceedings*.)

46. Morris, Marburg, and Willoughby, "Discussion," 141.

47. Moses, "Colonial Policy with Reference to the Philippines," 98.

48. Ford, "The Ethics of Empire," 505.

49. Morris, Marburg, and Willoughby, "Discussion," 141.

50. John W. Burgess, *Political Science and Comparative Constitutional Law*, vol. 1 (Boston: Ginn, 1890), 46.

51. Marburg in Morris, Marburg, and Willoughby, "Discussion," 141. Perhaps notably, Moses was just three years younger than Burgess. The German-educated Marburg was fifteen years Moses's junior.

52. Reinsch, *Colonial Administration*, 6, 1.

53. As this statement suggests, Reinsch was not especially committed to the most deterministic veins of scientific racism then circulating. In the same article, he admits the "fact" that among Africans the "cranial sutures" fuse early, foreclosing the possibility of significant "organic development of the faculties after puberty," but he denies that this difference is sufficient to explain disparities in civilization between Africans and Europeans. Rather, in his view, these were the result of "social, political, and economic conditions"; Reinsch, "The Negro Race and European Civilization," 148, 154–55.

54. Paul S. Reinsch, "Colonial Autonomy, with Special Reference to the Government of the Philippine Islands," *Proceedings of the American Political Science Association* 1 (1904): 123, 130.

55. Paul S. Reinsch, *Intellectual and Political Currents in the Far East* (Boston: Houghton Mifflin, 1911), 73.

56. An interesting parallel is the Jim Crow system established in Saudi Arabia by American oil interests beginning in the 1930s. See Robert Vitalis, *America's Kingdom: Mythmaking on the Saudi Oil Frontier* (Palo Alto, CA: Stanford University Press, 2006).

57. James D. Anderson, *The Education of Blacks in the South 1860–1935* (Chapel Hill: University of North Carolina Press, 1988), 50–51.

58. Reinsch, "Colonial Autonomy," 129, 118, 139.

59. In Robert Vitalis, "The Noble American Science of Imperial Relations and Its Laws of Race Development," *Comparative Studies in Society and History* 52, no. 4 (2010).

60. Reinsch, "Colonial Autonomy," 119.

61. Ford, "The Ethics of Empire," 503–4.

62. Moses, "Colonial Policy with Reference to the Philippines," 95.

63. Henry C. Morris, "Some Effects of Outlying Dependencies upon the People of the United States," *Proceedings of the American Political Science Association* 3 (1906), 205.

64. Jedidiah Kroncke, "An Early Tragedy of Comparative Constitutionalism: Frank Goodnow and the Chinese Republic," *Pacific Rim Law & Policy Journal* 21 (2012): 533.

65. Schmidt, "Paul S. Reinsch and the Study of Imperialism and Internationalism." "Open Door" refers to a tenet of U.S. foreign policy from 1899 to 1945 that all nations should have equal access to Chinese trading ports and that only the Chinese government should collect taxes on trade in those ports.

66. Reinsch, "Colonial Autonomy," 118.

67. Ford, "The Ethics of Empire," 505.

68. Paul S. Reinsch, Review of *Colonial Administration in the Far East: The Province of Burmah* by Alleyne Ireland, and Review of *Principes de Colonisation et de Legislation Coloniale* by Arthur Girault, *American Political Science Review* 3, no. 1 (1909): 113.

69. William Bennett Munro, "Some Merits and Defects of the French Colonial System," *Proceedings of the American Political Science Association* 4 (1907): 49, 55–56.

70. Paul S. Reinsch, *Public International Unions: Their Work and Organization* (Boston: Ginn, 1911), 67, 152–53.

71. Ibid., 2–3.

72. Ibid., 186, 8.

73. Reinsch, "The Negro Race and European Civilization," 146.

74. Paul S. Reinsch, Review of *Imperialism: A Study* by J. A. Hobson, *Political Science Quarterly* 18, no. 3 (1903): 533.

75. Reinsch, "The Negro Race and European Civilization," 148.

76. Stephen Skowronek, "The Reassociation of Ideas and Purposes: Racism, Liberalism, and the American Political Tradition," *American Political Science Review* 100, no. 3 (2006).

77. Woodrow Wilson, "The Reconstruction of the Southern States," *Atlantic Monthly* (January 1901), 15.

78. Skowronek, "The Reassociation of Ideas and Purposes," 387.

79. Woodrow Wilson, *Division and Reunion* (New York: Longman's, Green, and Company, 1893), 273.

80. Wilson, "The Reconstruction of the Southern States," 12, 14–15.

81. Wilson, quoted in Skowronek, "The Reassociation of Ideas and Purposes," 392–93.

Chapter 4

1. Paul S. Reinsch, "Colonial Autonomy, with Special Reference to the Government of the Philippine Islands," *Proceedings of the American Political Science Association* (1904): 130.

2. Robert Vitalis, "International Studies in America," *Items and Issues* 3 (2002); Richard P. Traina, *Changing the World: Clark University's Pioneering People, 1887–2000* (Worcester, MA: Chandler House Press, 2005).

3. Peter Filene, "The World Peace Foundation and Progressivism: 1910–1918," *New England Quarterly* 36, no. 4 (1963): 478.

4. Famously, Clark at Hall's behest hosted Freud's only lectures in the Americas, at a 1909 conference also featuring Carl Jung. See Dorothy Ross, *G. Stanley Hall: The Psychologist as Prophet* (Chicago: University of Chicago Press, 1972).

5. Thomas F. Gossett, *Race: The History of an Idea in America* (New York: Oxford University Press, 1997), 154.

6. For an account of the discovery that the *JRD* morphed into *Foreign Affairs*, see Robert Vitalis, *White World Order, Black Power Politics: The Birth of American International Relations* (Ithaca, NY: Cornell University Press, 2015); on the *JRD*'s place in the evolution of Development Studies, see Robert Vitalis and Marton T. Markovits, "The Lost World of Development Theory in the United States, 1865–1930" (presentation, American Historical Association Conference, San Francisco, CA, 2002), 7.

7. Ronald Rogowski, "International Politics: The Past as Science," *International Studies Quarterly* 12, no. 4 (1968): 400–401. On the further carving out of disciplinary space for international relations after World War II, see Nicolas Guilhot, ed., *The Invention of International Relations Theory: Realism, the Rockefeller Foundation, and the 1954 Conference on Theory* (New York: Columbia University Press, 2011).

8. On Du Bois's understandings of racial difference, see Judith Stein, "Defining the Race 1890–1930," in *The Invention of Ethnicity*, ed. Werner Sollors (New York: Oxford University Press, 1989), 83; Judith Stein, *The World of Marcus Garvey: Race and Class in Modern Society* (Baton Rouge: Louisiana State University Press, 1986), chap. 1; and Adolph L. Reed Jr., *W. E. B. Du Bois and American Political Thought: Fabianism and the Color Line* (New York: Oxford University Press, 1996). On Du Bois's underrecognized contribution to international relations theory, see Vitalis, *White World Order, Black Power Politics*.

9. George Blakeslee, "Introduction," *Journal of Race Development* 1, no. 1 (1910): 1, 4.

10. G. Stanley Hall, "The Point of View Toward Primitive Races," *Journal of Race Development* 1, no. 1 (1910): 6–7.

11. A small piece of evidence that Blakeslee and the *JRD* were understood to be advocates of nonwhite peoples is a 1914 review in the *American Journal of International Law* of a book edited by Blakeslee. The book in question is a collection of Japan essays from the *JRD*; the reviewer comments that, "as was to be expected, these lectures show

decided pacific leanings [with] pronounced emphasis on the factors tending to draw the United States and Japan together, and the effect of the whole is to leave the feeling that the various contributors are too sanguine"; Edward Krehbiel, Review of *Japan and Japanese-American Relations: Clark University Addresses* by George Blakeslee (Ed.), *American Journal of International Law* 8, no. 1 (1914): 180.

12. William S. Washburn, "A Worthy Example of the Influence of a Strong Man upon the Development of Racial Character," *Journal of Race Development* 1, no. 3 (1911): 373.

13. William E. Griffis, "A Literary Legend: 'The Oriental,' " *Journal of Race Development* 3, no. 1 (1912): 65–67. This article was included in the volume reviewed by Krehbiel (see note 11, above). It is worth noting that Griffis did not believe in racial equality, nor was he an advocate of all "Orientals." He believed that "Mongolians" were racially inferior and subscribed to the theory that the Japanese were, at least in part, of Aryan descent; Daniel E. Bender, *American Abyss: Savagery and Civilization in the Age of Industry* (Ithaca, NY: Cornell University Press, 2009), 94.

14. J. Macmillan Brown, "Ancient Race-Blending Region in the Pacific," *Journal of Race Development* 5, no. 2 (1914): 159.

15. On this split within Progressivism, see, for example, Mark Pittenger, *American Socialists and Evolutionary Thought, 1870–1920* (Madison: University of Wisconsin Press, 1993); Bender, *American Abyss*; Rogers Smith, *Civic Ideals: Conflicting Visions of Citizenship in U.S. History* (New Haven, CT: Yale University Press, 1997), 411, 19–24; Terrence Ball, "An Ambivalent Alliance: Political Science and American Democracy," in *Political Science in History: Research Programs and Political Traditions*, ed. John S. Dryzek, James Farr, and Stephen T. Leonard (New York: Cambridge University Press, 1995); and Douglas Torgerson, "Policy Analysis and Public Life: The Restoration of Phronesis?" in Dryzek, Farr, and Leonard, *Political Science in History*. It is also worth noting that while the reformist tradition in left Progressivism was much more likely to include women, the *JRD*'s writers are mostly male.

16. Blakeslee, "Introduction," 3.

17. William S. Washburn, "The Philippine Civil Service," *Journal of Race Development* 1, no. 1 (1910): 40–41.

18. John H. Hammond, "The Development of Our Latin-American Trade," *Journal of Race Development* 5, no. 1 (1914): 44–48; Hiram Bingham, "The Probable Effect of the Opening of the Panama Canal on Our Economic Relations with the People of the West Coast of South America," *Journal of Race Development* 5, no. 1 (1914): 64.

19. G. Stanley Hall, "The Point of View Toward Primitive Races," *Journal of Race Development* 1, no. 1 (1910): 6–7.

20. Federico A. Pezet, "Contrasts in the Development of Nationality in Anglo- and Latin-America," *Journal of Race Development* 5, no. 1 (1914): 12–13, 18.

21. Howard Odum, "Standards of Measurement for Race Development," *Journal of Race Development* 5, no. 4 (1915): 378– 79.

22. An unsigned "Notes and Reviews" section from 1915 is especially rich in this regard.

23. Washburn, "The Philippine Civil Service," 46, 53, 55.

24. W. Morgan Shuster, "Our Philippine Policies and Their Results," *Journal of Race Development* 1, no. 1 (1910): 61.

25. George W. Ellis, "Dynamic Factors in the Liberian Situation," *Journal of Race Development* 1, no. 3 (1911); Emmett J. Scott, "Is Liberia Worth Saving?," *Journal of Race Development* 1, no. 3 (1911): 301.

26. W. D. Boyce, "Advantages of Making the Canal Zone a Free City and a Free Port," *Journal of Race Development* 5, no. 1 (1914): 68–69, 83.

27. W. M. Davis, "Geographic Factors in South Africa," *Journal of Race Development* 2, no. 2 (1911): 139.

28. Dorothy Ross, *The Origins of American Social Science* (New York: Cambridge University Press, 1991), xv.

29. S. S. Visher, "Memoir to Ellsworth Huntington, 1876–1947," *Annals of the Association of American Geographers* 38, no. 1 (1948).

30. Ellsworth Huntington, *The Pulse of Asia* (Boston: Houghton Mifflin and Company, 1907).

31. Ellsworth Huntington, "Physical Environment as a Factor in Turkey," *Journal of Race Development* 1, no. 4 (1911); Ellsworth Huntington, "Geographical Environment and Japanese Character," *Journal of Race Development* 2, no. 4 (1912); Ellsworth Huntington, "A Neglected Factor in Race Development," *Journal of Race Development* 7, no. 2 (1917); Ellsworth Huntington, "The Adaptability of the White Man to Tropical America," *Journal of Race Development* 5, no. 4 (1915).

32. Huntington, "The Adaptability of the White Man to Tropical America," 187, 193. Bender notes that in the 1920s Huntington was enthralled by the development of climate-control technologies (such as humidifiers) and wondered if they might "in time overcome the evils of too great heat and thus enable civilization to move south once more?" Huntington, quoted in Bender, *American Abyss*, 65.

33. George W. Stocking Jr., *Race, Culture, and Evolution: Essays in the History of Anthropology* (1968) (Chicago: University of Chicago Press, 1982), 238–239.

34. See ibid.; Ross, *The Origins of American Social Science*; Reed, *W. E. B. Du Bois and American Political Thought*.

35. Stocking, *Race, Culture, and Evolution*, 242.

36. Bowler argues that a fully modern synthesis of genetics and Darwinian evolution did not emerge for more than another decade. This consensus, which held for most of the twentieth century, is now being challenged by epigenetics, which understands DNA to be in dynamic interaction with the environment. Peter J. Bowler, "Darwinism and Modernism: Genetics, Palaeontology, and the Challenge to Progressionism, 1880–1930," in *Modernist Impulses in the Human Sciences 1870–1930*, ed. Dorothy Ross (Baltimore: Johns Hopkins University Press, 1994).

37. Stocking, *Race, Culture, and Evolution*, 265, 232 (emphasis in the original).

38. Thorstein Veblen, "The Mutation Theory and the Blond Race," *Journal of Race Development* 4, no. 3 (1913): 492, 502.

39. See K. L. Anderson, "The Unity of Veblen's Theoretical System," in *Thorstein Veblen: Critical Assessments*, ed. John Cunningham Wood (New York: Routledge, 1993), 3.

40. Veblen, "The Mutation Theory and the Blond Race," 495, 504.

Chapter 5

1. One manifestation was a "eugenics-suffused exhibitionary complex" that "radiated across the nation" following the success of the eugenics displays at the 1915 World's Fair. Robert Rydell, Christina Cogdell, and Mark Largent, "The Nazi Eugenics Exhibit in the United States, 1934–43," in *Popular Eugenics: National Efficiency and American Mass Culture in the 1930s*, ed. Susan Currell and Christina Cogdell (Athens: Ohio University Press, 2006), 362.

2. Charles E. Merriam, *New Aspects of Politics* (1925) (Chicago: University of Chicago Press, 1972), 2.

3. Franklin H. Hankins, "Individual Differences and Democratic Theory," *Political Science Quarterly* 38, no. 3 (1923): 405.

4. Charles E. Merriam, *A History of American Political Theories* (New York: MacMillan Company, 1903); Charles E. Merriam, *American Political Ideas: Studies in the Development of American Political Thought, 1865–1917* (New York: MacMillan Company, 1920); Charles E. Merriam, *The Making of Citizens: A Comparative Study of Methods of Civic Training* (Chicago: University of Chicago Press, 1931); Charles E. Merriam, *Civic Education in the United States* (New York: C. Scribner's Sons, 1934); Charles E. Merriam, *Four American Party Leaders* (New York: MacMillan Company, 1926). By his own admission, he was trained "in the historical and comparative method, 'sitting at the feet of Gamaliel' " (the Jewish sage who taught the Apostle Paul "according to the perfect manner of the law of the fathers" [Acts 22:3]) "in Columbia University and later in the University of Berlin." Merriam, *New Aspects of Politics*, xi.

5. Jessica Blatt, "Lasswell, Harold Dwight (1902–78)" in *The Encyclopedia of Political Thought* ed. Michael T. Gibbons et al. (Hoboken, NJ: Wiley, 2014).

6. Michael T. Heaney and John Mark Hansen, "Building the Chicago School," *American Political Science Review* 100, no. 4 (2006), 589.

7. John G. Gunnell, "Continuity and Innovation in the History of Political Science: The Case of Charles Merriam," *Journal of the History of the Behavioral Sciences* 28 (1992): 134.

8. See Dorothy Ross, *The Origins of American Social Science* (New York: Cambridge University Press, 1991); and David Hollinger, "The Knower and the Artificer," in *Modernist Impulses in the Human Sciences, 1870–1930*, ed. Dorothy Ross (Baltimore: Johns Hopkins University Press, 1994).

9. Ellen D. Ellis, "The Pluralistic State," *American Political Science Review* 14, no. 3 (1920): 406.

10. Hollinger, "The Knower and the Artificer," 28.

11. Merriam, *New Aspects of Politics.* In fact, the book reprised themes, and many large chunks of text, from at least two earlier essays. However, it is the most expansive of Merriam's many programmatic statements.

12. In his "Reports of the Second National Conference on the Science of Politics" (Merriam was an organizer), A. B. Hall referred to the lessons of World War I with its "obliteration of lives" with a "chemical formula," positing as a counterweight a scientific "system of social control by which reason rather than passion will be the dominating power." *American Political Science Review* 19, no. 1 (1925): 110.

13. Albert Somit and Joseph Tanenhaus, *The Development of American Political Science* (New York: Irvington Publishers, 1982), 57–59, 102. According to Somit and Tanenhaus, exact figures are hard to come by since records are incomplete or unclear before the mid-1920s. They estimate that while fewer than forty political science students got PhDs between 1911 and 1921, most from Columbia and Johns Hopkins, the years between 1926 and 1935 saw 530 doctorates awarded in America, with fewer than 20 percent coming from those two institutions.

14. A. Gordon Dewey, Review of *The Science and Method of Politics* by George E. G. Catlin, *Political Science Quarterly* 42, no. 4 (1927): 617.

15. Merriam, *New Aspects of Politics*, 34, 10, xiii, 18. Anthropology was still, for many, primarily a natural science. This was reflected by the fact that when the National Research Council, established to mobilize American science for World War I, anthropology was represented while history, sociology, and political science were not.

16. Another term that sometimes substituted for one of these was *political technique.*

17. Barry Karl, *Charles Merriam and the Study of Politics* (Chicago: University of Chicago Press, 1974).

18. Merriam, *New Aspects of Politics*, viii.

19. The most famous exposition of this position came from Merriam's friend Walter Lippmann, in his *The Phantom Public* (New York: MacMillan Company, 1925).

20. See John G. Gunnell's discussion of Merriam in *Imagining the American Polity: Political Science and the Discourse of Democracy* (University Park: Pennsylvania State University Press, 2004).

21. Merriam, *New Aspects of Politics*, xi, 34, 133.

22. Ibid., v, 133.

23. John S. Dryzek, "Revolutions Without Enemies: Key Transformations in Political Science," *American Political Science Review* 100, no. 4 (2006): 487; see also William Y. Elliott, *The Pragmatic Revolt in Politics* (New York: MacMillan Company, 1928).

24. Dewey, Review of *The Science and Method of Politics*, 620.

25. M. Léon Duguit in France and Hugo Krabbe in Germany were the pluralists most often cited in U.S. commentaries.

26. Harold J. Laski, *Studies in the Problem of Sovereignty* (New Haven, CT: Yale University Press, 1917), 23.

27. E.g., F. W. Coker, "Pluralistic Theories and the Attack upon State Sovereignty," in *A History of Political Theories, Recent Times: Essays on Contemporary Developments in Political Theory*, ed. Charles E. Merriam and Harry Elmer Barnes (New York: MacMillan Company, 1924), 114; Merriam, *New Aspects of Politics*, vi; William Y. Elliott, "The Pragmatic Politics of Mr. H. J. Laski," *American Political Science Review* 18, no. 2 (1924): 258; William Y. Elliott, "Sovereign State or Sovereign Group," *American Political Science Review* 19, no. 3 (1925): 479. For Elliott, the association with fascism was clearly pejorative. Other U.S. political scientists in the period were more open-minded about the prospects of fascism before World War II. See Ido Oren, *Our Enemies and US: America's Rivalries and the Making of American Political Science* (Ithaca, NY: Cornell University Press, 2003).

28. Elliott, "Sovereign State or Sovereign Group," 493, 498; Elliott, "The Pragmatic Politics of Mr. H. J. Laski," 268.

29. Ellis, "The Pluralistic State," 404. Gunnell has written extensively about this controversy. See, for example, John Gunnell, "The Declination of the State," in *Political Science in History*, ed. John S. Dryzek, James Farr, and Stephen T. Leonard (New York: Cambridge University Press, 1995).

30. Ellen Ellis, "Political Science at the Crossroads," *American Political Science Review* 21, no. 4 (1927): 773; William B. Munro, *The Invisible Government and Personality in Politics* (New York: Arno Press, 1928), 10.

31. George E. G. Catlin, "The Doctrine of Power and Party Conflict," *American Political Science Review* 19, no. 4 (1925): 719.

32. George E. G. Catlin, "The Delimitation and Mensurability of Political Phenomena," *American Political Science Review* 21, no. 2 (1927): 255.

33. Dewey, Review of *The Science and Method of Politics*, 619.

34. Ellis, "Political Science at the Crossroads," 791.

35. For example, it was to this end that Merriam sponsored a monumental series of studies of "civic training" or "the production of citizens" in the United States (a volume he wrote himself), the Soviet Union, Italy, Germany, and elsewhere. Charles E. Merriam, *Civic Education in the United States*; Charles E. Merriam, *The Making of Citizens*.

36. Woodrow Wilson, "The Study of Administration," *Political Science Quarterly* 2, no. 2 (1887): 209.

37. Harry Elmer Barnes, "Some Contributions of Sociology to Modern Political Theory," in Merriam and Barnes, *A History of Political Theories, Recent Times*, 367.

38. Bertell Ollman, *The United States Constitution: 200 Years of Anti-Federalist, Abolitionist, Feminist, Muckraking, Progressive, and Especially Socialist Criticism* (New York: New York University Press, 1990), 4. Thanks to Doug Henwood for pointing me to the delightful Harding headline.

39. Ross, *The Origins of American Social Science*, 392.

40. Jonathan P. Spiro, *Defending the Master Race: Conservation, Eugenics, and the Legacy of Madison Grant* (Burlington: University of Vermont Press, 2009), 397.

41. George W. Stocking Jr., *Race, Culture, and Evolution: Essays in the History of Anthropology* (1968) (Chicago: University of Chicago Press, 1982), 139. In 1884, Boas wrote to his future wife that while in Germany he would be "restricted to my science and to teaching," a job in America offered greater chances to "further those ideals for which I live," including "equal rights for all." Quoted in Herbert S. Lewis, "The Passion of Franz Boas," *American Anthropologist* 3, no. 102 (2001), 452.

42. Boas briefly held a docentship at Clark, where he reportedly came into conflict with the domineering G. Stanley Hall.

43. Quoted in Lewis, "The Passion of Franz Boas," 450–51.

44. Reproduced in Franz Boas, "Scientists as Spies," *Anthropology Today* 21 (2005): 27. Boas's critics countered that it was Boas himself who, by exposing the spying, was creating a problem for international scientific work.

45. Stocking *Race, Culture, and Evolution*, 273. Boas's targets were not named at the time, but it has since emerged that all four of anthropologists to whom his letter referred were on the governing board of the AAA; three voted to censure, one abstained. Editor, "Editorial Note," *Anthropology Today* 21 (2005): 27.

46. In Stocking, *Race, Culture, and Evolution*, 276.

47. As Stocking reports, however, Boas had known about the spying for two years, and he waited until after the war to expose it.

48. The discussion of Boas's life and contribution to anthropology in this chapter relies on Stocking, *Race, Culture, and Evolution*, and also on Lewis, "The Passion of Franz Boas." Boas was not the first to begin to theorize a historical origin for culture, but his work and that of his students made the most powerful contribution to the development of the social sciences in the first half of the twentieth century.

49. The classic statement of this position is Lewis H. Morgan, *Ancient Society* (Cambridge, MA: Harvard University Press, 1877).

50. Also known as the U.S. Commission on Immigration, the Dillingham Commission was a joint Congressional Committee formed in 1907 in response to the increase in immigrants from Southern and Eastern Europe. It sponsored vast amounts of research and, despite Boas's contribution, mostly served the case for immigration restriction. According to Stocking, Boas occasionally allowed a neo-Lamarckian interpretation of some of these results, but his focus was on growth of the organism, not changes in the determinants of heredity; Stocking, *Race, Culture, and Evolution*, 184. It is also worth noting that the same study found that children's height correlated negatively with family size, which Boas attributed to nutrition differentials resulting from the socioeconomic pressures on larger families. On later controversies over the validity of Boas's findings, see Clarence G. Gravlee et al., "Heredity, Environment, and Cranial Form: A Reanalysis of Boas's Immigrant Data," *American Anthropologist* 105, no. 1 (2003).

51. Stephen Jay Gould, *The Mismeasure of Man* (New York: Norton, 1981).

52. Franz Boas, "Report Presented to the 61st Congress on Changes in Bodily Form of Descendants of Immigrants" (Washington DC: Government Printing Office, 1910), 5.

53. Stocking, *Race, Culture, and Evolution*, 178, 222.

54. Elazar Barkan, *The Retreat of Scientific Racism: Changing Concepts of Race in Britain and the United States Between the World Wars* (New York: Cambridge University Press, 1992), 68–69.

55. Spiro, *Defending the Master Race*, 293; see also Stocking, *Race, Culture, and Evolution*.

56. Boas's work had not gone unremarked before then—his early students had begun to publish significant work at least a decade earlier, and his *Mind of Primitive Man*, which brought together many of the threads outlined above, appeared in 1911. Moreover, Boas was on the editorial board of the *Journal of Race Development*. George Ellis and Boas's student Alexander F. Chamberlain often cited him therein, and *Mind of Primitive Man* received favorable review from the *JRD* in 1914. More generally, the Boasian perspective was noted in articles and reviews published in the *APSR*, *PSQ*, and other works before the 1920s, most often with respect to the "Negro" and immigration "problems" and occasionally with reference to colonialism. But this is the first extended consideration that I have discovered of the relationship of Boas's thought specifically to foundational questions of political theory. It is certainly ironic and perhaps telling that it should have appeared in the form of a tribute to the virulently racist Dunning.

57. Merriam and Barnes, *A History of Political Theories, Recent Times*.

58. Correspondence between the editors on the planning, execution, and eventual fate of the volume can be found in the Charles E. Merriam Papers, Series 2, Subseries 3, Box 25, Folder 15, University of Chicago Library, Department of Special Collections, Chicago, Illinois. In particular, in letters on January 20 and May 16, 1924, Barnes reports to Merriam that the book is set to "pulverize" a competing text then planned by Francis Coker. (Coker, who contributed a chapter on sovereignty to the Merriam and Barnes volume, may have agreed: His *Recent Political Thought*, Barnes's apparent referent in the letter, did not in fact appear for another decade.)

59. William A. Dunning, *A History of Political Theories, Ancient and Medieval* (New York: MacMillan Company, 1902); William A. Dunning, *A History of Political Theories, from Luther to Montesquieu* (New York: MacMillan Company, 1905); William A. Dunning, *A History of Political Theories, from Rousseau to Spencer* (New York: MacMillan Company, 1922).

60. George W. Stocking, *The Ethnographer's Magic and Other Essays in the History of Anthropology* (Madison: University of Wisconsin Press, 1992), 295. Goldenweiser did not eventually assume the stature of some of his fellow Boas students, probably because his brilliance was offset by a difficult personality and, it seems, tendencies both to drink too much and to fall in love "more often than was wise or very nice." Lewis, "The Passion of Franz Boas," 460.

61. Harry E. Barnes, ed., *The History and Prospects of the Social Sciences* (New York: Alfred A. Knopf, 1925).

62. Charles A. Ellwood et al., eds., *Recent Developments in the Social Sciences* (Philadelphia, PA: J. B. Lippincott Company, 1927).

63. T. V. Smith and Leonard Dupee White, *Chicago: An Experiment in Social Science Research* (Chicago: University of Chicago Press, 1929).

64. E. R. A. Seligman, ed., *The Encyclopedia of the Social Sciences* (New York: MacMillan Company, 1930).

65. Barnes, *The History and Prospects of the Social Sciences*, xv.

66. Barnes, "Some Contributions of Sociology to Modern Political Theory," 387. This essay was an updated version of an APSA address from 1921. The earlier version opened by commenting that the "fact that a sociologist has been asked to appear on the program of the American Political Science Association . . . is an admission that some political scientists have at last come to consider sociology of sufficient significance to students of political science"; Barnes, "Some Contributions of Sociology to Modern Political Theory," *American Political Science Review* 15, no. 4 (1921): 487.

67. Merriam would often repurpose blocks of text. For example, parts of his "Recent Tendencies" essay reappear in the first chapter of Merriam, *New Aspects of Politics*.

68. Charles E. Merriam, "Recent Tendencies in Political Thought," in Merriam and Barnes, *A History of Political Theories*, 23.

69. George W. Stocking Jr., *The Ethnographer's Magic*, 295.

70. A. A. Goldenweiser, "Anthropological Theories of Political Origins," in Merriam and Barnes, *A History of Political Theories, Recent Times*, 433, 455.

71. As against Victorian social evolutionism, which saw politics as emerging "upon the ruins of kinship organization." Ibid., 455.

72. Goldenweiser, "Anthropological Theories of Political Origins," 446, 454–55.

73. Charles Elmer Gehlke, "Social Psychology and Political Theory," and Herbert W. Schneider, "Political Implications of Recent Philosophical Movements," in Merriam and Barnes, *A History of Political Theories, Recent Times*.

74. The exception is Dewey student Schneider's "Political Implications of Recent Philosophical Movements," essentially a primer on pragmatism. It is worth noting that some other essays also touch on racial questions. Borchard, for example, notes that existing "idealist" theories of international law do not account for de facto asymmetries of power, as in colonial relationships. They simply do not make the category of race, or racial theories of politics, central to their argument.

75. Barnes, "Some Contributions of Sociology to Modern Political Theory," 365, 361.

76. Stocking, *Race, Culture, and Evolution*, 189.

77. Such overlap had in fact bedeviled race researchers for quite some time, but Boas took these observations to their logical conclusion, seeing them as reasons to abandon racial "types," rather than trying to salvage or soften the framework in the

face of counterevidence. One note here: Kamala Visweswaran has critiqued Boas for "legitimating" race science by "attempting to expunge race from social science by assigning it to biology." This seems to me wrong in the light of Boas's important biological work against race. But it does speak to the ways in which the separating out of race from the holistic category of "civilization" effected by the Boasian critique was in some measure a shared feature of both the new anthropology and the hard-line biological determinism of the 1920s. Kamala Visweswaran, "Race and the Culture of Anthropology," *American Anthropologist* 100, no. 1 (1998): 70.

78. Franklin H. Hankins, "Race as a Factor in Political Theory," in Merriam and Barnes, *A History of Political Theories, Recent Times*, 548.

79. C. G. Fenwick, Review of *A History of Political Theories, Recent Times* Edited by Charles E. Merriam and Harry E. Barnes, *American Journal of International Law* 19, no. 1 (1925): 242.

80. T. V. Smith, Review of *A History of Political Theories, Recent Times* Edited by Charles E. Merriam and Harry E. Barnes, *International Journal of Ethics* 35, no. 3 (1925): 312.

81. Raymond G. Gettell, Review of *A History of Political Theories, Recent Times* Edited by Charles E. Merriam and Harry E. Barnes, *American Historical Review* 30, no. 3 (1925): 575.

82. William Y. Elliott, Review of *A History of Political Theories, Recent Times* Edited by Charles Merriam and Harry Elmer Barnes, *American Political Science Review* 19, no. 1 (1925): 178; Mattoon M. Curtis, Review of *A History of Political Theories, Recent Times* Edited by Charles E. Merriam and Harry E. Barnes, *Philosophical Review* 34, no. 5 (1925): 499.

83. J. Grierson, Review of *A History of Political Theories, Recent Times* Edited by Charles Merriam and Harry Elmer Barnes, *American Journal of Sociology* 31, no. 1 (1925): 104; see also Smith, Review of *A History of Political Theories, Recent Times*, 313.

84. Hankins was at work on a longer treatment, published as *The Racial Basis of Civilization: A Critique of the Nordic Doctrine* (New York: Alfred A. Knopf, 1926).

85. Hankins, "Race as a Factor in Political Theory," 511, 514.

86. Ibid., 531, 534–35, 540–41.

87. Ibid, 508–9, 514, 521.

88. Ibid., 546–47.

89. Ibid., 547–48; Malcolm M. Willey, "Some Recent Critics and Exponents of the Theory of Democracy," in Merriam and Barnes, *A History of Political Theories, Recent Times*, 47; Barnes, "Some Contributions of Sociology to Modern Political Theory," 347; Gehlke, "Social Psychology and Political Theory," 424; Merriam, "Recent Tendencies in Political Thought," 20.

90. Hall et al., "Reports of the Second National Conference on the Science of Politics," 113. The first National Conference on the Science of Politics met in September 1923, with an attendance of about a hundred. Arnold Bennett Hall, "The First

Meeting of the National Conference on the Science of Politics," *Journal of Social Forces* 2, no. 3 (1924).

91. Franklin H. Hankins, "Individual Differences and Democratic Theory," *Political Science Quarterly* 38, no. 3 (1923): 405.

Chapter 6

1. E.g., Charles E. Merriam, "The Significance of Psychology for the Study of Politics," *American Political Science Review* 18, no. 3 (1924).

2. Merriam to Harry Elmer Barnes, November 23, 1923, and June 4, 1924, Series 2, Subseries 3, Box 25, Folder 15, Charles E. Merriam Papers, Department of Special Collections, University of Chicago Library, Chicago, Illinois.

3. Malcolm M. Willey, "Some Recent Critics and Exponents of the Theory of Democracy" in *History of Political Theories*, ed. Charles E. Merriam and Harry Elmer Barnes (New York: MacMillan Company, 1924): 59–61. Interestingly, Willey himself was in some measure associated with "the Boas group," having recently coauthored a survey article on the culture concept with Melville Herskovits, "The Cultural Approach to Sociology," *American Journal of Sociology* 29, no. 2 (1923). He thought the Boasians had done fatal damage to theories of inherent racial difference but believed that individual differences of all kinds were biologically determined.

4. John Carson, *The Measure of Merit: Talents, Intelligence, and Inequality in the French and American Republics 1750–1940* (Princeton, NJ: Princeton University Press, 2007), 231.

5. Charles E. Gehlke, "Social Psychology and Political Theory" in Merriam and Barnes, *History of Political Theories*, 424.

6. Harry E. Barnes, "Some Contributions of Sociology to Modern Political Theory" in Merriam and Barnes, *History of Political Theories*, 378.

7. Charles A. Beard, "Conditions Favorable to Creative Work in Political Science," *American Political Science Review* 24, no. 1, Report of the Committee on Policy of the American Political Science Association (1930): 28.

8. T. V. Smith, Review of *The New History and the Social Studies* by Harry E. Barnes, *American Political Science Review* 19, no. 4 (1925): 827.

9. These were otherwise wildly diverse figures—Smith was suspicious of ethical absolutes, for example; Elliott was suspicious of those who questioned them.

10. Dorothy Ross, *The Origins of American Social Science* (New York : Cambridge University Press, 1991), 405.

11. Minutes of the Meeting of the Sociological Conference Group, Committee on Scientific Problems of Human Migration, Offices of the National Research Council, March 29, 1923, Box 84, Folder 9, Mary Van Kleeck Papers, Sophia Smith Collection, Smith College, Northampton, Massachusetts, p. 23.

12. More accurately, Crane was part of a group organized by the group trying to organize the SSRC; the SSRC had not yet been formally constituted.

13. Arnold Bennett Hall, "The First Meeting of the National Conference on the Science of Politics," *Journal of Social Forces* 2, no. 3 (1924): 373.

14. A. B. Hall et al., "Reports of the Second National Conference on the Science of Politics," *American Political Science Review* 19, no. 1 (1925): 106.

15. Yerkes's IQ tests were used in conjunction with occupational tests. D. J. Kevles, "Testing the Army's Intelligence: Psychologists and the Military in World War I," *Journal of American History* 55, no. 3 (1968).

16. Memorandum Regarding Request of National Research Council through Its Division of Anthropology and Psychology for a Grant and for Other Cooperation from the Russell Sage Foundation in a Study of Problems of Human Migration, November 1, 1922, Box 84, Folder 10, Mary Van Kleeck Papers.

17. Haraway is wonderful on Yerkes's primate research and its connections to his larger social vision. Donna Haraway, *Primate Visions: Gender, Race, and Nature in the World of Modern Science* (New York: Routeldge, 1989).

18. Kevles, "Testing the Army's Intelligence," 574–75; Carson, *The Measure of Merit*, 253.

19. John M. O'Donnell, *The Origins of Behaviorism: American Psychology 1870–1920* (New York: New York University Press, 1985).

20. Carson, *The Measure of Merit*, 109.

21. Carl C. Brigham, *A Study of American Intelligence* (Princeton, NJ: Princeton University Press, 1922), xx. See also Robert M. Yerkes and Clarence Stone, eds., *Army Mental Tests* (New York: Henry Holt and Company, 1920); Robert M. Yerkes, ed., "Psychological Examining in the United States Army," *Memoirs of the National Academy of Sciences* 15 (1921).

22. Ibid., xx, 80.

23. Ibid., 119, 50.

24. This statement substantially contradicts Brigham's position in the rest of the book. For example, earlier he had explained a correlation between years of schooling and intelligence scores by arguing that higher intelligence caused longer schooling. Brigham, *A Study of American Intelligence*, 63.

25. Brigham, *A Study of American Intelligence*, 192.

26. Ibid., 93, 113.

27. Ibid., 178.

28. Ibid., 188.

29. "We . . . face a possibility of racial admixture here that is infinitely worse than that faced by any European country today, for we are incorporating the negro into our racial stock, while all of Europe is comparatively free from this taint." Brigham, *A Study of American Intelligence*, 210, 209. In Brigham's (partial) defense, it must be noted that he later acknowledged that the tests had been faulty and prejudicial, and he publicly disavowed the idea that they demonstrated innate, racial differences in intelligence. C. C. Brigham, "Intelligence Tests of Immigrant Groups," *Psychological Review* 37, no. 2 (1930).

30. Charles E. Merriam, *New Aspects of Politics* (1925) (Chicago: University of Chicago Press, 1972), 79–80.

31. Letter to William C. Bagley, April 16, 1922, Series 2, Subseries 3, Box 25, Folder 13, Charles E. Merriam Papers, University of Chicago Library, Department of Special Collections, Chicago, Illinois.

32. Walter Lippmann, "A Future for the Tests," *New Republic* 33 (1923): 11.

33. Walter Lippmann to Charles E. Merriam, February 17, 1923, Series 2, Subseries 3, Box 34, Folder 12, Charles E. Merriam Papers.

34. Correspondence on this topic may be found in Charles E. Merriam Papers. For letters to and from Yerkes, see Series 2, Subseries 3, Box 43, Folder 16; to and from Bingham, see Series 2, Subseries 3, Box 26, Folder 2.; see also Thurstone, Series 2, Subseries 3, Box 41, Folder 11.

35. Harold F. Gosnell, "Some Practical Applications of Psychology in Government," *American Journal of Sociology* 28, no. 6 (1923): 735.

36. Yerkes to Charles Merriam, February 2, 1923, Series 2, Subseries 3, Box 43, Folder 16, Charles E. Merriam Papers.

37. R. C. Brooks, Review of *Boss Platt and His New York Machine* by Harold F. Gosnell, *American Political Science Review* 18, no. 3 (1924): 627–29.

38. Charles E. Merriam, "Political Research," *American Political Science Review* 16, no. 2 (1922): 320.

39. Merriam to Yerkes, January 19, 1923, Series 2, Subseries 3, Box 43, Folder 16, Charles E. Merriam Papers.

40. Clark Wissler, "Final Report of the Committee on Scientific Problems of Human Migration," *Reprint and Circular Series of the National Research Council* (1929).

41. E.g., Report and Recommendations of Committee on Scientific Problems of Human Migration, Presented to the Division of Anthropology and Psychology [of the NRC], April 8, 1925, Box 84, Folder 11, Mary Van Kleeck Papers.

42. Beardsley Ruml to Robert M. Yerkes, April 16, 1926, Series 3, Subseries 6, Box 59, Folder 632, Laura Spelman Rockefeller Memorial Archives, Rockefeller Archive Center, N. Tarrytown, New York.

43. Robert Mearns Yerkes, "Autobiography of Robert Mearns Yerkes" in C. Murchison, ed., *History of Psychology in Autobiography* 2 (Worcester, MA: Clark University Press, 1930). See also correspondence between Yerkes and Van Kleeck in 1925, Box 84, Folder 7, Mary Van Kleeck Papers. For example, in a letter dated July 10 of that year, Yerkes remarked, "I am deeply disappointed by the failure of our plans."

44. The timing renders it doubtful that the committee itself played a role, even if figures associated with it may have. Indeed, it may be that the political success of the nativist movement may have taken some of the wind out of its scientific wing's sails.

45. Elazar Barkan, *The Retreat of Scientific Racism: Changing Concepts of Race in Britain and the United States Between the World Wars* (New York: Cambridge University Press, 1992), 112–13.

46. Brigham went on to help develop the Scholastic Aptitude Test, for example. Matthew Downey *Carl Campbell Brigham: Scientist and Educator* (Princeton, NJ: Educational Testing Services, 1961).

47. Ross, *The Origins of American Social Science*, 401; Martin Bulmer, "Some Observations on the History of Large Philanthropic Foundations in Britain and the United States," *Voluntas* 6, no. 3 (2006): 283.

48. The SSRC proved particularly useful to foundations that had been burned by political controversy surrounding their work. Rockefeller philanthropy had proved especially vulnerable to this, given the publicity around the brutal labor practices of the foundations' benefactors. For example, in the wake of the 1914 Ludlow Massacre, Rockefeller attempts to fund "industrial relations" research aroused understandable suspicion. But turning funds over to independent experts provided a measure of political cover. These concerns are addressed specifically in early LSRM letters to the SSRC announcing approval of funding requests. Such letters often contained language specifying that when the SSRC disbursed funds to researchers, grantees should be discreet about the original source of funds. Carnegie had met with similar skepticism in its early efforts to fund social science research and proved reluctant to reenter the field through much of the 1920s; Martin Bulmer and Joan Bulmer, "Philanthropy and Social Science in the 1920s: Beardsley Ruml and the Laura Spelman Rockefeller Memorial, 1922–1929," *Minerva* 19, no. 3 (1981); Donald S. Fisher, *Fundamental Development of the Social Sciences: Rockefeller Philanthropy and the United States Social Science Research Council* (Ann Arbor: University of Michigan Press, 1993); Raymond B. Fosdick, *The Story of the Rockefeller Foundation* (New York: Harper and Brothers,1952.; Kenton W. Worcester, *Social Science Research Council, 1923–1998* (New York: Social Science Research Council, 2001), 145–46.

49. Charles Merriam to Yerkes describes the SSRC resolutions, November 20, 1923, Series 1, Box 34, Folder 644, Robert M. Yerkes Papers, Manuscripts and Archives, Yale University Library, New Haven, Connecticut.

50. Shortly after arriving at the LSRM, Ruml began advocating for that organization to begin directly supporting the NRC, which until then had been largely underwritten by Carnegie money. See Vernon Kellogg to Beardsley Ruml, June 28, 1922, Series 3, Subseries 6, Box 57, Folder 617, Laura Spelman Rockefeller Memorial Archives.

51. He did not work directly with Yerkes but rather assisted Walter Dill Scott as codirector of the Division of Trade Tests; this was a somewhat rival initiative to Yerkes's, emphasizing occupational rather than intelligence testing.

52. The Carnegie Corporation of New York was (and remains) distinct from the Carnegie Institute of Washington (which the elder Merriam chaired), more recently known as the Carnegie Institution for Science. Angell, who recommended Ruml to the Rockefellers, would soon leave Carnegie to assume the presidency of Yale. He also served briefly as chair of the NRC and had been an adviser to the army mental testing program.

53. See Bulmer, "Some Observations on the History of Large Philanthropic Foundations"; Bulmer and Bulmer, "Philanthropy and Social Science in the 1920s"; Kersten Jacobson Biehn, "Psychobiology, Sex Research, and Chimpanzees: Philanthropic Foundation Support for the Behavioral Sciences at Yale University 1923–41," *History of the Human Sciences* 21, no. 2 (2008); Raymond B. Fosdick, *The Story of the Rockefeller Foundation*, chap. 11; Alice O'Connor, *Poverty Knowledge: Social Science, Social Policy, and the Poor in Twentieth-Century U.S. History* (Princeton, NJ: Princeton University Press 2002), chap. 1; also, Ross, *The Origins of American Social Science*, 393–96.

54. Biehn, "Psychobiology, Sex Research, and Chimpanzees," 21.

55. James Angell to Beardsley Ruml, January 16, 1923; and Ruml to Raymond Fosdick, December 21, 1923, Series 3, Subseries 6, Box 71, Folder 756, Laura Spelman Rockefeller Memorial Archives.

56. Ruml to Fosdick, July 16, 1923, Series 2, Box 3, Folder 39, Laura Spelman Rockefeller Memorial Archives.

57. Ruml, General Memorandum by the Director, LSRM, October 1922, Series II, Box 2, Folder 31, Laura Spelman Rockefeller Memorial Archives, pp. 9–11. See also correspondence in Record Group 2, Series 0, Box 53, Folder 549, Rockefeller Archive Center, Rockefeller Foundation Collection, N. Tarrytown, New York.

58. Comments by Mary Van Kleeck and Robert M. Yerkes, respectively. Minutes of Meeting of Committee on Scientific Problems of Human Migration, Washington DC, January 25, 1923, Series 2, Box 73, Folder 1398, Robert M. Yerkes Papers.

59. "Reorganization of state government in relation to research as a state function," Annual Meeting of the Division of States Relations Agenda, NRC, May 27, 1921, Series 2, Subseries 3, Box 35, Folder 20, Charles E. Merriam Papers; and John C. Merriam to Charles Merriam, March 10, 1922, Series 2, Subseries 3, Box 35, Folder 20, Charles E. Merriam Papers.

60. See Mary Van Kleeck to Robert M. Yerkes, February 2, 1923, Box 84, Folder 10, Mary Van Kleeck Papers; Yerkes to Charles Merriam, February 2, 1923, Series 2, Subseries 3, Box 43, Folder 16, Charles E. Merriam Papers; Van Kleeck to C. Merriam, February 7, 1923, and reply February 13, 1923, Box 84, Folder 4, Mary Van Kleeck Papers.

61. Merriam describes resolutions to this effect at planning meetings for the SSRC in a November 20, 1923, letter to Yerkes, Series 1, Box 34, Folder 644, Robert M. Yerkes Papers.

62. Merriam to Ruml, November 1 and November 20, 1923, Series 2, Subseries 3, Box 39, Folder 10, Charles E. Merriam Papers. See also November 16 letter, same folder, as well as Charles Merriam to Yerkes, November 20, 1923, Series 1, Box 34, Folder 644, Robert M. Yerkes Papers, for a description of the SSRC resolutions.

63. Yerkes to Van Kleeck, November 13 and December 14, 1923, Box 84, Folder 6, Mary Van Kleeck Papers.

64. The minutes of the Committee on Scientific Problems of Human Migration (CSPHM), Biological Conference Group, are appended to the main funding request.

In that meeting, apropos of proposed studies of immigrant groups, Yerkes comments that

> this is, of course, largely, if not, primarily, a sociological matter and had been referred to a conference group, of which Miss [Mary] Van Kleeck is in charge. That group met last week for preliminary discussion. . . . The group represents sociology, economics, government. They recognize their dependence upon other interests, on the several biological sciences—they want help from anthropology, and psychology. . . . It happens that two or three organizations have recently made a move looking toward the organization of a National Research Council for the social sciences. Professor Charles Merriam of the University of Chicago is, I think, the prime mover.

Appendix 1, Biological Conference Group to the CSPHM, Submitted in support of the NRC's funding request to the LSRM, Series 3, Subseries 6, Box 59, Folder 634, Laura Spelman Rockefeller Memorial Archives.

65. Ross, *The Origins of American Social Science*, 402.

66. The "Agenda for the Meeting of the Social Science Research Council," held on February 16, 1924, notes that the proposed International Communication study was "referred to us for consideration . . . on the suggestion of Dr. Ruml of the Spelman Foundation." Series 3, Subseries 6, Box 64, Folder 682, Laura Spelman Rockefeller Memorial Archives.

67. Gamio was a biologically minded anthropologist with a fraught relationship to Boas. The project in question was what became Manuel Gamio's *Mexican Immigration to the United States* (1931) (New York: Arno Press 1969), and both the idea for a Mexican study and of attaching Gamio to it came from Leonard K. Frank of the LSRM, probably in consultation with Gamio's friend, John Merriam. After a long series of memos and letters boosting the project, in late 1925 Frank wrote to Charles Merriam to say that "in talking over the project Dr. Ruml has pointed out what I neglected to note, namely that I had put myself in the position of seeming to urge this project upon you and the Council," and to urge him to "consider the situation as one between the Council and Dr. Gamio." Merriam's reply noted that the Gamio proposal was with the council "and in all probability will be approved. . . . I do not consider that either you or my brother was urging the matter on us, but thought you were merely showing us an excellent opportunity. My brother was especially emphatic in calling attention to the advantages of the proposed plan, especially as it involved a certain amount of cooperation on the part of the Carnegie Institution." Just over a month later, Frank wrote to Gamio himself to say that he was happy to hear that the proposal was progressing and admonishing him that "if you are asked to undertake this work it will be for the Council and not for the Memorial and I believe it would be wiser if no mention of the Memorial's interest or participation were made by you." Leonard K. Frank to Charles Merriam, December 14, 1925, and reply December 16,

1925; Frank to Manuel Gamio, January 29, 1926, Series 3, Subseries 6, Box 56, Folder 603, Laura Spelman Rockefeller Memorial Archives.

68. "Roundtable I: Psychology and Political Science," *American Political Science Review* 18, no. 1 (1924): 122–25.

69. Hanover Conference, Social Scientists' Report, 1925, Series 3, Subseries 6, Box 52, Folder 563, Laura Spelman Rockefeller Memorial Archives, p. 17. The conferences took place at Dartmouth, in Hanover, New Hampshire.

70. Richard C. S. Trahair, "Elton Mayo and the Early Political Psychology of Harold D. Lasswell," *Political Psychology* 3 no. 3/4 (1981). Merriam had, in fact, tried unsuccessfully to bring Mayo to Chicago. See Ross, *The Origins of American Social Science,* 456–57.

71. Report to LSRM on Comparative Civil [sic] Training, July 1 through December 1925, Series 3, Subseries 6, Box 70, Folder 747, Laura Spelman Rockefeller Memorial Archives.

72. Funding Proposal, Comparative Civic Training, 1925, Series 3, Subseries 6, Box 70, Folder 747, Laura Spelman Rockefeller Memorial Archives.

73. Lasswell to Merriam, November 1, 1926, Series 2, Subseries 3, Box 34, Folder 4, Charles E. Merriam Papers.

74. Merriam to Ruml, July 20, 1927, Series 3, Subseries 6, Box 70, Folder 748, Laura Spelman Rockefeller Memorial Archives.

75. Trahair, "Elton Mayo and the Early Political Psychology of Harold D. Lasswell,"180–81.

76. That book offers a psychoanalytic interpretation of the appearance in society of "agitators," "administrators," and "theorists," arguing in effect that the early experiences of people of each of these distinct types in effect shape them so profoundly as to determine the course of their later engagement with politics.

77. Local Community Research Committee Annual Report 1928–1929 to the Laura Spelman Rockefeller Memorial, undated, Series 3, Subseries 6, Box 71, Folder 753, Laura Spelman Rockefeller Memorial Archives.

78. Charles E. Merriam and Harold F. Gosnell, *Non-Voting: Causes and Methods of Control* (Chicago: University of Chicago Press, 1924); Harold F. Gosnell, "An Experiment in the Stimulation of Voting," *American Political Science Review* 20, no. 4 (1926); Harold F. Gosnell, "Non-Naturalization: A Study in Political Assimilation," *American Journal of Sociology* 33, no. 6 (1928).

79. Local Community Research Committee Annual Report 1928–1929 to the Laura Spelman Rockefeller Memorial, Series 3, Subseries 6, Box 71, Folder 753, Laura Spelman Rockefeller Memorial Archives.

80. Harold Gosnell, *Negro Politicians: The Rise of Negro Politics in Chicago* (Chicago: University of Chicago Press, 1935). The first book by a white political scientist on African American politics appears to have been William F. Nowlin's *The Negro in American National Politics* (Boston: Stratford Company, 1931). African American writers had, of course, already done important work on black political life, much of it

under the rubrics of history and sociology. Gosnell's work drew particularly on the young Ralph Bunche's "The Negro in Chicago Politics," published in *National Municipal Review* 18 (May 1928): 261–64.

81. See Charles Merriam, "An Institute of Politics for the University of Chicago," undated memo (presumably from the mid-1920s), Series 4, Subseries 5, Box 122, Folder 3, Charles E. Merriam Papers. A Public Administration Clearing House, under Louis Brownlow, came later.

82. Quoted in Martin Bulmer, "The Early Institutional Establishment of Social Science Research: The Local Community Research Committee at the University of Chicago, 1923–30," *Minerva* 18 (1980): 81.

83. The Social Sciences Building was constructed in part as the culmination of an effort to move the LCRC toward political science and economics, and away from sociology, history, philosophy, and social work, all of which were seen to be pursuing more "descriptive" and less "scientific" methodological agendas. However, by the time the LCRC had realized its greatest triumph—the inauguration of the Social Science Research Building in 1930—the university's academic leadership was changing with the elevation of Robert Maynard Hutchins to the presidency. Hutchins was much less sympathetic to the program of Merriam and his colleagues, with the somewhat ironic result that by the postwar period, when the Chicago School's model began to see wide acceptance in political science as a whole, it was rapidly losing ground in its home institution. See Bulmer, "The Early Institutional Establishment of Social Science Research."

84. Carson, *The Measure of Merit*. All the same, some of the sharpest and most thorough critiques of mental testing eventually emerged from the *Journal of Negro Education* after its launch in 1932.

85. Thurstone, in Hall et al., "Reports of the Second National Conference on the Science of Politics."

86. Hall et al., "Reports of the Second National Conference on the Science of Politics," 106–7.

87. Ibid., 150.

88. Ibid., 116–23.

Epilogue

1. Malcolm Willey, "Some Recent Critics and Exponents of the Theory of Democracy" in *History of Political Theories, Recent Times*, ed. Charles E. Merriam and Harry E. Barnes (New York: MacMillan Company, 1924): 47, 51.

2. John S. Dryzek notes a pattern through much of the discipline's history in which "revolutionaries" of one sort or another rail against disciplinary enemies who often remain unidentifiable. See John S. Dryzek, "Revolutions Without Enemies: Key Transformations in Political Science," *American Political Science Review* 100, no. 4 (2007).

3. Gordon Dewey, Review of *The Science and Method of Politics* by George E. G. Catlin, *Political Science Quarterly* 42, no. 4 (1927): 617.

4. Robert H. Wiebe, *The Search for Order 1877–1920* (New York: Hill and Wang, 1967), 295; Albert Shaw, "Presidential Address: Third Annual Meeting of the American Political Science Association," *American Political Science Review* 1, no. 2 (1907): 181.

5. Theodore M. Porter, *Trust in Numbers: The Pursuit of Objectivity in Science and Public Life* (Princeton, NJ: Princeton University Press, 1995), 7. Porter notes that "mechanical objectivity" as a communication strategy (as opposed to quantification as a tool more generally) is linked to institutional weakness and fragmentation. Quantitative analysis is useful for understanding all sorts of things. But if you have actual power, you can make your understanding "stick" without showing the spreadsheets.

6. On mechanical objectivity and the cultural resonance of intelligence testing in the United States, see John Carson, *The Measure of Merit: Talents, Intelligence, and Inequality in the French and American Republics, 1750–1940* (Princeton, NJ: Princeton University Press, 2007).

7. Nicolas Guilhot, ed., *The Invention of International Relations Theory: Realism, the Rockefeller Foundation, and the 1954 Conference on Theory* (New York: Columbia University Press, 2011).

8. Mark Solovey, *Shaky Foundations: The Politics-Patronage-Social Science Nexus in Cold War America* (New Brunswick, NJ: Rutgers University Press, 2013), 4.

9. See also Ido Oren, *Our Enemies and US: America's Rivalries and the Making of American Political Science* (Ithaca, NY: Cornell University Press, 2003), chaps. 3 and 4. Two of the most prominent theorists of pluralism in the 1950s, David Truman and Robert Dahl, were also leading behavioralists.

10. David Easton, *The Political System: An Inquiry into the State of Political Science* (New York: Alfred A. Knopf, 1953).

11. Dryzek, "Revolutions Without Enemies," 490.

12. Ellen Ellis, "Political Science at the Crossroads," *American Political Science Review* 21, no. 4 (1927): 791.

13. Solovey, *Shaky Foundations*, especially introduction and chap. 1.

14. See George Stocking Jr., ed., *Malinowski, Rivers, Benedict and Others: Essays on Culture and Personality* (Madison: University of Wisconsin Press, 1986).

15. On anthropology, see George Stocking Jr., *Race, Culture, and Evolution: Essays in the History of Anthropology* (1968) (Chicago: University of Chicago Press, 1982); and Lee Baker, *From Savage to Negro: Anthropology and the Construction of Race, 1896–1954* (Berkeley: University of California Press, 1998). On sociology, Stephen Steinberg, *Race Relations: A Critique* (Palo Alto, CA: Stanford University Press, 2007); Davarian Baldwin, "Black Belts and Ivory Towers: The Place of Race in U.S. Social Thought, 1892–1948," *Critical Sociology* 30 no. 2 (2004); Alice O'Connor, *Poverty Knowledge: Social Science, Social Policy, and the Poor in Twentieth-Century U.S. History* (Princeton, NJ: Princeton University Press, 2002); and Leah Gordon, *From Power to Prejudice: The*

Rise of Racial Individualism in Midcentury America (Chicago: University of Chicago Press, 2015). On criminology, see Kahlil Gibran Muhammad, *The Condemnation of Blackness: Race, Crime, and the Making of Modern Urban America* (Cambridge, MA: Harvard University Press, 2011); and Jeannette Covington, "Racial Classification in Criminology: The Reproduction of Racialized Crime," *Sociological Forum* 10 no. 4 (1995). On economics, see Thomas C. Leonard, "Eugenics and Economics in the Progressive Era," *Journal of Economic Perspectives* 19, no. 4 (2005); on psychology, see Graham Richards, *Race, Racism, and Psychology: Toward a Reflective History* (New York: Routledge, 1997); for a perspective on the co-construction of race and the social sciences more broadly, see Howard Winant, "Race, Ethnicity, and Social Science," *Ethnic and Racial Studies* 38, no. 13 (2015).

16. On the racial commitments of international relations, see especially Robert Vitalis, *White World Order: Black Power Politics: The Birth of American International Relations* (Ithaca, NY: Cornell University Press, 2015); Robert Vitalis, "The Graceful and Generous Liberal Gesture: Making Racism Invisible in American International Relations," *Millennium—Journal of International Studies* 29, no. 2 (2000); David Long and Brian C. Schmidt, eds, *Imperialism and Internationalism in the Discipline of International Relations* (Albany: State University of New York Press, 2003); Brian C. Schmidt, "Political Science and the American Empire: A Disciplinary History of the 'Politics' Section and the Discourse of Imperialism and Colonialism," *International Politics* 45 (2008); and Alexander Anievas, Nivi Manchanda, and Robbie Shilliam, eds, *Race and Racism in International Relations: Confronting the Global Colour Line* (New York: Routledge, 2015). For a similar perspective regarding international relations in the U.K., see Duncan Bell, "Beyond the Sovereign State: Isopolitan Citizenship, Race and Anglo-American Union," *Political Studies* 62, no. 2 (2013).

17. Gordon, *From Power to Prejudice.*

18. Baldwin, "Black Belts," 400; see also Stanford Lymans, "Race Relations as Social Process: Sociology's Resistance to a Civil Rights Orientation" in *Race in America: The Struggle for Equality*, ed. Herbert Hill and James E. Jones Jr. (Madison: University of Wisconsin Press, 1993).

19. Gunnar Myrdal, *An American Dilemma* (New York: Harper and Row, 1944).

20. Gordon, *From Power to Prejudice*, 22. As Gordon and others emphasize, when *American Dilemma* was published, several African American scholars on the left objected to the volumes' framing. Oliver Cox, for example, chided Myrdal's focus on whites' irrational attitudes by pointing out that "if beliefs per se could subjugate a people, the beliefs which Negroes hold about whites" would have made a good deal more difference. More substantively, he described the book as "the finest expression" of "practically all the vacuous theories of race relations which are acceptable among the liberal intelligentsia and which explain race relations away from the social and economic order." Cox, "An American Dilemma: A Mystical Approach to the Study of Race Relations," *Journal of Negro Education* 14 (1945): 143, 132.

21. Mack H. Jones and Alex Willingham, "The White Custodians of the Black Experience: A Reply to Rudwick and Meier," *Social Science Quarterly* 51, no. 1 (1970), 31–32.

22. Rogers M. Smith, "The Puzzling Place of Race in American Political Science," *PS: Political Science and Politics* 37, no. 1 (2004); Charles W. Mills, *The Racial Contract* (Ithaca, NY: Cornell University Press, 1997), 18.

23. Smith, "The Puzzling Place of Race," 41.

24. Ibid.

25. Joseph Lowndes, Julie Novkov, and Dorian T. Warren, eds., *Race and American Political Development* (New York: Routledge, 2008), 3.

26. For example, Michael K. Brown, *Race, Money, and the Welfare State*. (Ithaca, NY: Cornell University Press, 1999); Ira Katznelson, *When Affirmative Action Was White* (New York: Norton, 2006); Jill Quadagno, *The Color of Welfare: How Racism Undermined the War on Poverty* (New York: Oxford University Press, 1994); and O'Connor, *Poverty Knowledge*. On urban development, see Adolph L. Reed Jr., *Stirrings in the Jug: Black Politics in the Post-Segregation Era* (Minneapolis: University of Minnesota Press, 1999); and Preston H. Smith II, *Racial Democracy and the Black Metropolis* (Minneapolis: University of Minnesota Press, 2012). On bureaucratic practices, see Melissa Nobles, *Shades of Citizenship: Race and the Census in Modern Politics* (Palo Alto, CA: Stanford University Press, 2000); Victoria Hattam, *In the Shadow of Race: Jews, Latinos, and Immigrant Politics in the United States* (Chicago: University of Chicago Press, 2007); and Claire Jean Kim, "The Racial Triangulation of Asian-Americans," *Politics & Society* 27, no. 1 (1999). On law, see Pamela Brandwein, "Slavery as an Interpretive Issue in the Reconstruction Congresses," *Law and Society Review* 34, no. 2 (2000); and Kimberlé Crenshaw, Neil Gotanda, and Gary Peller, *Critical Race Theory* (New York: The New Press, 1996). On race and modern movement conservatism, see Joseph E. Lowndes, *From the New Deal to the New Right: Race and the Southern Origins of Modern Conservatism* (New Haven, CT: Yale University Press, 2009).

27. Michael Dawson and Cathy Cohen, "Problems in the Study of the Politics of Race," *Political Science: The State of the Discipline*, ed. Ira Katznelson and Helen V. Milner (New York: Norton, 2002): 490. Also see Task Force on Political Science in the 21st Century, "Report" (Washington, DC: American Political Science Association, 2011); and, e.g., Taeku Lee, "Race, Immigration, and the Identity-to-Politics Link," *Annual Review of Political Science* 11 (2008).

28. Dorothy Ross, *The Origins of American Social Science* (New York: Cambridge University Press, 1991), 471.

Index

abolitionism, 22, 23, 47
Adams, Herbert Baxter, 3, 26–27, 29, 35, 41, 57, 113, 154n4, 155n15, 159n63
Adcock, Richard, 9, 10
administration, study of, 18, 36, 41–43, 45; and colonial governance, 52, 54–56, 59–62, 67–68, 70, 71–73, 76
African Americans, 45, 65, 136, 190n20; characterizations of, 13, 46, 49, 51, 81, 123, 139
African-American politics, analyses of, 2, 11, 140, 163n38, 187n80
Africans, characterizations of, 22, 80, 104, 169n53
Algeria, French colonialism in, 67
Allport, Floyd, 118
Almond, Gabriel, 94
alt-right, *see* white supremacy
American Anthropological Association (AAA), 103, 106, 128, 177n45
American Council of Learned Societies (ACLS), 129, 131
American Economic Association (AEA), 31, 161n12
American Eugenics Society, 74, 85, 102
American Historical Association (AHA), 38, 47, 158n52, 161n12
American Historical Review (AHR), 85, 112
American Indians, characterizations of, 13, 33, 76, 83, 105, 166n6; intermarriage of whites and, 78
American Journal of International Law, 112, 171n11

American Journal of Psychology, 73
American Missionary Association, 64
American Museum of Natural History, 91, 106
American Political Science Association (APSA), 5–6, 47, 96, 100, 102; and African Americans, 46–49; and Association for Politics and the Life Sciences, 149n3; colonial scholarship in, 54, 59–61, 63 66, 67, 72, 75, 163n30; Committee on Political Research, 108, 118, 128; and crossover with AHA, 161n12; and empiricism, 42; founding of, 38, 41, 46, 161n15; National Conferences on the Science of Politics, 29, 108, 115, 119, 133, 136, 175n12, 180n90; Politics section of, 60; and reform, 43, 45, 72, 79
American Political Science Review (APSR), 1, 2, 46–50, 59, 100, 109, 112, 126, 141, 178n56
American Revolution, 28, 29
Angell, James Rowland, 129–31, 184n52
Anglo-Saxonism, *see* Teutonism
Annals of the American Academy of Political and Social Sciences (AAAPSS), 164n50, 165n67
anthropogeography, *see* climate theory
anthropology, 8, 12, 26, 71, 86; and Boasian turn, 11, 12, 90–115, 117, 177n48, 179n77; historiography of, 9, 86, 144; as source of insights for political science, 8, 26, 71, 96–97, 107–9, 112–14, 120, 141, 175n15,

anthropology (*continued*)
186n64; and World War I, 103,
175n15, 177n44 and n45
anthropometry, 105
Anti-Imperialist League, 59
area studies, 73–75, 88
Armstrong, Samuel Chapman, 64
Aryanism, 17, 26, 33, 36, 38, 113–14,
172n13. *See also* Teutonism
assimilationism, 64–65, 92
Atlantic Monthly, 35
authoritarianism, 3, 10, 31; and racial
difference, 7, 93, 95, 97, 107, 111, 115,
117
autonomy, colonial, 67–68, 70–71, 82

Bagehot, Walter, 38
Bagley, William C., 125
Baldwin, Simeon, 161n12
Baptist, Edward, 157n47
Barkan, Elazar, 128
Barnes, Harry Elmer, 108–12, 116–18,
178n58, 179n66; *History and Prospects
of the Social Sciences*, 108–9; *History of
Political Theories. Recent Times*,
108–109
Barrows, David P., 74, 82
Beard, Charles A., 101–2, 118, 161n12;
*An Economic Interpretation of the
Constitution*, 101
Beckwith, John, 2
behavioralism, 2, 128, 139, 142–44;
"behavioral revolution," 90
Bell, Daniel, 153n17, 158n 57, 190n16
Bentley, Arthur, 98, 101–2; *The Process of
Government*, 98
Bingham, Harold C., 126
Bingham, Hiram, 79
Bingham, Walter Van Dyke, 129
biological determinism, 2–3, 11, 55,
86–87, 92, 103, 106–7, 111, 121, 128,
136, 169n53, 179n77. *See also* eugenics
biology, 2; compared to political science,
7–8, 12, 27, 75, 96, 97, 119, 120
Blakeslee, George Hubbard, 5, 6, 73, 77,
79, 92, 101, 102, 171n11

Boas, Franz, 7, 102–3, 177n41 and n48,
178n56; critique of race formalism, 7,
101, 179n77; and idea of innate racial
differences, 7, 92, 102, 104–5, 107,
111–12, 141, 177n50, 179n77, 181n3;
influence on political science, 7, 93,
107–8, 110–11, 117, 143; *Mind of
Primitive Man*, 178n56; and NRC,
106–7, 128; and separation of nature
and culture, 11, 104–105; and
students, 7, 12, 74, 91, 102, 103, 104,
107–108, 110–11, 115, 178n56; and
World War I, 103, 177n44, 177n45,
177n47
Boyce, W. D., 83
Bretton Woods Conference, 129
Brigham, Carl C., 113, 122–24, 136,
182n24 and n29, 184n46
Broca, Paul, 113
Bryan, William Jennings, 40, 59
Bryce, James, 17, 22, 25, 37, 47, 53, 84,
156n26, 158n56; *The American
Commonwealth*, 25–26, 37
Buell, Raymond C., 60–61, 68
Bulmer, Martin, 128
Bunche, Ralph, 163n38, 187n80
Burgess, John W., 3, 5, 16, 20, 92, 139,
154n1, 158n60, 159n76; and civil
service, 16–18; and Columbia
University, 21, 24–25, 154n3; and
empire, 6, 32–33, 59, 63, 65, 163n30;
as founder of political science, 13,
15–17, 35–36, 45, 52, 59, 94, 154n2,
156n21, 159n63; "The Ideal of the
American Commonwealth," 30–31;
and the judiciary, 28, 45–46, 160n85;
*Political Science and Comparative
Constitutional Law*, 27, 35; and Reconstruction, 13–14, 19, 23–25, 39, 154n4,
155n12; rejected by second generation
of political scientists, 38–39, 41–44, 52,
57, 88, 99, 113; and slavery, 22–23; and
Teutonism, 25–27, 29, 32, 33, 71, 75,
87, 101, 159n66
Burr, Clinton Stoddard, 113

Calkins, Gary N., 47
Carnegie Corporation of New York, 130, 184n52
Carnegie Institute of Technology, 129
Carnegie Institute of Washington, 91, 106, 184n52
Carson, John, 136
Catlin, George E. G., 100
Chamberlain, Alexander F., 178n56
Chamberlain, Houston Stewart, 113
Charney, Evan, 2
Chicago School of Political Science, see University of Chicago
Chicago School of Sociology, see University of Chicago
China, 57, 61, 67, 73, 77
Chinese Americans, 51, 52, 65, 170n65
civil service reform, 16–18
Civil War, U.S., 3, 15, 19, 21–24, 30, 34, 44, 70, 95, 154n1, 156n16
civilization, concept of, 3, 14, 32, 37, 62, 65, 75; and climate theory, 83, 85; critique of "universal civilization," 63–64
class differentiation, in evolutionary theory, 17–18
class struggle, 101
climate theory, 22, 74, 83–85
Cohen, Cathy, 146
Coker, Francis W., 162n27, 178n58,
Cold Spring Harbor Laboratory, 106
Cold War, 98, 142, 143
colonialism, 6, 7, 178n56; and APSA, 59–61, 72, 75, 163n30; and autonomy, 67–68; European-style colonialism, 77, 79; and Jim Crow, 54, 61; and the Philippines, 59–60; "progressive" colonialism, 62
"color line," 53
Columbia University, 5, 16, 21; Law School, 21; Political Science at, 16, 18, 24, 32, 38, 46, 96, 154n3, 175n13; Trustees of, 21, 102
Committee on Political Research, see APSA
Committee on Public Information, 90

Committee on Scientific Problems of Human Migration, see Migration Committee (NRC)
Committee on Social Trends, 129
communications research, 94
Congress, United States, 25, 58, 68–70, 129, 168n22; Committee on Immigration and Naturalization, 123, 177n50; committee system, 44, 57; "Congressional supremacy," 44; in the work of Woodrow Wilson, 35, 44–45
Constitution, United States, 26, 28, 99
Corwin, Edward, 118
Council on Foreign Relations, 74
Cox, Oliver, 190n20
Crane, Robert T., 119–21, 181n12
craniometry, 121
Crick, Bernard, 10
criminology, 9, 144, 152n22, 189n15
Croly, Herbert, 41
culture, modern concept of, 11–12, 87, 91, 95, 105, 107, 111, 181n3; older concept, 12, 75, 80, 87–89, 103–4, 145
Curtis, Mattoon M., 112–13

Dahl, Robert A., 189n9
Darwinism, 26–27, 56, 86–88, 167n14 and n19, 173n36
Davenport, Charles B., 106
Davis, W. M., 84
Dawson, Michael, 146
democracy, 3, 4, 10; conceptions of, 6, 8, 25, 27, 38–39, 52, 95, 96–100; limits of, 15, 18, 28, 30, 43, 57, 67, 72, 117, 123–25, 157n41
Department of Experimental Biology, see Cold Spring Harbor Laboratory
Dewey, Gordon, 96–97, 100, 140
Dewey, John, 74, 94
differential psychology, 8, 116, 118, 121, 123, 124, 133
Dillingham Commission, 105, 177n50
disciplinary objectivity, 142. See also mechanical objectivity; Porter
Dixon, Thomas, 13, 154n4
Dryzek, John, 9, 143, 188n2

Du Bois, W. E. B., 47, 53–54, 58, 74, 77, 111, 164n50, 166n4, 171n8; *The Souls of Black Folk*, 53
Duguit, Léon, 175n25
Dunning, William A., 13, 24–25, 46, 47, 50, 57, 108–9, 112–13, 116–17, 158n52, 161n12, 178n56; "Dunning School," 46, 50, 155n10, 158n52

Easton, David, 142
École Libre des Sciences Politiques (Sciences Po), 16, 156n21
education, 17, 65, 66, 73; and colonization, 59–60, 64–65, 82, 88; and intelligence testing, 123, 125, 136
Elliott, William Yandell, 99–101, 112, 118, 176n27, 181n9
Ellis, Ellen, 100–101
Ellis, George W., 82, 178n56
Ely, Richard T., 17, 31
empire, 55, 61–62. *See also* imperialism
empirical biopolitics, 1–2, 4, 138, 149n3. *See also* genes
empiricism, 42, 54, 95–96, 140
Encyclopedia of the Social Sciences, 108, 165n68
ethnic cleansing, 31. *See also* genocide
ethnicity, 30, 31, 67, 102; concept of, 40, 146, 162n18
ethnology, 3, 27, 29, 92, 95, 113, 158n60
eugenics, 3, 91, 102, 106–7, 112–14, 116, 120, 124, 128, 136, 140, 143, 144, 168n30, 174n1
Eugenics Record Office, *see* Cold Spring Harbor Laboratory
Eugenics Research Association, 102
evolution, 27, 57–58, 83, 86–89, 91–92, 94, 95, 106, 124, 138, 147, 173n36; Boasian critique of social evolutionism, 107, 109–12, 143; of institutions, 25–27, 57, 71, 75, 92, 139, 159n66; of races, 6–8, 72–77, 104–5. *See also* Darwinism; Lamarckianism
executive, the, 45, 57; in writings of Henry Jones Ford, 58; in writings of Woodrow Wilson, 44, 45, 161n7

Farabee, William Curtis, 74
Farr, James, 9
fascism, 10, 99, 111, 166n11, 176n27
Fichte, Johann Gottlieb, 113
Filipinos, conceptions of, 64–65, 81–82. *See also* Moros, conception of
Finley, John P., 82
Ford Foundation Behavioral Sciences Program, 142
Ford, Henry Jones, 5, 35, 52, 56–58, 61, 63–67, 69, 92, 101, 167n19, 168n22 and n35; *Natural History of the State: An Introduction to Political Science*, 57; *Rise and Growth of American Politics*, 56
Foreign Affairs, 74, 76, 171n6. *See also* Council on Foreign Relations; *Journal of International Relations*; *Journal of Race Development*
formalism, *see* legalism; race formalism
Foucault, Michel, 149n2
foundations, charitable, 8, 119, 120, 127, 128, 130, 131, 140–42, 184n48. *See also* Carnegie Corporation of New York; Carnegie Institute of Technology, Carnegie Institute of Washington; Laura Spelman Rockefeller Memorial; Russell Sage Foundation
Franco-Prussian War, 20
Frank, Leonard K., 186n7
Freedmen's Bureau, 64
Freeman, E. A., 25
French colonialism, 67–68
Freud, Sigmund, 94, 171n4

Galton, Francis, 113
Galton Society, 102, 106
Gamio, Manuel, 133, 186n67
Garvey, Marcus, 91
Gehlke, Charles Elmer, 110, 117
genes, 1–3, 138, 149n5, 150n8; history of the word, 151n14
genetics, 1–2, 86, 88, 138, 149n1, 150n8, 173n36
genocide, 136. *See also* ethnic cleansing
genomics, 138

geographic determinism, 22, 23, 85, 88, 113
German idealism, see Hegel
German universities, 20, 21, 26, 158n60
Gettell, Raymond, 112
Gilded Age, 17–18, 26, 43
Ginn, Edward, 73, 75, 102
Gobineau, Arthur de, 113
Goddard, Henry H., 122
Goldenweiser, Alexander, 108, 109–10, 113, 178n60
Goodnow, Frank, 35, 38, 41, 42, 43, 67, 162n28
Gordon, Leah, 145, 190n20
Gosnell, Harold F., 94, 126, 134–35, 140, 187n80; Negro Politicians, 135, 187n80
Gould, Charles W., 124,
Gould, Stephen Jay, 105
Grant, Madison, 102, 106, 113, 124
Great Depression, 107
Great Society, 146
Griffis, William Elliot, 78, 172n13
Griffith, D. W., 113; The Birth of a Nation, 113, 154n4
Gunnell, John, 9, 10, 94, 154n2

Haeckel, Ernst, 74
Hague Tribunal, 68
Hall, Arnold Bennett (A. B.), 119, 136, 175n12
Hall, G. Stanley, 5, 6, 73–74, 77, 78, 80, 81, 87, 122, 171n4, 177n42
Hammond, John Hays, 79
Hampton Institute, 64–65
Hankins, Franklin Hamilton, 110, 112–15, 116, 117, 180n84
Hanover Conferences on the Social Sciences, see Social Science Research Council
Hansen, John, 94
Haraway, Donna, 182n17
Hart, Albert Bushnell, 47–48, 51, 161n12
Harvard University, 47, 50, 55, 96, 163n38
Haskell, Thomas L., 15
Hayes, Rutherford B., 70; and Hayes-Tilden Compromise, 24

Heaney, Michael, 94
Hegel, Georg Wilhelm Friedrich, 56, 113; Hegelian idealism, 20, 26, 27, 34, 95, 159n66
hereditarianism, 3, 74, 86, 105, 107, 124, 177n50
higher education, history of, 15, 16, 18, 20, 41, 130
historicism, 4, 7, 15, 36, 110, 141. See also idealism; legalism
History of Political Theories, Recent Times, 108–15, 116–17, 178n58
Hitler, Adolf, 55
Hoffman, Frederick, 47
Hoover Institute, 94
human measurement, 7. See also anthropometry; craniometry; psychometrics
human sciences, 91–92
Huntington, Ellsworth, 74, 84–85, 173n32; Pulse of Asia, The, 85. See also climate theory

Ickes, Harold, 97
idealism, 5, 20, 26; critiques of, 36, 58, 90; in international relations, 55, 166n7, 179n74
ideology, 9–10, 142; sources of, 1, 138, 146
illiberalism, 10, 153n28
immigration, 17, 18, 25, 31–32, 40, 52, 65, 101, 127, 178n56; restriction of, 50–51, 91, 106, 117, 120–21, 123, 124, 128, 136, 144, 177n50. See also Johnson-Reed Act; Migration Committee (NRC)
imperialism, 14, 52, 54, 59–60, 62, 69–70, 74, 92, 163n30, 166n6
inductivism, 39, 41, 42, 52, 57, 101, 111
Institute for Government Research, 126
institutionalist economics, 31
intelligence testing, 117, 121, 123–24, 127, 184n51; by U.S. Army, 7–8, 116–17, 120, 122, 182n15; controversies about, 118, 125, 138–39, 182n29; and intelligence quotient (IQ), 122

intermarriage, 78. *See also* miscegenation
International Bureau of Students, 79
International Journal of Ethics, 112
international organization, 55, 68
international relations theory, 22, 55, 72, 73, 75–76, 88, 163n38, 166n7, 171n8; historiography of, 5, 9, 55, 144, 151n17, 167n12 and n13, 190n16. *See also Journal of Race Development*
international trade, 59, 62, 67, 79–80, 83, 170n65
Ireland, Alleyne, 60, 61–62, 168n30

James, William, 87, 94, 122
Japan, 73, 74, 77, 171n11, 172n13
Jim Crow, *see* segregation; suffrage
Johns Hopkins University, 38, 73, 96, 161n11 and n15, 175n13
Johnson, Alvin, 51–52, 165n68
Johnson-Reed Immigration Act, 128. *See also* immigration, restriction of
Jones, Mack, 10–11, 145
Journal of International Relations, 74
Journal of Physical Anthropology, 107
Journal of Race Development (JRD), 5, 72–89, 139, 171n11, 178n56
Journal of Theoretical Politics, 1
judiciary, the, 42; in writings of John W. Burgess, 16, 28, 30, 45
Jung, Carl, 171n4

Kellogg, Vernon, 133–34
Key, V. O., 94
Knox, Robert, 22
Knox College, 155n12
Krabbe, Hugo, 175n25
Kroeber, Alfred, 74, 109
Ku Klux Klan, 50, 70, 91

labor movement, 32, 41, 99
Labour Party, 98
laissez-faire, 31
Lake Mohonk conferences, 54, 166n6,
Lamarck, Jean-Baptiste, 86
Lamarckianism, 74, 86–88; neo-Lamarckianism, 86, 88, 177n50

Langdell, Christopher Columbus, 157n41
Langdon, William Chauncy, 46
Lapouge, Georges Vacher de, 113, 124
Laski, Harold, 6, 95, 98–99, 101
Lasswell, Harold D., 93–94, 100–101, 134–35, 138; *Psychopathology and Politics*, 134
Latin America, 73, 79–81, 83–84
Laura Spelman Rockefeller Memorial (LSRM), 127, 129–35, 184n48
League of Nations, 63, 70, 71
League to Enforce Peace, 63
legalism, 4, 35, 41, 55, 90, 115
legitimacy, 5, 16, 25, 26, 28, 41, 99
liberalism, 1, 3, 4, 10, 15, 43, 53, 54, 70, 93, 98, 101, 111, 115, 117, 128, 136; technocratic impulses in, 10, 62, 90, 95, 130, 133, 141, 142, 147
Liberia, 82
Lieber, Francis, 15, 24, 26, 29, 154n2, 155n15
Lincoln, Abraham, 44
Lippmann, Walter, 125
Local Community Research Council (LCRC), 108, 130–31, 134–35, 188n33. *See also* University of Chicago
Lodge, Henry Cabot, 50, 52
Lowie, Robert, 103, 107, 110
lynching, 49–51, 165n61, 165n67

Mac-Mahon, Patrice de, 20–21, 157n37
manifest destiny, 23
Marburg, Theodore, 63, 169n51
Martin, John, 49
Marxism, 98, 142
Mayo, George Elton, 134, 187n70
Mayo-Smith, Richmond, 31–32
McDougall, William, 113
McGerr, Michael, 40
McKinley, William, 40
mechanical objectivity, 142, 189n5 and n6. *See also* disciplinary objectivity; Porter
Merriam, Charles E., 5, 90; as academic entrepreneur, 91–93, 119–21, 128–35, 176n35; and Boas, 101, 107, 143; and

Burgess, 29, 94; and Chicago School of Political Science, 6–8, 91, 93–94, 134, 188n83; and determinism, 137, 138–40; and eugenics, 116; and Gamio, 186n67; *History of Political Theories, Recent Times*, 108–12, 116, 117, 178n58; and intelligence testing, 117–18, 124–29; *New Aspects of Politics*, 95–97, 99, 175n11, 179n67; and pluralism, 99–101; political ambitions of, 97; and reform, 97–98, 100, 117, 141; and Ruml, 130–35, 144

Merriam, John C., 106–7, 120, 130, 132, 136, 184n52

methodological individualism, 143, 147

Mexico, 103; and immigration, 133, 186n67

Migration Committee (NRC), 120–21, 126–29, 131–33, 183n54

Mills, Charles, 145

miscegenation, 105, 124. *See also* intermarriage

modernity, 41, 84

Mormons (Church of Jesus Christ of Latter-Day Saints), 33

Moros, conceptions of 59, 82. *See also* Filipinos, conceptions of

Morris, Henry, 59, 66

Moses, Bernard, 62–63, 66, 169n45 and n51

Mulford, Elisha, 29

Munro, William B., 67–68, 100

Myrdal, Gunnar, 145, 190n20

Nation, The, 85, 103

National Academy of Sciences (NAS), 122, 123, 132, 140

National Association for the Advancement of Colored People (NAACP), 111, 165

National Conferences on the Science of Politics, *see* APSA

National Research Council (NRC), 7, 91, 103, 106–7, 119–20, 128–29, 131–32, 133, 135, 140, 175n15, 184n50 and n52, 185n64. *See also* Migration Committee

National Resources Planning Board (NRPB), 129

National Science Foundation (NSF), 142

National Socialism (Nazism), 107, 136, 174n1

national soul, *see* state theory

nationalism, 15, 16, 23, 25, 33, 53, 69, 110, 142, 153

natural law, 36, 61, 95

natural rights theory, 16, 22, 23, 28–29, 32

natural sciences, 8, 20, 33, 57, 92–94, 102, 109, 118, 129, 132, 140, 144; anthropology as a natural science, 120, 175n15

New Deal, 2, 91, 129

New Republic, The, 125, 165n68

New School for Social Research, 110, 165n68

Niagara Falls conference, 165n62. *See also* Du Bois; National Association for the Advancement of Colored People (NAACP)

Nineteenth Amendment, 164n50

Nordicism, *see* Teutonism

North American Review, 47, 50

Odum, Howard, 81

Ogburn, William F., 135

Open Door Policy, 67, 170n65

Oren, Ido, 10

organicism, 93, 143

Orientalism, 78

Origin of the Species, 86

Osborn, Henry Fairfield, 106

Pan-Africanism, 77

Paris Commune, 157n37

Park, Robert E., 74, 145

Pearson, Karl, 94

Pendleton Act, 18. *See also* civil service reform

peoplehood, racialized conceptions of, 8, 28, 39, 34, 36, 39, 45, 64, 67, 71, 95, 99, 101, 114

Pezet, Federico A., 80–81, 84
Philippine Commission, U.S., 59, 62–63
Philippines, the, 32, 56, 59–60, 64–66, 70, 73, 76, 77, 79, 82, 163n30, 165n71, 166n6
Philosophical Review, 112
physical anthropology, 105
Plessy v. Ferguson, 164n59
pluralism, 6, 8, 53, 94–95, 98–101, 141, 142, 143, 175n25, 189n9
policy studies, 94
political culture, 144
political psychology, 8, 94, 134
political science in the United States, historiography of, 5, 9, 10–11, 15, 16, 18, 22, 40, 43, 53, 55, 69, 70, 74–75, 84, 94, 118, 128, 142, 144, 145–46, 147, 149n3, 152n23, 154n2, 155n15, 159n66, 160n88, 175n13
Political Science Quarterly (PSQ), 32, 42, 46–47, 50, 59, 61, 109, 154n3, 165n68, 178n56
political sociology, 94
Populism, 30, 40
Porter, Theodore, 142, 189n5
Proceedings of the American Political Science Association, 42
progress, 3, 4, 74, 76, 94–95, 104; and colonialism, 6, 33, 54, 62, 77, 83, 88; and immigration, 32; "progressionism," 26–27, 54, 56–57, 83, 167n14; and race, 14, 23, 25, 33, 37, 62, 75, 79, 81, 104, 105, 124; and technology, 41, 68
progressivism, 39–41, 43, 62, 73, 78–79, 84, 141, 172n15
Progressive Era, 17, 39, 74, 75, 97, 130, 141
Progressive Party, 90
psychology, 7, 8, 73, 96, 97, 99, 109, 119, 120, 129, 136, 146, 189n15; military psychology, 121
psychometrics, 121, 128, 141. *See also* differential psychology; human measurement
Puerto Rico, 56, 63, 165n71

race formalism, 111; critiques of, 105. *See also* Boas, Franz
race theory, 9–12, 89, 91, 96, 115, 139, 145–47; debates about race in the 1920s, 11, 90–115; Victorian race theory, 3, 12, 104–105, 179n71. *See also* race formalism; race relations; racial hierarchy; race science; racism; scientific racism
race relations, 51, 145–46, 190n20
race riots, 91
race science, 5, 7, 11, 92, 139, 140–41, 143, 179n77. *See also* scientific racism
"race war," 50, 84
racial hierarchy, 4, 10, 14, 40, 42, 69, 71, 75, 83, 111, 118, 122, 145, 147; critique of, 78; racial hierarchy in United States, 43–45, 70. *See also* imperialism; scientific racism; white supremacy
racial individualism, 145. *See also* Gordon
racially specific medicine, 2, 151n10
racism, 2, 4, 10–11, 140, 144; Burgess and, 13–14, 113, 155n12; Davenport and, 106; intelligence testing and, 125, 136; Stoddard and, 55, 166n11. *See also* Teutonism; white supremacy
Radical Republicans, 25, 45
RAND Corporation, 94
Ranke, Leopold von, 26, 59n164
rational choice, 2
realism, 55, 166n7
recapitulationism, 74
Reconstruction, 13, 15, 17, 24, 34, 39, 44–45, 47–48, 64–65, 164n50; and lynching, 50–51. *See also* Burgess; Dunning; Wilson, Woodrow
Red Scare, 91
Reed, Adolph, Jr., 53
reform, 6, 39, 40, 54, 72, 172n15; and the AEA, 31; and empire, 58, 62, 72, 76, 79, 84, 166n6; Hankins and, 113; Merriam and, 92, 97, 141; and Ruml, 130; Wilson and, 43–44, 52, 70, 99, 161n7. *See also* civil service reform
regulation, economic, 30, 31, 43, 161n7

Reinsch, Paul, 60, 92, 169n53; and assimilationism v. colonial autonomy, 64–65, 67–68, 71, 72, 80; and the Philippines, 60, 64–65; *Public International Unions: Their Work and Organization*, 68–69; and trade, 62, 67

Rensselaer School, 15, 155n13

Republican Party, 2, 23. *See also* Radical Republicans

republicanism, 21, 40, 47, 80–81, 84

research funding, 8, 120, 121, 129, 132, 142, 184n48; and Merriam as academic entrepreneur, 91, 119, 127, 130–31; and Ruml, 133–34

Rodgers, Daniel, 16, 160n88

Roosevelt, Franklin Delano, 129, 154n1

Roosevelt, Theodore, 54, 81, 154n1, 156n26, 166n6

Rose, John, 48–49, 52

Rosenwald, Julius, 97

Ross, Dorothy, 9, 10, 15, 84, 118, 128, 147, 155n15, 159n66

Rowe, Leo Stanton, 36

Ruml, Beardsley, 127, 129–35, 138, 140, 144, 184n50 and n52, 186n66 and n67

Russell Sage Foundation, 120

Sapir, Edward, 110

Saudi Arabia, 169n56

Save-the-Redwoods League, 102, 106. *See also* Grant; Merriam, John C.

Scaife Foundation, 149n3

Schmidt, Brian, 5, 60

Schneider, Herbert, 110, 179n74

scientific racism, 55, 91, 102, 144, 151n10, 169n53. *See also* race science

scientism, 90, 94, 102, 138–39, 142

Scopes trial, 91

Scott, Emmett J., 82

Scott, Walter Dill, 184n51

sectionalism, U.S., 19, 22, 30

Seelye, Julius, 20

segregation, 46, 48–49, 65, 70, 164n59; and intelligence testing, 125; and progressivism, 40

self-government, 21, 27–28, 52, 58, 61, 65–66, 81, 138

Seligman, E. R. A., 31

settlement house movement, 32, 78

Shaw, Albert, 35, 41, 43, 71, 161n12

Shikai, Yuan, 67

Shuster, W. Morgan, 82

Skowronek, Stephen, 16, 18, 43, 69, 70

slavery, 14, 19, 22–23, 49, 121, 157n47

Smith, Rogers, 10, 11, 40, 145–46

Smith, Thomas Vernor (T. V.), 108, 112, 118, 181n9

Smithsonian Institution, 91; Bureau of Ethnology, 80

social contract theory, 3, 16, 21, 23, 28, 29, 56

social control, 7, 97, 117, 121, 125, 137, 141, 143, 175n12

Social Science Research Council (SSRC), 6–7, 108, 119–20, 128–29, 131–33, 135, 144, 181n12, 184n48, 185n61; Hanover Conferences on the Social Sciences, 108, 133, 187n59

social sciences, historiography of, 9, 10, 11, 15, 86, 108, 109, 152n22

socialism, 53, 78, 98, 99, 101; fear of, 30–31, 41

Society of Friends (Quakers), 166n6

sociology, 43, 99–100, 109, 112, 145, 146, 175n15, 188n83; historiography of, 9, 12, 86, 144, 152n22, 189n15

Solovey, Mark, 142, 144

Somit, Albert, 149n3, 154n2, 175n13

Sorel, Georges, 99

sovereignty, 5, 15, 21, 25, 26–27, 36, 37, 39, 41, 95; popular sovereignty, 28, 29, 58, 117, 143, 167n19

Spanish-American War, 32, 52, 56

Spencer, Herbert, 27, 108

Spiro, Jonathan, 102

State Department, U.S., 73

state theory, 26, 28–34, 36–37, 39, 41, 42, 52, 56, 95, 98–100, 141, 159n66, 161n5, 162n27; "national soul" as "state," 14

statistics, 97, 109, 141, 158n60

Stephenson, Gilbert T., 49, 52, 164n59

sterilization laws, *see* eugenics

Stocking, George, Jr., 11, 86–87, 111, 177n50

Stoddard, Lothrop, 55, 106, 113, 166n11

suffrage, 17, 23, 47–48, 164n50; debates about, 13–14, 30; suppression of, 47–49. *See also* segregation

Supreme Court, 160n85, 164n59

Taft, William Howard, 59, 102

technocracy, *see* liberalism

technology, 7, 68, 97–98, 117–18, 121–22, 125–27, 135, 138–39, 142, 173n32. *See also* intelligence testing; mechanical objectivity

teleology, 7, 41, 55, 56, 58, 83, 93, 95, 109, 139

Terman, Lewis, 122, 124–25

Teutonism, 4–5, 14–15, 25–27, 30–32, 36, 54, 56, 57, 71, 87, 93, 101, 113; Anglo-Saxon "genius for liberty," 5, 17, 33, 42, 44, 159n66; Anglo-Saxonism in Britain, 25, 153n17, 158n 57, 190n16; Nordicism, 110, 113; Teutonic germ theory, 3, 4, 27, 29. *See also* Aryanism

Thiers, Adolphe, 20, 157n37

Thomas, Franklin, 110

Thurstone, L. L., 126, 135

Treat, Payson, J., 74, 82

Truman, David, 94, 189n9

Tuskegee Institute, 49–50, 64, 165n61

University of Chicago, 38, 90, 128; Chicago School of Political Science, 6, 94, 96, 130, 134–35, 188n83; Chicago School of Sociology, 145. *See also* Merriam, Charles E.

University of Wisconsin, 38, 96, 161n11 and n15

uplift, racial, 6, 51–52, 62–63, 72, 75, 76, 79–82, 87–88, 139

urbanization, 40

van Kleeck, Mary, 120, 185n64

Veblen, Thorstein, 74, 87–88

vigilantism, *see* lynching

Vineland Training School for Feeble-Minded Boys and Girls, 122

Vitalis, Robert, 5, 9, 22, 55, 74–75, 152n23

Volksgeist, see state theory

Wade, Nicholas, 3, 151n10

Wallis, Wilson D., 78

Wappäus, Johann Eduard, 158n60

Washington, Booker T., 64

Watson, John, 94, 129

Weismann, August, 86

White, Andrew, 155n15

whites, conceptions of, 17, 23, 24, 42, 50, 51, 70, 145, 190n20. *See also* Teutonism; white supremacy

white supremacy, 2, 7, 52, 55, 61, 77, 92, 103, 107, 113, 114–15, 124, 139, 151n10, 155n12. *See also* racism; Teutonism

Willey, Malcolm, 116–17, 139, 181n3

Willingham, Alex, 10–11, 145

Wilson, Ernest J., III, 11

Wilson, Woodrow, 5, 43, 69–71; and administration, 36, 42; and Bryce, 37; and Burgess, 35–36, 39, 46; and changes in ethnic composition of U.S., 101; *Congressional Government*, 44; *Constitutional Government*, 45, 70; and League of Nations, 71; as part of second generation of political scientists, 5–6, 33, 39, 41, 43, 52, 55; and Reconstruction, 44, 46, 47, 50, 69–70, 154n4; *The State*, 36–37

Woolsey, Theodore Dwight, 155n15

World Peace Foundation, 73, 75, 102

World War I, 6, 7, 14, 89, 90–91, 95, 103, 113, 175n12 and n15

World War II, 55, 73, 107, 142

Yerkes, Robert, 7, 93, 106, 113, 115, 120–22, 125–28, 130, 131, 132, 136, 182n15 and n17, 183n43, 184n51, 186n64

Yoakum, Clarence Stone, 122

Acknowledgments

This project has been through so many iterations that a true accounting of my debts is too daunting to attempt. The only easy thing is where to start: Adolph L. Reed, Jr. has been there from the very beginning. His work and teaching have shaped how I think about power, race, hierarchy, and the role of social science in American politics and culture in almost every respect and he has been unfailingly generous with his help and astonishingly vast knowledge at every stage. Another important influence is Robert Vitalis, who pointed me to this topic in the first place, and who has provided valuable comments, references, and encouragement over many years.

At the New School for Social Research I was lucky enough to benefit from guidance and support from David Plotke, Victoria Hattam, Oz Frankel, Elzbieta Matynia, and the Transregional Center for Democratic Studies, among many others; at Sarah Lawrence College from Elke Zuern and other generous colleagues; at Marymount Manhattan College from my supportive colleagues in the Division of Social Sciences and Humanities and particularly from Lauren Brown, Andreas Hernandez, Erin O'Connor, Michelle Ronda, Rosemary Nossiff, and Kent Worcester, who read and commented on portions of the manuscript. This project was also facilitated by a junior fellowship leave from Marymount. The Faculty Resource Network and especially Anne Lydia Ward and Nikhil Singh, as well as the Department of Social and Cultural Analysis at New York University provided support and resources during my leave. Andrew Seal did meticulous work on the index. Essential research assistance came from Molly Ward and Seth Ackerman, as well as from archivists at the Rockefeller Archive Center and special collections libraries at the University of Chicago, Yale University, Smith College, and the University of Kentucky.

Among the many institutions that made this project possible, perhaps none is more important than the New York City school system. The teachers, staff, afterschool caregivers, and parent community at my children's wonderful Brooklyn public school were essential supports for a family in which two parents were writing books and on the tenure track at the same time.

Material in Chapters 1 and 4 is derived in part from articles published in *Ethnic and Racial Studies*, available online at www.tandfonline.com/doi/abs/10.1080/01419870.2012.730623 and www.tandfonline.com/doi/abs/10.1080/0141987042000246309. I am grateful to the anonymous readers for that journal. Other chapters have been improved by discussions at meetings of the American Political Science Association, the Social Science History Association, the Southern and Western Political Science Associations, the American Studies Association, and Cheiron: The International Society for the History of the Behavioral Sciences. I am particularly thankful for incisive feedback from Wilbur Rich and Nikol Alexander Floyd on the paper that eventually became Chapter 1; from Alice O'Connor who asked hard questions about the paper that became Chapter 6; and from Joe Lowndes who took the time to read and comment on several chapters. Others who have been generous with readings, publishing suggestions, cheerleading, and/or writing companionship include Katie Kilroy-Marac, Gary Younge, Penny Lewis, Rachel Schwartz, Alissa Levin, Nicolas Guilhot, Leah Gordon, Anwen Tormey, Anne Pitcher, Hillary Frey, and Elliot Ross.

Priscilla Yamin did me the great favor of suggesting that I contact Peter Agree at the University of Pennsylvania Press. I could not have asked for a kinder, wiser, or more responsive editor. It has been a pleasure to work with him; his capable colleagues, including Lily Palladino, Amanda Ruffner, and Kathy McQueen; and the supportive editors of Penn's American Governance series. Rick Valelly's comments on an early portion of the manuscript helped me to think through the framing of the study, as did generous reports from Dorothy Ross and an anonymous reviewer. Pamela Brandwein's thorough reading of the entire manuscript pushed me toward sharper arguments and clearer organization. This book is much better for all their help.

My closest comrades in this writing process have been the members of the "brain trust," the incomparable Kim Phillips-Fein, Caitlin Zaloom, and Liza Featherstone. They insist I could have written this book without them, but I know better. Thinking happens in communities, and they have been mine. Their insight and friendship made all the difference.

And finally, my family. My brilliant mother, Joan Blatt, never doubts. Neither does my husband and very tolerant partner, Sean Jacobs, whose absolute confidence in me means more than he knows. His endless curiosity and intellectual energy are sources of continuous inspiration and pride; his steadfastness is a constant comfort. Our kids, Leo and Rosa Jacobs, have grown up with this book. I like to think it has taught them patience. They are my greatest joy.